DOORWAY

Remember that *frisson* as you step through a doorway: into a crowded party or a silent church; for a job interview, or into your own home after a long journey. Though we take them for granted, doorways impinge on our lives in many ways. Their thresholds divide up the world, punctuating our movements from place to place and creating 'fault-lines' in our experience. Their mystery intrigues and challenges us. We measure ourselves against them and they set down the geometry of our relationships. Doorways affect our emotions and influence how we behave; sitting on a doorstep, we can find peace just watching the world go by. Framing the transient moment, doorways stand as reminders of the 'between' in which we live. It is no wonder that through human history and across all cultures, doorways have possessed great symbolic power and had ceremonies and rituals associated with them.

Doorway is a profound but accessible and entertaining exploration of the ways our built surroundings set out the spatial matrix of our existence. Using examples from archaeology to the present, and from all around the world, this book provides a fresh and revealing perspective on architecture and its poetry.

Simon Unwin is Professor of Architecture at Dundee University. He has lived and taught in Britain and Australia, and lectured on his work in China, Israel, India, Sweden, Turkey and the United States. His book *Analysing Architecture* has been translated into Chinese, Japanese, Persian and Spanish.

Related titles by Simon Unwin:

Analysing Architecture
An Architecture Notebook: Wall

DOORWAY

Simon Unwin

Routledge
Taylor & Francis Group

LONDON AND NEW YORK

First published 2007
by Routledge
2 Park Square, Milton Park, Abingdon, Oxon, OX14 4RN

Simultaneously published in the USA and Canada
by Routledge
270 Madison Ave, New York, NY 10016

*Routledge is an imprint of the Taylor & Francis group, an informa
business*

Printed and bound in Great Britain by
The Cromwell Press, Trowbridge, Wiltshire.

Publisher's Note.
This book has been prepared using camera-ready copy supplied by
the author.

British Library Cataloguing in Publication Data
A catalogue record for this book is available from the British
Library.

Library of Congress Cataloging in Publication Data
Unwin, Simon, 1952–
Doorway / Simon Unwin
    p. cm
  Includes bibliographical references and index.
  ISBN 978-0-415-45880-1 (hbk : alk. paper)
  ISBN 978-0-415-45881-8 (pbk : alk. paper)
  1. Doorways. 2. Doorways – Psychological aspects. 3. Space
(Architecture) I. Title
NA3010.U59 2007
721'.822–dc22   2007033039

ISBN10: 0–415–45880–3 (hbk)
ISBN10: 0–415–45881–1 (pbk)

ISBN13: 978–0–415–45880–1 (hbk)
ISBN13: 978–0–415–45881–8 (pbk)

for Mary, David and Jim

'*All the golden land's ahead of you and all kinds of unforeseen events wait lurking to surprise you and make you glad you're alive to see.*' **Jack Kerouac** (*On the Road*, 1957)

CONTENTS

DOORWAY

INTRODUCTION

The doorway is one of the most powerful instruments available to the architect. It is even richer in its powers than the wall, upon which it almost always depends. Where the power of the wall is to *deny* (to keep things apart), that of the doorway is to *permit* (to allow passage). And permission usually has more dimensions of possibility – risks as well as rewards – than denial.

Doorways and the doors by which they may be closed are so common a feature of our surroundings that we rarely give conscious thought to what they do, to us as well as for us. Until we encounter a door that is locked against us, or one that has been violated and failed to protect our belongings from thieves, they seem just part of the background, a mere component of the stage-set within which we act out the small and grand dramas of our lives.

We cannot exactly ignore them – we pass through doorways probably hundreds of times every day – but neither do we pay them much attention. Because our minds are taken up with more immediate concerns – buying food, talking to friends, getting our work done… – we tend to acknowledge doorways only at a subliminal level.

But the powers of the doorway pervade our lives. There is hardly a culture on earth that does not use the doorway. It is an essential element in the organisation of space, a key part of the common language of architecture.

This book will be of interest to readers wanting to understand the powers architecture has to determine the use and experience of space. In particular it looks at the parts the doorway plays in organising the settings for life. The book is less concerned with the appearance of doorways and doors (as elements in a decorative scheme) than with how they are used to organise space, and the ways encountering them and passing through them impinges upon our experience of the world.

In the following pages we shall explore various aspects of the doorway as an element in spatial organisation and experience. We shall consider the doorway from the point of view of the architect – for whom it is an element in the language of design – as well as from the point of view of everyone who experiences buildings – for whom the doorway punctuates movement between one place and another, influencing perceptions, relationships and even behaviour.

Passing through doorways affects our states of being; who we think we are as well as where we find ourselves. Often these effects are small, but sometimes they can be dramatic. It will be seen that in dealing with the powers of the doorway we shall be dealing in issues that are psychological, philosophical and poetic (symbolic), as ingredients of the architectural.

The aim of the book is to enrich understanding of the general powers of architecture by looking in detail at those of one element: the doorway. It will help those who act architecturally (design and make places) to appreciate the variety of dimensions they have at their disposal. It should also help all those who inhabit 'architected' space (i.e. everyone) become more aware of the ways settings condition our relationship with the world, the way architecture sets the spatial matrix within which we live.

The chapters of the book are grouped into five sections.

The first section, *The Powers of Doorways*, looks at the 'doorway' as a key concept (along with 'pathway' and 'domain') in the way we make sense of our surroundings. It speculates on the origins of doorways in our relationships with the world and at the parts played by doorways when we begin to make places for ourselves in the landscape.

The second section describes *The Geometry of Doorways*. It explains why doorways tend to be rectangular and how their sizes relate to the things that pass through them. This section looks too at the power of the doorway axis, and at how architects have sought to exploit and sometimes contain that power in their designs.

The third section explores *Experiencing Doorways*. Beginning by drawing attention to the psychological power of the threshold and at how doorways can offer points of escape or refuge, it goes on to look too at how passing through a doorway can change how we see the world and our sense of identity. This section discusses the idea of the 'in-between' and how doorways establish places where we experience a transitional state of being. This section also explores the sensual experience of doorways.

The fourth section looks at the roles played by doorways in *Organising Space*. It illustrates examples where doorways are points of contact between different 'worlds', and at how they are used as points of discrimination and control. It considers the temptation of transgression, the use of illicit doorways, and relationships between doorways and the organisation of routes. Finally it illustrates examples of entrances composed as labyrinths.

The fifth section discusses the possibility of *Architecture without Doorways*. It looks at the symbolic association of doorways with death; and at specific attempts to reduce the role of the doorway as an element of architecture, especially in association with breaking open the box-like room.

The book concludes with an overview of the doorway as an element of architecture, drawing together some general observations about the roles played by doorways in our organisation of space and experience of the world.

The book contains many photographs and drawings of specific examples; some that are grand and well known, many taken from the ordinary background within which most of us live. All have been included to illustrate subtleties of the common language of architecture as it relates to doorways.

Architecture is not solely a visual art. It involves all the usual senses in addition to sight: touch, hearing, smell and sometimes even taste. It involves our sense of movement and time as well as many emotional senses: trepidation, fear, comfort, security, shock, astonishment, exposure, resignation, attachment, exclusion, rejection… and so on. Architecture also involves our more complex and subtle senses, of: history, nostalgia, safety, romance, comfort, domination, possession, struggle, status, subjugation, exploitation, intimidation….

In order to discuss such issues in relation to the powers of the doorway, words are necessary. But the core content of this book lies in the drawings. These are usually the plans or sections of buildings. Because drawing – whether on paper, within the space on the other side of a computer screen, or directly on the ground – is the medium through which architects design, it is also the best medium through which to understand how architecture works.

THE POWERS OF DOORWAYS

This book is about the doorway; it is also about threshold, transition, the in-between and the experience of passing through. To begin we need to pick apart our usual understanding of a doorway. We can do this by imagining how doorways might have emerged into our experience of the world.

The doorway has not always existed but it clearly has a very long history. At some time in the distant past someone somewhere must have been the first to build a wall and leave a small gap in it for access. We cannot really say that this person invented the doorway because he or she would likely have seen the entrances animals make into their dens, blinked while emerging from the darkness of a cave into bright sunlight, or perhaps wondered about the possibly mysterious consequences of squeezing through the crack in a tree split open by lightning.

Even so, we can assume that those who walked through the first built doorway must have felt they had acquired some sort of magic: a device that allowed transportation from one world into another – maybe from the danger of the plains into the safety of a protective enclosure, or from being battered by wind and rain into the seclusion of a dry shelter – in an instant.

It is likely that these people quickly became aware of what we would call the psychological power of the doorway. Maybe they experienced the sort of threshold shock we sometimes feel when we propel ourselves, too quickly for our brains to keep up, into a new and different situation: from a bright open beach into a small tent; from a quiet dressing room onto a stage in front of an audience; or from the bustle of a busy street into the quiet sanctuary of a church.

We cannot say, and it hardly matters, whether the doorway came before the discovery of fire or the invention of the wheel. But though less acknowledged, it was a step of equivalent magnitude in humanity's progress towards changing the world to accord with its own needs and desires. Our present responses to doorways seem like dim echoes of distant chords; we need to tune in to those echoes to understand the simple and the subtle ways that doorways punctuate our lives and orchestrate our experience.

The first doorway

We cannot know what form the first doorway took. Archaeologists find ancient examples built of stone but these are likely to have been preceded by generations of doorways built of less permanent materials of which little or no archaeology survives.

In this book we shall look at some of the oldest surviving doorways on earth (as well as many from other periods of history)

The mouth of a cave is a natural prototype for the doorway. It provides access into the cave and a point of transition between two distinctly different situations: one open and light – an 'outside' – and one dark and enclosed – an 'inside'. It has physical and psychological dimensions.

and analyse what they do and how they work. But we do not need to look to prehistory to find origins for the doorway; they persist in the ways we relate to the world now. When we stop somewhere in the landscape, even if only for a short while, we situate ourselves in relation to our surroundings. We find or make a home for ourselves, even if that home is no more than a patch of grass under a tree. Often the home we find or make has some sort of threshold or rudimentary doorway. We might take advantage of a 'doorway' we find amongst the rocks or between two trees, or we might make one for ourselves.

TWO RUDIMENTARY DOORWAYS (one found, one made)

As we walk across moors, through woods, along the beach… we constantly interpret, make sense of, the land in which we find ourselves. Part of that 'making sense' involves tracing a pathway, first with our eyes and then with our feet. But making sense of the world around also involves recognising places: places where we might stop and sit down for a moment to rest; places where we might shelter from the wind and rain; places where we could light a fire to cook some food.

In a varied landscape, where we have a choice of different kinds of location, we seem to have an instinct about where to set a fireplace. We choose such places for practical reasons but also for social and psychological ones too. We particularly like hollows with a clear direction of approach; we can nestle into them with our companions, slightly concealed but able to see people coming – whether friends or enemies.

A dell

On the right is a sketch of a rocky dell deep in a forest near where I live. It has been used as a place for a fire so many times over so many years that there is a mound of consolidated black ash under the fireplace. The dell is popular for the social event of a campfire because it is like a room in the landscape. The rock outcrop, undergrowth and surrounding trees provide the room with 'walls' and a 'roof' partly open to the sky. The rocks provide sitting places around the fire. The room has two clear points of entry – a 'grand front entrance' and a small 'back door'. The back door is no more than a steep narrow channel down through the rocky outcrop. The front door is defined by undergrowth encroaching on the path and by a group of trees like a porch or portico. These sentinel trees together with the undergrowth frame the approach and entrance of the room. People's hands have

We are good at recognising places in the landscape; places we can use like 'rooms'. Often these rooms have 'doorways'.

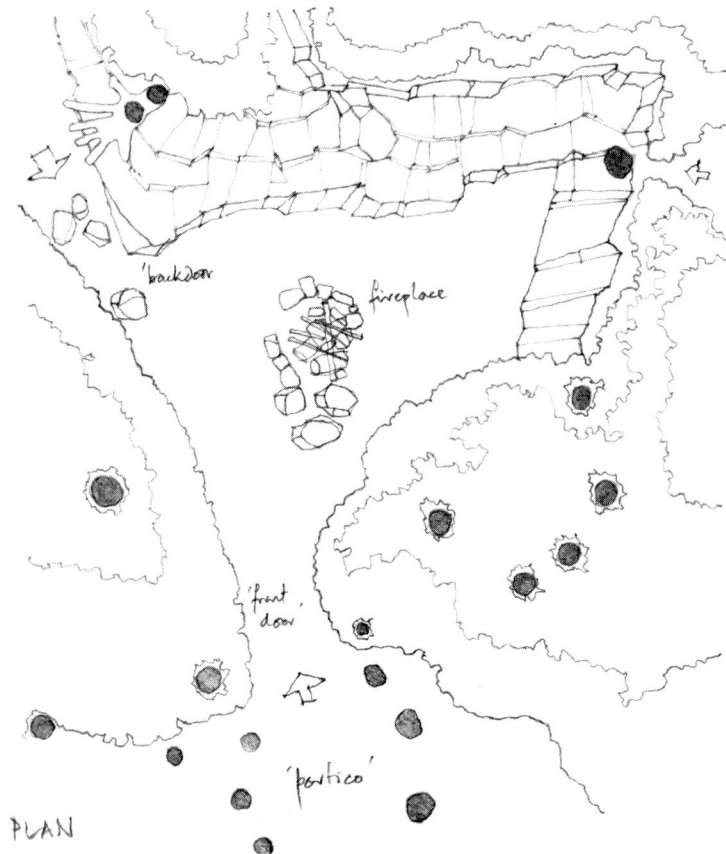

PLAN

made the fireplace with a circle of stones, and their treading feet have kept the pathway clear of brambles, but it is our sense-making minds that turn the dell into a 'room' and the trees into its 'doorway' and 'portico'.

Inside – outside

The human faculty for making sense of the world registers the transition from outside to inside too. When you pass through the natural constriction of the dell's portico and front door (see the drawing above) you feel you are stepping over a threshold between two distinctly different sets of conditions: from the gloomy woods into the sky-lit dell; from an endless confusion of trees into a distinct and definite *place*. And as you make this transition your state of being changes. You move from being a 'person outside' into

a 'person inside', from being a 'person at large' into a 'person at home', from being a 'person lost' into a 'person who knows where they are'. The catalyst of this transformation is the doorway.

And when you are on one side or the other, the doorway gives you a view into another place. From outside in the woods you look in and wonder what the dell is like inside. From inside you look out and see the dark woods and imagine what is out there. The doorway divides your world, and in doing so, provokes a sense of 'otherness'.

The plan of the dell (above) illustrates the enclosure it provides and the constriction at its doorway. The heart of this natural room is the fireplace. And the trees at its entrance provide it with a porch or portico.

A Masai night camp

The dell is a found place, modified only slightly by the building of a fireplace and the placing of logs to sit by the fire. But we construct such places from scratch too. The drawings alongside depict the sort of night camp that Masai tribesmen build to protect themselves when away from their village on a hunting expedition. It is an artificial dell – a home for the night. Like the dell in the woods this night camp has social and psychological as well as practical dimensions: it defines the place of a small group of insiders (who sleep by the fire within its enclosing form); and it provides the wandering hunters with a temporary but stable centre (focused on a fireplace and anchored to a tree) amongst the endless bushland. But unlike the dell, which provides little shelter from the elements and no real protection against intruders, this camp is built specifically to exclude. It has a wall of branches with sharp spikes, made to keep out predatory animals. Its doorway is a small gap left for the hunters to go in and out. When plugged with a clump of the same spikey branches to complete the ring of protection, the doorway becomes indistinguishable from the wall. The doorway with its 'door' is a simple and precise point of control, like a switch that can turn access into the camp on and off.

SECTION

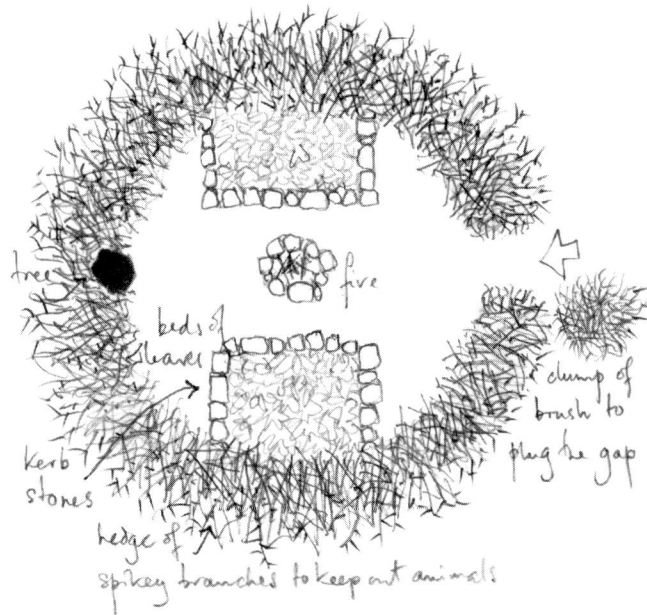

PLAN

The rudimentary examples of the dell and the Masai night camp illustrate a characteristic that is fundamental to the doorway. It is a characteristic that may at first seem obvious and not worth attention but it is nevertheless essential to the doorway's power. The doorway is an absence that we register as a presence; it is a 'nothing' – a gap – that is useful and has meaning.

This intriguing characteristic was recognised some two and a half thousand years ago by the Taoist philosopher Lao Tzu. In his *Tao Te Ching* there is a well-known passage. It mentions doorways, and reads:

> *'Thirty spokes meet in a hub;*
>> *but it is on the hole at the centre that*
>> *the use of the wheel depends.*
> *'Turn clay into a pot;*
>> *it is the space within that makes the*
>> *pot useful.*
> *'Build doorways and windows into a room;*
>> *the spaces where there is nothing make*
>> *the room usable.*
> *'So, although what we make is Something,*
> *it is the Nothing that makes it useful.'*

To the Masai builders of the spikey wall of their night camp the doorway is where they leave a gap. It is the only point around their protective circle where, initially at least (until they decide to plug it), they do not put any branches. And when I draw the plan of the night camp, the doorway is where I leave the paper untouched. It would be easy therefore to interpret the doorway as a negative (an absence) in contrast to the positive (presence) of the wall. But in our experience of space, in our moving around, the opposite is the case: it is the wall that is a negative because it stops us moving from one place to another (it says 'no'); the doorway is a positive because it lets us through.

The killing of Remus

The positive–negative dichotomy of the wall and doorway is illustrated by the following story.

According to legend, when Rome was founded, Romulus ordered first that its boundary be drawn on the ground by the furrow of a brass plough pulled by a white bull. Where the city gates were to be, the plough was lifted to leave a gap in the line.

From the moment it was drawn, this line became the defensive wall of the city, and the gap the gateway through it. Romulus's twin brother Remus made fun of these 'defences' and jumped over the line. He was promptly killed for violating the new city's boundaries. If he had walked respectfully through the gap he would have been safe.

Sometimes on the beach we do the same as Romulus. The man in the photograph on the next page is sitting in a patch of

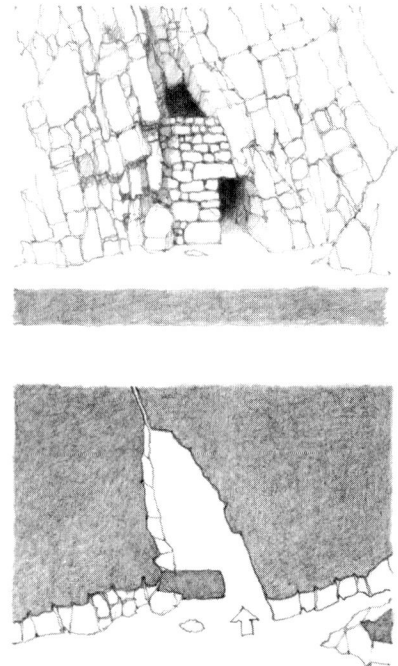

A doorway is an absence that we register as a presence.

ground defined by a furrow. It is his family's own small 'city', and all their possessions have been coralled within the loop. As in my drawing of the Masai night camp, a gap has been left for a doorway; here it has been marked with sandcastles to add emphasis to the break. It is interesting to muse on what this simple arrangement of line and gap means.

The line is clearly intended to define and take possession of a place. And though the line is not much of a physical barrier to movement, it certainly presents a psychological one. If you were a member of the man's family you could no doubt cross it with impunity; but as a stranger you would treat it with respect and walk around. If you did cross the line, and walk straight through the family's place, you would be thought delinquent; your transgression would cause affront and an argument or even a fight might ensue. Such is the power of a line.

The doorway adds a subtlety to this arrangement. It is not needed for physical reasons; there is no real wall around this place, only a line in the sand. But the doorway mitigates the psychological negative presented by the line. It symbolises the possibility of entrance and exit. By breaking the line which cuts the family off from the world outside, the doorway implies a dialogue: it suggests that the family is open

both to adventure (at the moment of the photograph most of the family are away having a swim while the father guards the fort) and to visitors, if they were to approach respectfully and seek permission to enter. Such is the power of a gap.

All this might be treated as a game and thought inconsequential. But with its simple line in the sand, and by the gap left in that line, the family has laid down some spatial rules for its relations with other people – people who are metaphorically and literally outside its circle.

And such is the hold of this rudimentary work of architecture, even over those who made it, that, by the evidence of the footprints in the sand, the doorway is actually used. (Though one suspects that this family also has its Remus, eager to subvert the spell by jumping over the line.)

We make places for ourselves on the beach. Sometimes we do this by drawing a line around a patch of sand. In this example the separation from the world implied by the line is mitigated by the provision of a 'doorway'.

We might assume that the doorway had to be invented to solve the problem of the wall, as a hole cut through a barrier for access. But if we ask the question 'which came first, doorway or wall?' we get an unexpected answer. It is the doorway, or at least its threshold, that bears the seed of the wall.

It seems obvious to say that a doorway links two places divided by a barrier; but a doorway also accentuates the division. Rather than reducing the dimensions of separation implied by a barrier, a doorway adds to them. A doorway may draw attention to a division that might otherwise not be noticed. A doorway reminds you of the place beyond the barrier, and offers the possibility of passing through from here to there.

A doorway can be the generator of a division that otherwise would not exist or at least would have no tangible manifestation. And whilst identifying a point of transition a doorway is also the location for defending that transition against transgression. Here are some examples that illustrate these properties of doorways.

A doorway to enter into darkness

In 1972 the designer Ettore Sottsass built some doorways in the desert. On the right is a drawing of one that he called a 'Doorway to enter into darkness'.

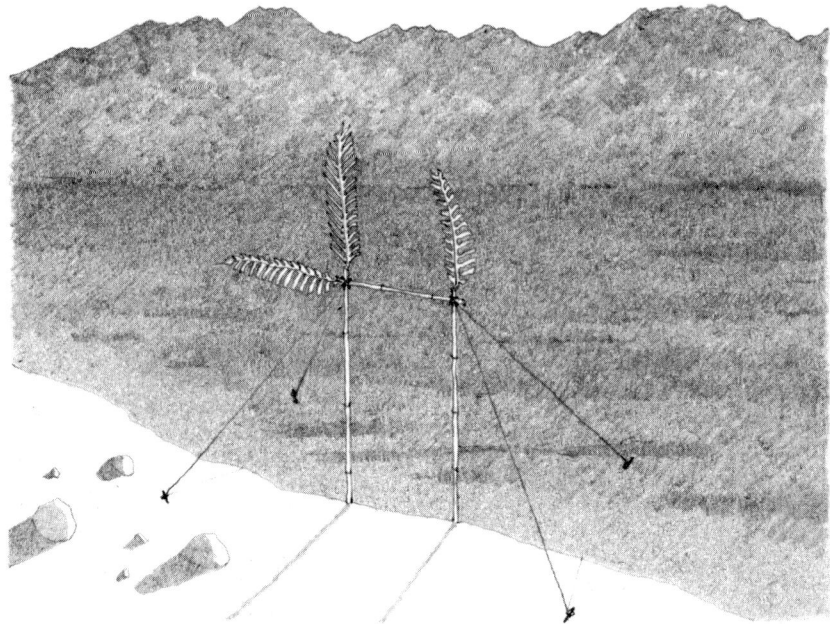

Made of sticks held in place with guy ropes and decorated with palm fronds, this doorway was positioned on the edge of a great shadow cast across the land. It was a doorway from sunlight into shade.

I did not experience this doorway in reality but, putting aside its possible poetic interpretation as a portal into 'the valley of the shadow of death', I know its presence would have changed my perception of the desert landscape, and affected my behaviour. Even as an idea recorded in a photograph* I can imagine Sottsass's doorway doing various things.

First, the doorway draws attention to a division of the land, between sunlit and

A photograph of Sottsass's 'Doorway to enter into darkness' may be found in Design Metaphors *(1988, edited by Barbara Radice) pp. 16–17. The other doorways he built in the desert included: 'There is always a door someone doesn't let you through' which was similar but decorated with leaves and criss-crossed with string (ibid. p. 18); and 'There is sometimes a door through which you are meeting your love' which was decked with flowers and framed a picturesque view of a craggy mountain across a romantically calm lake (ibid. p. 19).*

shadowed, that I might otherwise not have noticed.

Second, being a doorway (rather than just a marker or series of markers), it implies that the division between light and shadow could be registered as some sort of barrier.

Third, the doorway suggests a particular point at which that barrier of shadow might or should be penetrated. Like the doorway in the beach place (p. 15) it provides the line of division with a specific threshold or crossing point.

And fourth, whilst evoking a barrier that I might otherwise not have noticed, the doorway also tacitly invites me to step through it. But, because the doorway has made the division between sunlight and shadow seem portentous, this becomes in my mind more a challenge or a dare than an invitation. If I had been there to experience this doorway, crossing its threshold would have provoked a *frisson* of trepidation, as if something might have happened to me as I passed through into the shade. Such is the power of a threshold.

Sottsass's doorway is a small work of architecture. It is a work of architecture, rather than just sculpture, in that it potentially accommodates me (or anyone else) as an active user, inhabitant, occupant, transient… rather than merely a viewer or witness who stands outside and detached. His doorway

distinguishes between a zone of light and a zone of shadow and identifies a place for me to cross from one into the other. In doing so it evokes the idea of 'another place' or ' place beyond' and suggests that I might aspire to cross through, from here to there. This is an architectural device that we shall see has been used many times.

In all these effects it is the doorway that is the instrument of change. The doorway and its tacit invitation to pass through, creates a division that would otherwise not be there. A doorway draws together and yet keeps apart what it stands between. The wall is child of the doorway.

Doorway as parent of the wall

When houses are built, a rectangular frame of timber is positioned in the prescribed position on the edge of the floor slab to preserve the gap for the doorway whilst the walls are being built (right). As soon as the door frame is there, the walls come into existence, if only in the imagination.

Similarly, in Sicily, when someone takes possession of an unfenced parcel of land, their first task is to erect the gateway and gate. This may stand alone for a long time before the fence is built. The gate stands for and represents the barrier and establishes that the land is owned by someone.

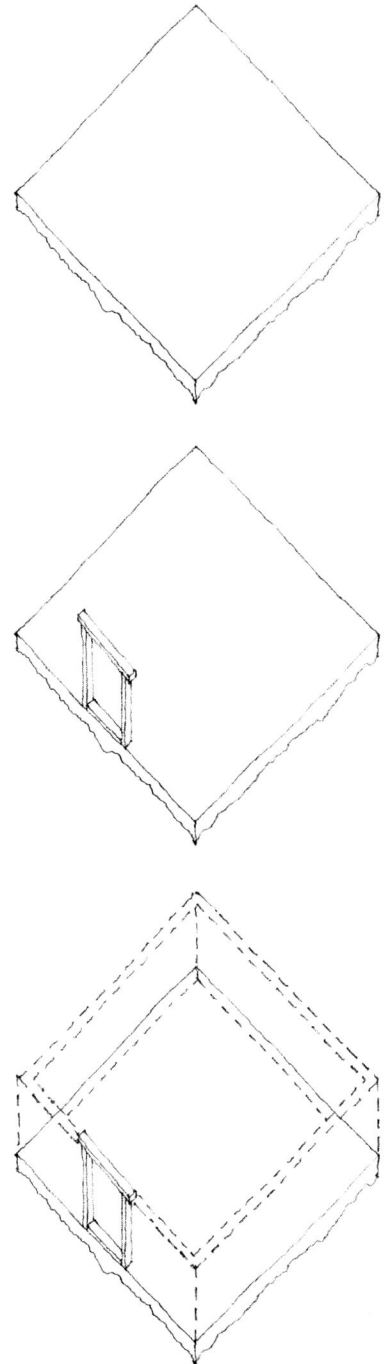

The recluse

When I encountered the place in this photograph, I drew it as a plan in my notebook (below). I took the photograph from the base of the cairn at the bottom of the plan.

This is a place where a recluse has chosen to live. The core of the place is his old caravan which is positioned close to the lowest part of a large bowl of land and near the point where a track crosses a small stream. (Alongside it is the wreckage of a previous caravan broken by a storm. The man was to die a few months after my visit, in another storm.)

At first sight it might seem that the only doorway shown is the one into the caravan. This is the entrance into the cell at the heart of the place, but there are two other, more interesting doorways in the photograph.

The man who has settled in this spot has obviously chosen it because of the seclusion and shelter of the bowl of land, the access allowed by the track, the water provided by the stream and a wonderful view of the sea and sunsets (to the left of the photograph). It is an isolated place (on the coast of one of the islands off the west coast of Scotland) the extent of which is partly defined by the surrounding hills and the cliffs down to the sea. The man's caravan

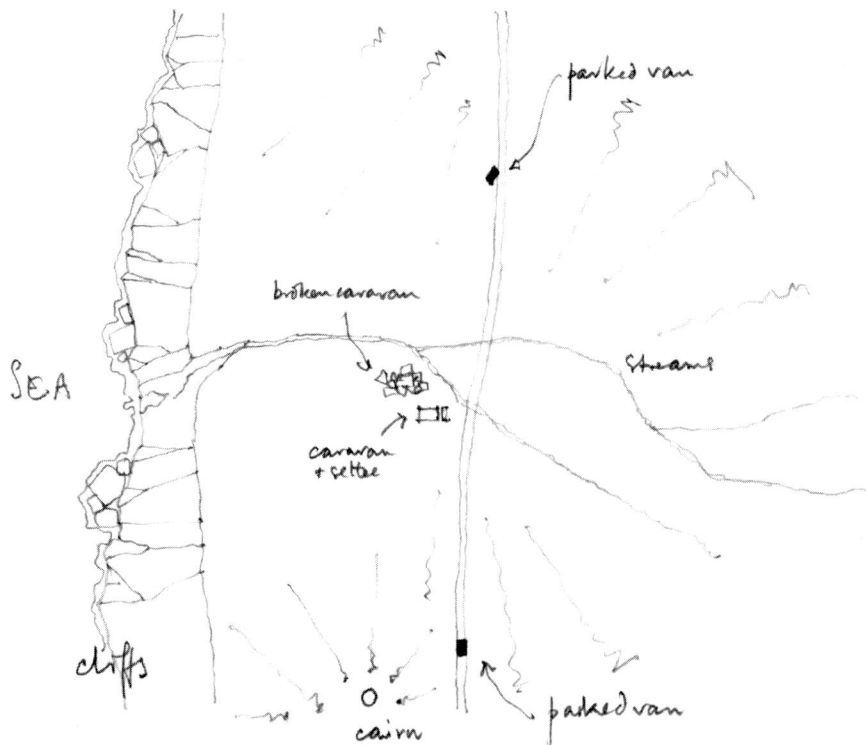

at the centre makes it clear that he considers this to be his patch of ground. It stands like a country house at the centre of its park.

But, to assert his presence and occupation of the land, the man has done more. He has parked two old trucks just where the track begins to descend into the bowl of land. (The farther one is circled in the photograph.) Like the gate lodges of a park these trucks clearly mark the limits and entrances of what the man considers to be his domain. The architecture of the place is constituted by the caravan and these two outlying trucks within the topography of the landscape.

With these trucks the man has made it clear that visitors are not welcome to pass through the 'gateways' into his land. The farther truck stands to one side of the track but the truck in the foreground clearly establishes a gateway and slams it firmly shut at the same time. The two trucks together conjure up a great circle, an implied boundary around the place, protecting the man's seclusion.

Here, even more so than in the case of Sottsass's doorway in the desert, it is the gateway that is the generator of the line of division, which though in some places vague and insubstantial is nevertheless powerful. Here even the gateway itself has no substance; it is the truck by which it is closed that conjures it into existence.

Establishing thresholds

Establishing thresholds – the evocation and construction of doorways – is one of the key ways in which we organise and manage the space of the world. Barriers establish possession and keep people, things and places apart; doorways make us aware of the place beyond, and invite us to pass through, or tell us to keep out.

Sottsass's doorway in the desert, the Sicilian landowner's gateway and the recluse's trucks are not isolated examples; they illustrate themes that can be found in all parts of the world and in all periods of human history.

Like the recluse's truck this door indicates that one should keep out of its garden (which is in Turkey), even though it would be easy enough to clamber through the gap alongside (photograph – David Unwin).

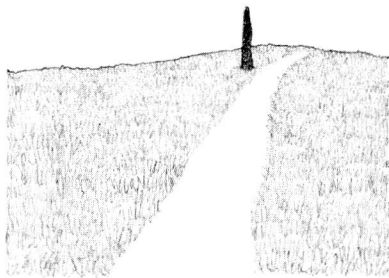

People define the gateways into their territories in different ways.

The way the recluse has used his trucks is a device for the management of space that stretches back into prehistory. It seems a core part of the language of architecture by which we impose our stories of possession and inhabitation on the land. In ancient times standing stones were similarly positioned beside pathways on boundaries to warn wandering strangers that they were entering land that belonged to a particular chief or tribe (above). Presumably the standing boundary stones also served to indicate to exiles the limits of the territory to which they were not allowed to return. These standing stones identified gateways and, like the recluse's trucks, projected boundary lines laterally across the landscape.

In more recent times both Catholic and Protestant communities in Northern Ireland have painted slogans and images on the gable ends of houses at the edges of their territories (above right). These created gateways that either admitted or excluded people according to religious allegiance. In doing so they also projected and drew attention to lines of sectarian division that stretched through the city.

Soccer on the beach

Making a doorway is easy. Boys playing soccer on a beach make a 'doorway' when they put down a pair of shoes as goalposts (below). In a small way, for the duration of the game, they change the world.

What they do is mysterious and engaging, though they treat it as nothing special. They create a fault-line in the fabric of space. By identifying its ends with shoes they generate a threshold where, if the ball goes over it, a goal is scored.

The goals in a game of football are like magnets pulling the opposing teams in opposite directions. It is not difficult to interpret them as the portals of enemy cities under

A soccer game on the beach; and the moment of transformation when one boy is belatedly made goalkeeper to protect the goal marked by a pair of training shoes (which is under imminent threat).

simultaneous attack by opposing forces. It is as if they are a single doorway split and pulled apart to create a battlefield – a zone of conflict – in the space between. During the game two of the boys are transformed into special guards – goalkeepers – stationed in the goals to stop the ball crossing the sacred threshold.

As doorway markers the two shoes on the sand are one step on from the ancient standing stone marking a territorial boundary, but they are close to the minimum needed to define a threshold precisely. (Two dots would do.)

Like the standing stone or the recluse's trucks the shoes imply not only the doorway of the goal, which transforms the ball into a score, but also the 'wall' in which it stands – the goal line that kills the ball dead.

From the shoes we infer vertical posts stretching upwards into space; but the height of the goal is left vague (and no doubt subject to occasional dispute). In a proper game of soccer both the width and height of the goal are defined exactly by the goalposts and crossbar (to obviate dispute), and the threshold itself is marked with a white line on the ground.

When the boys nonchalantly pick up the shoes at the end of the game the doorway vanishes, the fault-line in space is healed and the goalkeepers return to normal.

In Philip Pullman's trilogy *His Dark Materials* a 'subtle knife' is needed to cut openings between parallel worlds. In our real world, we generate the mystery of a threshold every time we put down a pair of shoes as goalposts.

The West Bank Wall

When the guerrilla artist Banksy wanted to question the wall Israel was in the process of building around the West Bank in 2005 he dotted onto it the shape of a soccer goal (right), complete with a pair of scissors indicating that a new gateway could be 'cut here'. If it were to be cut, it would be like the two opposing goals of the normal soccer field reunited at the half-way line between the 'teams'.

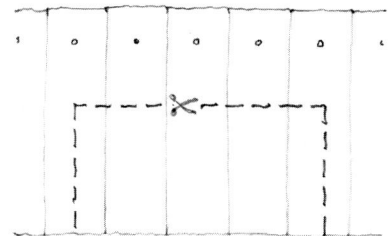

In 2005 the guerrilla artist Banksy painted the outline of a goal on the wall Israel was building around the West Bank. Like a chain, a wall is only as strong as its weakest link. If Banksy's goal was cut, the whole of the wall might as well be removed.

THE GEOMETRY OF DOORWAYS

TENDING TO THE RECTANGULAR

Built doorways are some of the most insistently rectangular elements in the world. Why? We can all think of some non-rectangular doorways: gaps in the stones of a burial chamber; arched ones in churches; circular ones in Chinese gardens; ones with a corner missing squeezed into a tight loft-space…. But, generally speaking, doorways tend towards the rectangular: with vertical sides (jambs); a horizontal threshold; and a horizontal or arched head.

There are a number of reasons for this tendency. They impinge on the issue from two different directions: the geometry of making; and the geometry of human form and movement. Neither of these takes priority. Together they exert influences that pull the doorway towards being rectangular. And together they illustrate that the doorway is an instance where the human being is in an especially close relationship with the architecture it makes to frame its being.

The geometry of making

There is a discussion of 'the geometry of making' and its influence on the form of architectural elements in *Analysing Architecture*. Briefly the expression refers to the ways in which the inherent geometry of materials influences the geometry of the forms made from them. An example is the way rectan-

gular bricks lend themselves to construction into straight and vertical rectangular walls with right-angled corners. Any deviations from this, such as the introduction of curves, inclination away from the vertical or non-right-angled corners, may not be impossible but certainly cause problems because they do not resonate with the inherent geometry of the brick.

Doorways are subject to the influence of the geometry of making.

Two challenges face the builder of a doorway in a wall. First, if the doorway is to be closable then the construction and mechanism of a door has to be taken into account. Second, if the wall is to continue above the height of the doorway then it must be supported in some way.

The door

In the Masai night camp (p. 13) the issue of building the wall above the doorway does not apply. And the door by which the access through the wall is closed is no more than another clump of the same spikey branches. The issue of harmonising the shape of the gap with the geometry of the door hardly arises; nor does that of providing a mechanism by which it can be opened or closed; it is no more than a matter of pulling the clump into the gap or pushing it back out.

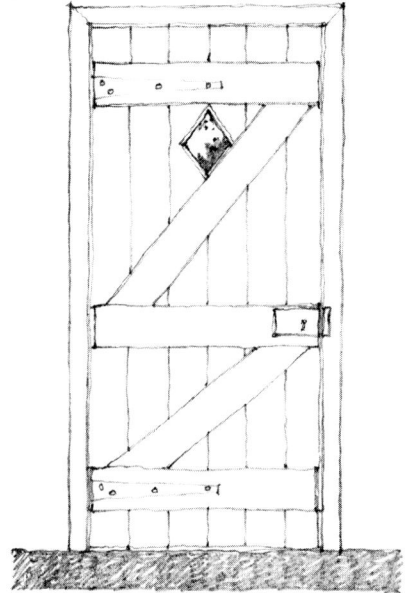

Doorways and their doors tend to be rectangular partly because of the geometry of making.

In the natural world, examples of 'doors' are rarer than 'doorways'. It is plausible to suggest that at a moment in the distant past someone did invent the door. Its principles are: that it should fit its doorway; that it should allow through and keep out what it is supposed to; that it be openable and closable; and that it be light enough to move. Two other factors also come into play: the desirability of it being fixable in place, so that it cannot be opened by whom or what it is intended to keep out; and the geometry of making the door itself.

These principles and factors are illustrated by the simple gate in the photograph alongside. Taking them in reverse order:

– the gate is constructed of reasonable straight pieces of timber; seven uprights fixed to two horizontal ledges with a diagonal brace to stop it going out of shape;

– it is fixable in place by its hinges and by a catch (hidden from view);

– the construction means the gate is light and easy to move;

– its hinges mean that it can be opened and closed;

– and it is fit for purpose in that it keeps sheep out of the garden whilst allowing the gardener through.

Four out of five of these principles and factors lead to the gate being rectangular. It is easier to make that way, and the hinges

would not work if it was not.

This gate closes against the side of a house but the wall against which the gate is hung responds to the rectangularity of the gate with a vertical edge. The ground plane and threshold are horizontal so that the gate can swing open.

Most doors follow these principles and take into account these factors. Through history, until large sheets of material were available, doors have been constructed of combinations of vertical and horizontal pieces of timber. Many still are. And hinges remain the simplest, most efficient and reliable means of keeping a door in place whilst allowing it to be opened and closed.

A simple gate illustrates the basic principles of the geometry of making a door.

Lintols and arches

The second challenge is to support the wall above the doorway. There are subtle variations to the structural response to this challenge but they resolve down into two alternatives: the beam (lintol) and the arch.

Some of the oldest doorways on earth have lintols. It is the most straightforward way to span across a gap.

The upper photograph on this page illustrates a lintol at the temple of Hagar Qim on the island of Malta. Because the stone has been carved into shape this is quite a sophisticated example. It would have been preceded by many instances of rough boulders being balanced on uprights. Nevertheless this Maltese example is reputed to be more ancient than the pyramids – some five thousand years old and maybe two and a half thousand years older than the classical temples of Greece.

Together with the ground or threshold, the horizontal lintol completes the rectangle of the doorway. Bearing in mind the geometry of making it is a relatively straightforward opening to close with a door. This holds true whether the wall is made of stone, timber, steel, concrete, straw bales, glass or of whatever else walls may be built. (The example on the right is from the house alongside the gate on the previous page.)

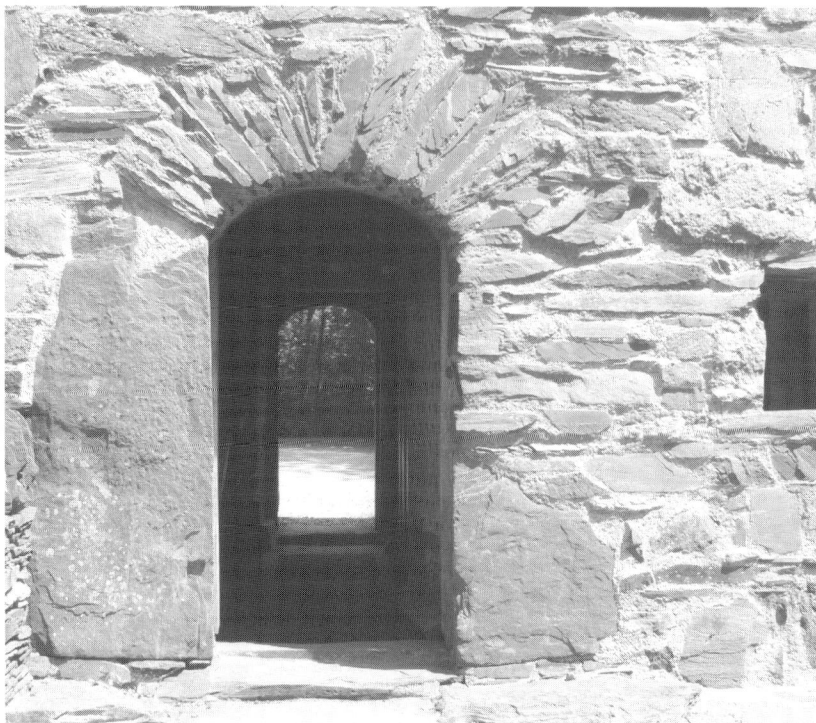

The alternative way to span the opening of a doorway is with an arch. Its invention involved more imagination than that of the lintol. It depends on realising that if you wedge small stones into the top of a doorway they will not fall into the opening and will support weight above.

Building an arch presents a few problems. First, temporary support (centring) is needed to keep the small stones (voussoirs) from falling until the last (the key-stone) is in place. Second, because the voussoirs want to fall to the ground they push on the walls on either side of the opening, hence there needs to be substantial mass in the wall to resist this tendency of the arch to spread. And third, the natural shape of an arch is curved, so the rectangle of the doorway is lost; this conflicts with the geometry of making of a door.

It is slightly harder to make a door with a curved head than a rectangular one. The upper photograph alongside shows a rough arched doorway built of large and small pieces of slate. (It is from the same house illustrated on the title page of this chapter.) Notice how the large irregular stones have been shaped along one side to provide the opening with vertical jambs. Smaller stones form the arch.

The lower photograph shows the interior of the same doorway. Here the head of the opening has been made square (supporting the wall above with a lintol) so that a rectangular (easier to make) door will fit.

An arch is not the most straightforward shape for a door.

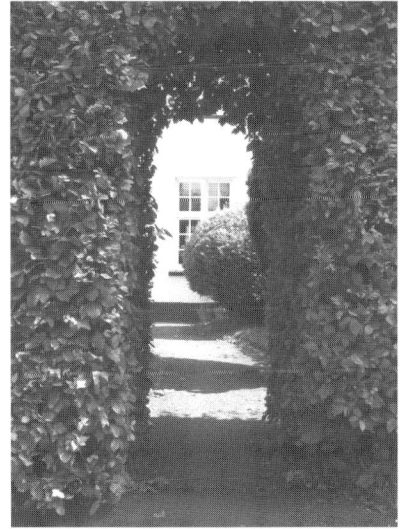

Books through the literature of architecture have discussed the relative characteristics of the lintol and the arch. Nowadays there are many variations on doors and their mechanisms for hinging and fixing. There are doors that do fit arches, sliding doors, roller shutter doors, revolving doors, automatic doors…. There is a mass of technical literature on hinging and locking mechanisms. It would be a diversion to discuss any of these issues further. Here the intention is to look at the geometry of doorways as it relates to the organisation of space, rather than fabric and construction, and how it affects our experience of the places we make.

Human form and movement

Doorways do not tend to be rectangular only because of the way in which they and their doors are made and work. Doorways tend to be rectangular even when their shape is not influenced by the geometry of making. The photographs on the right show three doorways: a doorway cut through living rock (in Cappadocia); another through a slab of stone (in the same Maltese temple of Hagar Qim); and a third the arch through our front hedge (B in the plan on p. 170). None has a door or gate. And in none does the material of the wall necessarily suggest, through the geometry of making, that the opening should be rectangular. Some other influence is coming into play.

The primary purpose of a doorway is to let us through. Its shape relates to ours and the way we interpret the world. In the

The geometry of making is not the only reason why doorways tend to be rectangular.

case of the goal marked by the training shoes we assumed that they projected posts vertically into the air. The vertical seems right; there is an infinity of possible projections at angles but there is only one vertical. We assume that a shoe implies this one vertical.

Also, in the case of Romulus's gateway, when we replaced the furrows with courses of stone, we would tend to make them vertical so that they would be stable (their weight would act directly down through the always vertical line of gravity). (This is another aspect of the geometry of making.)

When we encounter a doorway which does not have a horizontal ground plane or vertical or nearly vertical sides we find it feels uncomfortable. It seems in conflict with our sense of horizontality and verticality.

The cave opening in the photograph is wide enough and high enough to pass through easily. But as we walk through we might be inclined to lean a little to the right. We would be concerned about hitting our heads on the rock on the left or tripping on the rock at the bottom right. In that this 'doorway' is in conflict with our own innate geometry, walking through it feels less than comfortable.

From the beginning of doorways there has been a tendency to make them rectangular and their sides vertical not only because of the influence of the geometry of

making but also to make them in accord with our own form and movement.

The picture opposite is of the interior of West Kennet Long Barrow in Wiltshire (UK). It is thought to have been built a few hundred years earlier than the Maltese temple on p. 27, around 3700 BC. Despite the irregularity of the stones from which this doorway is built, its nascent rectangularity and verticality is apparent.

Human beings apply geometry to the world. Architecture is a prime vehicle of human geometry. And doorways are a particular manifestation of it.

'Doorways' with sloping sides conflict with our presumption of verticality and make us feel uncomfortable.

Imposing our geometry on the world

West Kennet was apparently built as an artificial cave. But its architect replaced the geologically determined geometry of caves with one that is in accord with our own.

The ubiquity of the doorway rectangle is a subtle and frequent reminder of the orthogonal dimensions of our being. (In *Analysing Architecture* I called them 'the six directions plus centre'.) The sides of a doorway resonate with our sides; the lintol is above our heads and the threshold under our feet. Its opening is a frame for our form and our passage forward. As we move through it (in time) the doorway is first in front of us and then behind. The doorway implies a three-dimensional cross – with six rather than four arms – and is a direct representation of the three space dimensions and one temporal by which we situate ourselves in the world.

The orthodox doorway represents our presence even when we are not using it. Sottsass's doorway in the desert (p. 16) is built of sticks rather than stones but by its rectangularity and its verticality (as well as its dimensions) it tells us who it is for; it is specifically a doorway for a human being to 'enter into darkness'.

Even so, some architects choose to distort the geometry of doorways as a challenge to orthodoxy (right).

Distorted geometry

The photograph (right) shows one of the doorways into the Fire Station at the Vitra Factory in Switzerland. It was designed by Zaha Hadid and built in 1994. Throughout the building, orthogonal geometry is distorted, as a challenge to orthodox ways of thinking about form and space. The challenge is also to the geometry of making and to the relationship between people and the spaces they occupy. This doorway, however, illustrates a slight compromise with the geometry of making: the head and threshold have to be parallel so that the door will slide.

The geometry of a built doorway emanates from and resonates with our own... or not.

All the examples in this chapter are taken from the building in the photograph above. It is called La Congiunta and stands in the Swiss countryside near the small town of Giornico. It was designed by Peter Märkli and built in 1992. It is a gallery for the exhibition of the work of sculptor Hans Josephsohn.

The building is made of concrete and has one floor raised about 600mm (2') from the ground level around, so you have to step up into it. It has only one door from the outside and is divided into seven compartments. All the doorways between the compartments appear to be the same size, rectangular with raised thresholds, and proportioned for the passage of human beings. None has a door.

The entrance door has an industrial metal door bolted onto the outside. The roofs of the compartments are of various heights. None of them has a window. All are lit by clerestory or skylight. The plan is alongside. The proportions of the building are apparently dictated by musical harmonic ratios. (To get into the gallery you have to collect a key from a bar in the town.)

Because the building is very simple (yet subtle) it demonstrates some of the powers of doorways very clearly. In this chapter we will look at doorways as picture frames, as points of view and as reference points or datums. I shall leave you to work out where on the plan each photograph was taken.

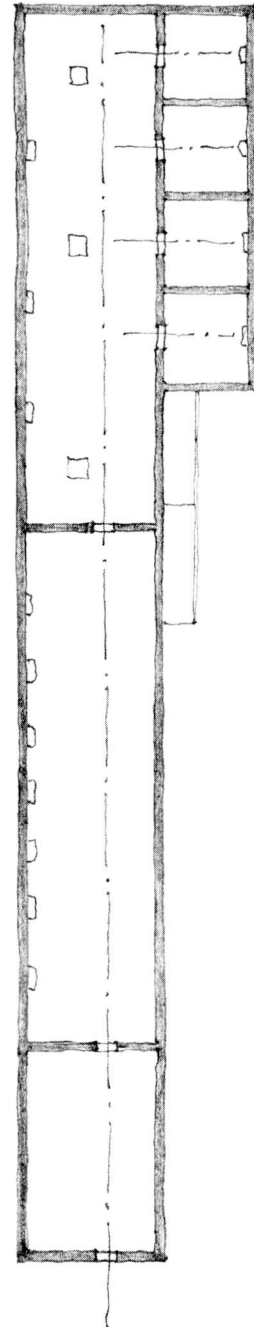

Doorway as picture frame

Once you have made a doorway you realise that it does various things that maybe you had not predicted. One of these is that it frames what you see through it. The rectangle it makes separates the place on the other side of the doorway from where you are; it also makes it into a picture, as if painted or projected onto a screen stretched across the opening. One can imagine playing this game with Sottsass's doorway in the desert, framing various picturesque views of the distant mountains.

The metaphors are compelling: the doorway was probably the archetype of the picture frame; the word *camera* is the Italian for room, and a camera's shutter is a doorway that lets the picture in to strike the photosensitive film or screen; the pupil of the eye is a doorway that allows in the image of the outside world, projects it onto the retina and into the brain within the cell of the skull.

The doorway is a fulcrum between the space you occupy and the 'other world' you can see through it. Its rectangle creates a geometric datum against which what one sees is measured. The doorway imposes its straight lines and rightangles, counterpointing the perspective or natural irregularity of the picture it frames. It mediates between here and there, and between the natural – the world distorted by perspective – and the intellectual – the perfect rectangle of the doorway.

A doorway also frames what stands on its threshold. When we take photographs, particularly at weddings it seems, we pose people either on the threshold of a doorway or framed by the rectangle of the doorway in the background. Apart from the symbolic connotations (which will be discussed later in this book), this device of the photographer has the effect of putting the subjects of the photograph in their place. The doorway provides a specific point on or in relation to which they can stand. (It also has the effect of creating a visual resonance between the rectangle of the doorway in the picture and that of the picture itself.)

The geometric regularity of a doorway imposes a controlling frame on what it contains. An architect can use the frame of a doorway to compose a particular picture of the world on the other side.

Doorway as point of view

A doorway is a fixed point; its threshold is specific, a place where you know where you are – you are standing in the doorway. It is where you first enter a room. It is the point at which you get your first full view of the place you are entering. An architect can compose things accordingly; so that a person's first view of the place they have entered is the most affecting.

Doorway as point of reference

Because a doorway is a specific point and one through which we enter a place, we tend to use it as a datum, a reference point according to which we know where we are and how to get out. In La Congiunta there is no possibility of getting lost. It is always easy to move to a point where you can see the doorway through which you entered from outside. That doorway, bright with light, is a constant datum.

The view of the entrance doorway is possible because the doorways of the main compartments of the gallery are aligned through the length of the building with the way in/out: they share an axis.

DOORWAY AXIS (making linkages)

It is part of the innate geometry of a doorway that it creates an axis. The axis created by a doorway is one of the most powerful and one of the most frequently encountered ways in which doorways are used architecturally. Determining who discovered the effect is as impossible as determining who invented the doorway or the door. The discovery is undoubtedly a human one; it depends on a sophisticated combination of eye and mind to recognise that a doorway generates an axis.

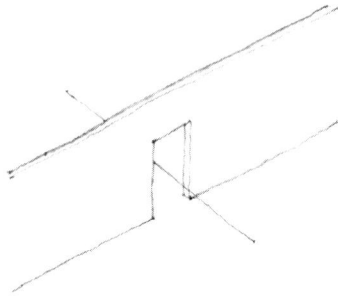

Skara Brae

Whenever and wherever the doorway axis was discovered it had become established in the common language of architecture by five thousand years ago. By that time it is found even in examples geographically distant from the regions usually considered to be the sources of human civilisation.

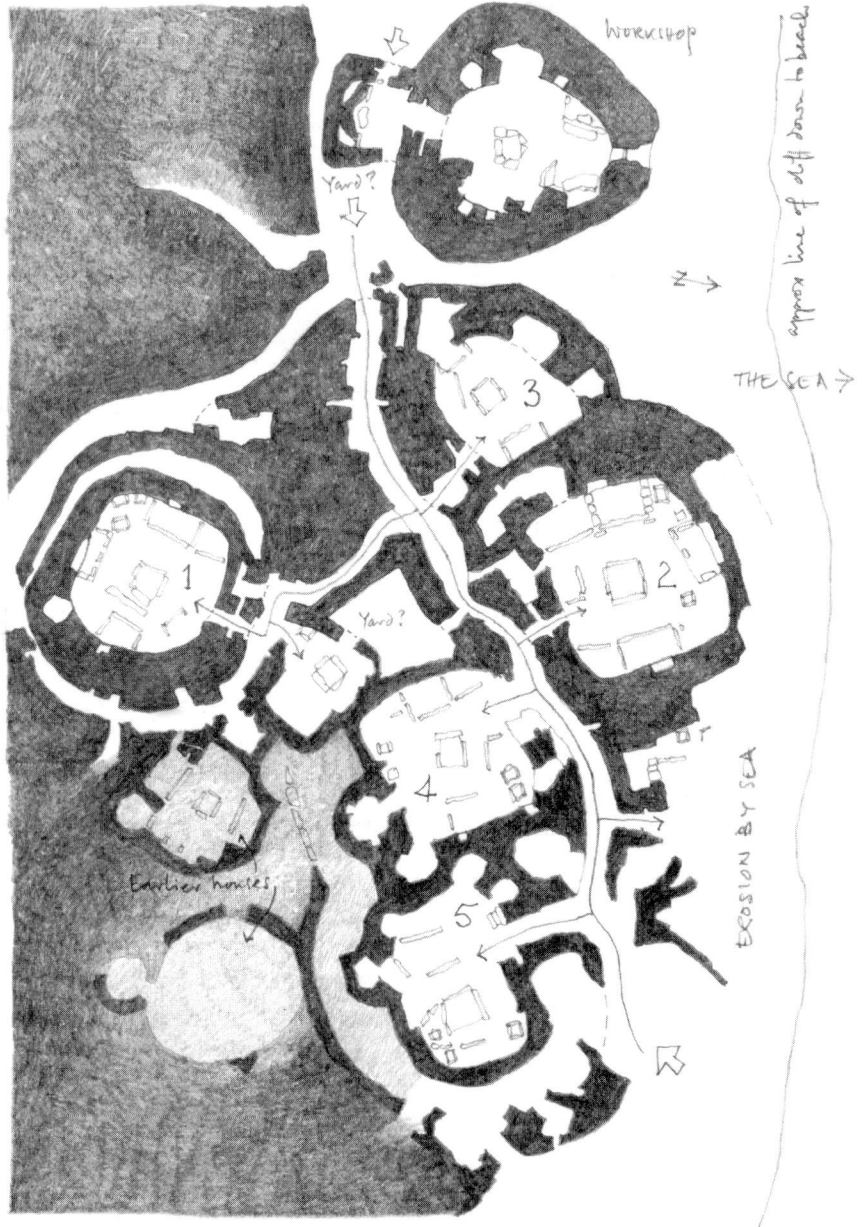

The houses at Skara Brae on Orkney were built around 2500 BC. Five surviving dwelling units are shown in the plan above. The variety of their layouts suggests that the

Some of these Stone Age houses exhibit the architectural idea of the doorway axis.

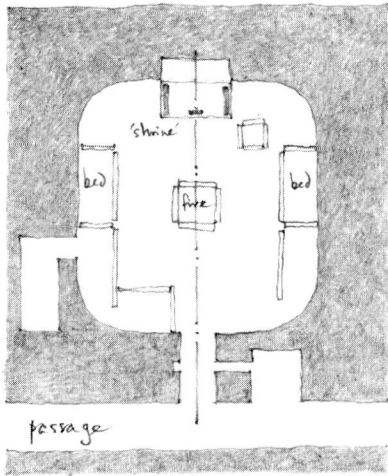

idea of the doorway axis may have been for these builders a fairly recent acquisition. Two of the houses (3 and 5 on the plan) do not have axial plans; their elements are irregularly disposed according to use. One (4) has a plan that is verging on the axial. And two (1 and 2) have plans that are clearly intended to be axial. Access to all the houses is by way of a covered crawl passage. The doorways of houses 1 and 2 are approximately on axis with their central fireplaces and, against the wall opposite the doorway, a stone 'dresser' which may have been a shrine or storage place for valuable items.

An idealised version of the plan is shown above. The arrangement of the plans of these two houses makes them seem more important than the other houses in the group. By their alignment, the dresser shrine, fireplace and doorway give the internal spaces of these houses an organising architectural idea that the other houses do not share. The plans of the other houses are more irregular; less formed according to a geometric discipline.

It might be thought that the dresser shrine (shown in the photograph above right) was the generator of the axis, just as we might think of the altar as the generator of the axis of a church or temple; but it is more likely that, with the fireplace occupying its customary position at the centre of the room, the dresser shrine was deliberately positioned opposite the doorway; i.e. the generator of the axis was the doorway. It places the person entering the room in a specific position, and the dresser shrine is purposefully positioned in relation to that human axis as a reminder, to anyone entering the house, of the wealth and status of the inhabitants.

Two other observations may be made. First, the axis is not an axis of approach to the dresser shrine; the fireplace is in the way so you have to walk around it. The linkage between the doorway and the dresser shrine was conceived as a visual and abstract axis rather than one of continuity of pathway. And second, the tightness of the passage outside the house makes it clear that the doorway axis was conceived as an internally directed one. It does not project outwards from the room to anything outside, but is contained within.

Left: the idealised plan of an axial Skara Brae house.

Right: a 'dresser shrine' with a fireplace in the centre of the floor in front of it.

The doorway axis

The axis that a doorway creates depends on the geometry given it by the human form. It is as if we make doorways in our own image. Just as the axial symmetry of a human body, reinforced by its forward-dominant line of sight and direction of movement, introduces an axis into the world, so too does the body's image – the doorway. When a body stands in a doorway its axis is coincident with that of the doorway. In this position not only is the person standing on the threshold between one place another but is aligned with the axis of its own frame.

The doorway's axis persists without the presence of the person. The person's axis is mobile but the doorway's is fixed. It establishes a fixed line that stretches through space in both directions. The doorway makes the person's axis permanent. Though the doorway axis persists without the person, its power derives from the person's presence. The axis becomes a datum to which the person may relate themselves at any point inside or outside the doorway.

The doorway axis establishes a linkage between the spaces into which it stretches. It can be used to establish a linkage between specific things or places. When an object (such as a Skara Brae dresser shrine) is placed on a doorway axis the architectural

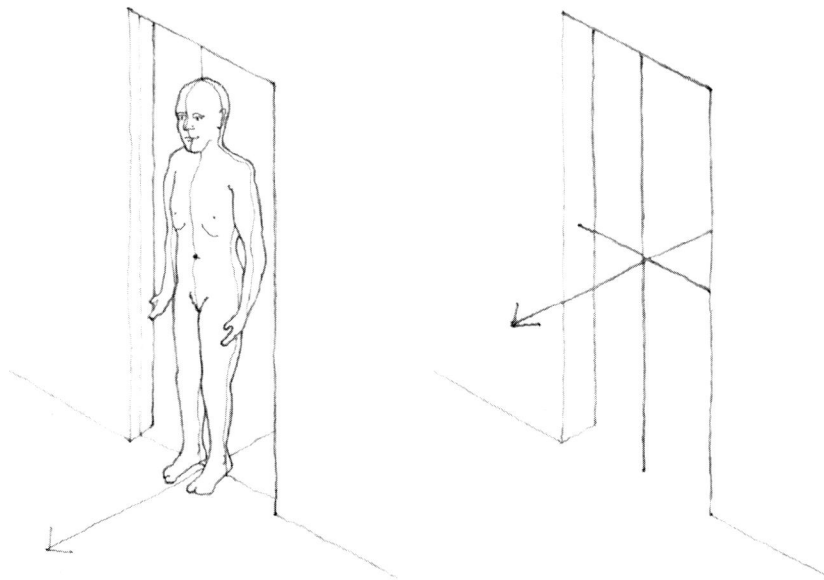

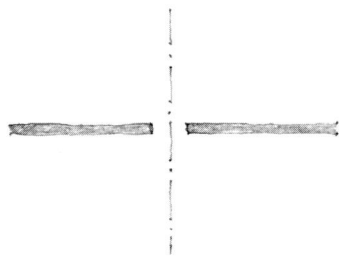

ESTABLISHMENT OF AXIS

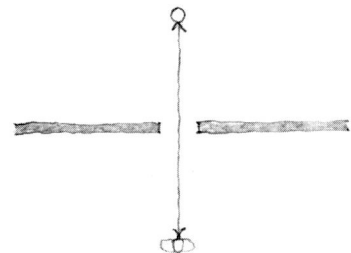

AXIAL LINKAGE

A doorway is in the image of the human being for whom it is made. It establishes the six directions plus centre in its own form.

relationship imbues it with importance. When a person is in the doorway, or has just passed through it, they are, by the instrument of the doorway, placed in a special relationship with the object. See alongside:

1. If the doorway is large enough for a person to see the important object through it then the special relationship can extend through the doorway to the world outside. The doorway is like a 'sight' (a gunsight) holding the axis in place.

2. The doorway can be like a 'gun' in that its axis can act to project the presence of an important person or a sacred object out into the world. This is a device that is often used in churches and temples. The doorway axis of an ancient Greek temple projected the presence of the god within to the distant horizon and specifically to the rising sun.

3. The doorway can imply that the person might approach or aspire to approach the important object. This is a device often used in art galleries where important paintings are placed on axis with a doorway, drawing viewers in towards that particular painting.

The doorway axis is one of the most powerful devices in architecture. It has been used through history in all cultures. It has been used so often that one might feel that it has become a cliché. Even so it has many subtleties and variations.

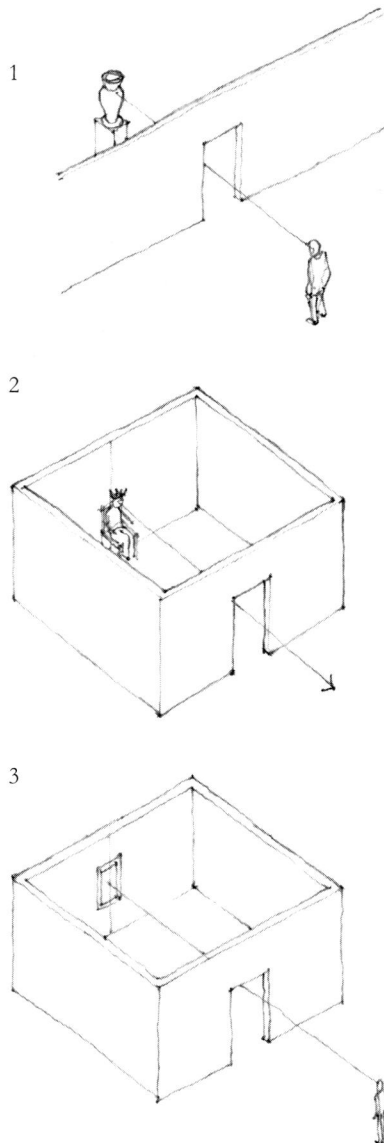

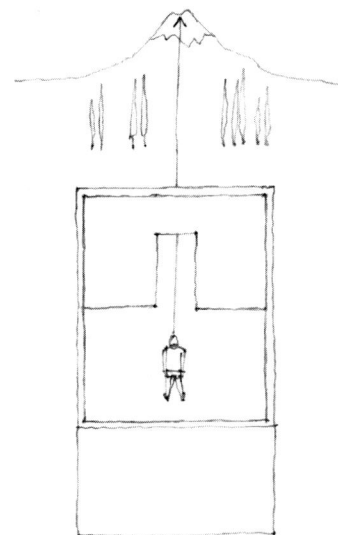

1

2

3

A doorway axis can establish a linkage between a room and an important object (maybe a sacred mountain) in the distance.

Here are some examples from the many thousands available. Each of these selected examples illustrates an extra subtlety attaching to the use of the doorway axis.

Maltese temple – progress to a goal

The temple at Tarxien (right), like that of Hagar Qim on pp. 27 and 29, dates from around 3000 BC. In these and other Maltese temples, doorways seem to have held special significance. It is as if they were built as ceremonial sequences screened from the world outside by their megalithic walls banked around with earth. Archaeological understanding of these temples is limited.

The sequential doorways of a Maltese temple are arranged along their collective axis. One doorway leads to the next, and the doorway axis of one doorway is reinforced by those of the others. A person is irresistibly drawn forward from one section of the temple to the next.

A complexity in Tarxien is that two sequences of doorways collide in a seemingly unresolved way. Nevertheless it has the longest axial doorway sequence in any Maltese temple. The sequence begins at the uncomfortable collision of axes near the centre of the plan and stretches through three doorways to a fourth, which is the altar at the focus and culmination of the axis. This composition of doorways creates a strong sense of progression towards a goal.

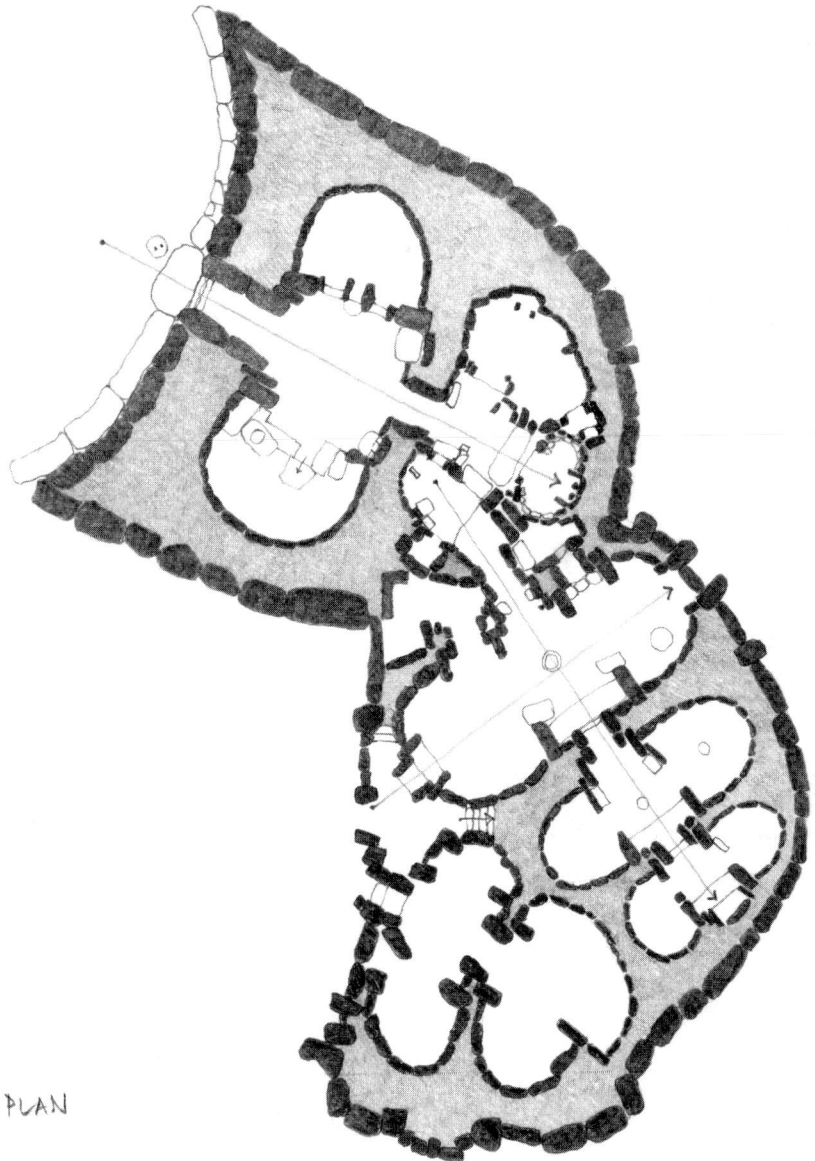

As in the Skara Brae houses, the sequential doorways of Maltese temples create an internally directed axis. There is little evidence to suggest that the Maltese temple builders considered that their doorway axes could stretch outwards into the landscape. The magnetic pull they create

PLAN

The importance of the threshold to Maltese temple builders is evident in the high sills they sometimes gave their doorways and their occasional choice of special stones (maybe with strange markings) as sill stones.

is inwards, towards the focal altar. Passing through each doorway may have been associated with different stages in initiation ceremonies, or different levels of spiritual separation from the outside world.

Beach place – the axis breaks free

On p. 15 we saw a picture of a man sitting inside his family's place on the beach. It was anchored to a rock, marked with a loop of line in the sand and provided with a doorway. His family's possessions were protected within it. The photograph on the right shows another place on the beach. It too is anchored to a rock, marked with a line and provided with a doorway. But this place is different in that it is laid out according to the discipline of a doorway axis.

The plan of this place is very similar to that of an axial Skara Brae house except that the rock has taken the place of the dresser shrine, and the towel that of the fireplace. Here, in contrast to Skara Brae and the Maltese temples, the doorway axis is not contained within the room but projects out into the world, in the direction of the sea and the distant horizon. The rock, from being a nondescript rock on the beach, has been transformed; the doorway has generated a special relationship between it and the sea. The towel lies on this axis too.

This beach place is a contemporary example of a primitive idea. For a very long time people have been fascinated by the magical sense of linkage that can be generated by a doorway. Ancient burial mounds and henges have their entrances aligned with sunrises and sunsets. Greek temples have their doorways facing the rising sun or the peak of some distant sacred mountain. And mosques are oriented to Mecca.

A doorway, even if only a line in the sand, can, by its axis, create a linkage between an object or a person and the distant horizon.

Mihrab – an axis to the unseen centre

In contrast to the beach place on the previous page, the dominant axis of a mosque is generated by a symbolic rather than an actual doorway. The focus of a mosque is its *mihrab*, positioned in the *qibla* wall to indicate the precise direction of Mecca. It tells worshippers the direction in which they should pray.

The doorway axis established by the *mihrab* is not one through which a person may look or pass. It is an abstract axis established by the architecture of the mosque. In some cases, on the opposite side of the world from Mecca, these axes may stretch for thousands of miles curving around the surface of the earth. The power of these symbolic doorways is to establish a relationship, a linkage, between the worshipper and the focus of the Islamic faith, the *Ka'ba* in Mecca.

The plan on this page is of the Shah mosque in Isfahan, Iran. It illustrates various instances of the power of the doorway axis. First, as in all mosques, the *mihrab* indicates the direction of Mecca. Second, this is a mosque of the Persian type, which means that it has a courtyard at its centre with a large doorway – an *iwan* – leading from the courtyard into the room with the *mihrab*; in this arrangement the *mihrab* itself becomes a point of focus on the doorway axis of the *iwan*.

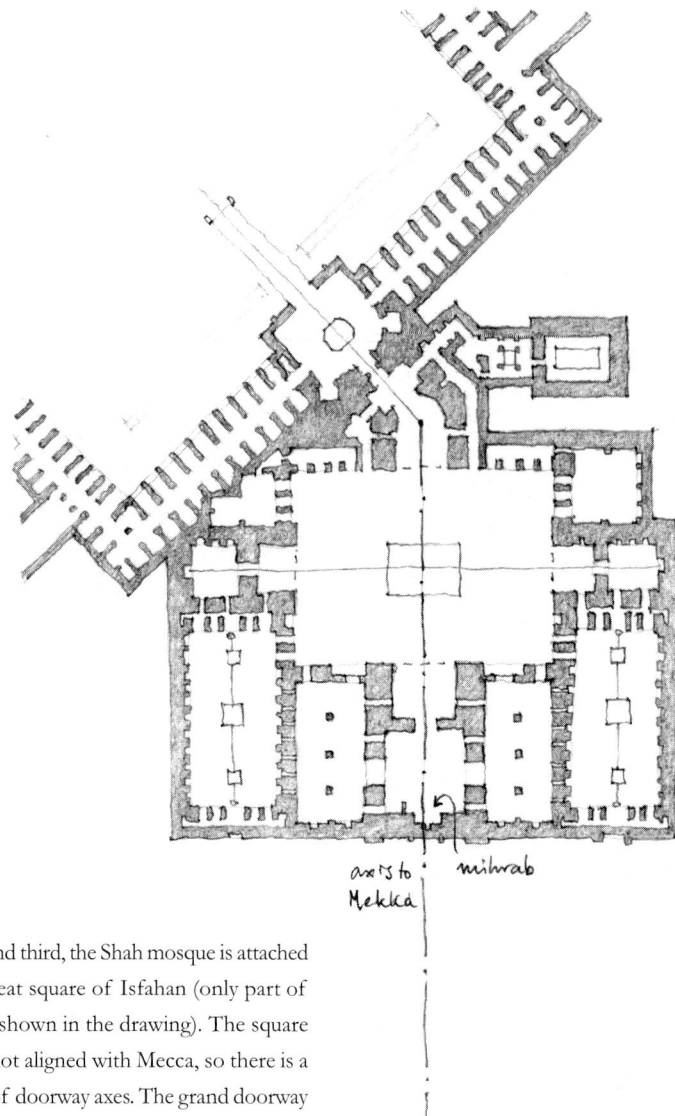

And third, the Shah mosque is attached to the great square of Isfahan (only part of which is shown in the drawing). The square itself is not aligned with Mecca, so there is a conflict of doorway axes. The grand doorway between the square and the mosque has to accommodate a change in direction, one that links the city to Mecca.

The doorway axis is not solely an architectural device but an axis of religious devotion too. In *The Art of Islam* (1976) Titus Burkhardt wrote that:

> '*the* mihrab *is the gateway to the unseen, and the* iwan *which stands before it is its face, while the gateway to the mosque summarizes the entire sanctuary, since the function of the sanctuary is precisely to be a gateway to the hereafter.*'

At its junction with the great square of Isfahan, the Shah mosque manages a change of direction by means of doorway axes.

ELEVATION

Projecting the human axis

The doorway axis has been used frequently in religious architecture. It can establish a linkage between the individual and a sacred object or place – an altar, the image of a god or a sacred place in the distance. Where it projects the sacred power of an object or place out into the world, the architectural device of the doorway axis becomes an instrument of religious dominion. It represents an assertion and manifests a proposition: that such-and-such a god or religion holds sway across the land.

In deference to religion, political and military leaders have been more circumspect about using the doorway axis to express their personal power. Nevertheless, sometimes those who have felt themselves to be deserving have used doorway axes to project their status and presence out into the world.

In his design for the Villa Rotonda (right, 16thC, near Vicenza in Italy) the architect Andrea Palladio did this for all human beings. With its plan determined by a concentric series of squares and circles, the villa establishes a centre point to be occupied by a person. The villa's four doorways, reinforced by their porticoes and steps, project axes out across the Italian landscape. They imply that the power of the human being stretches to the horizon and beyond.

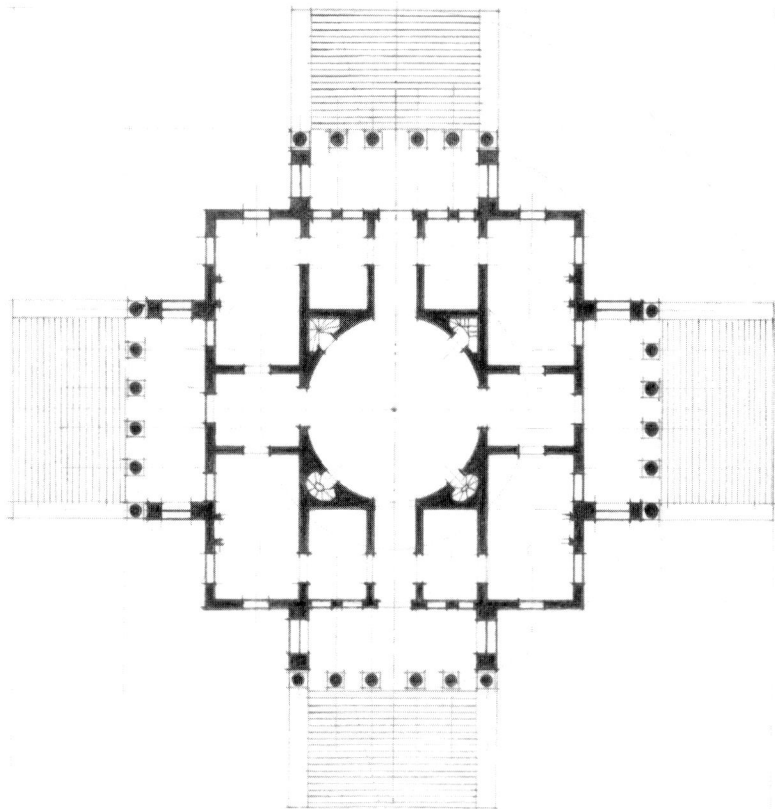

PLAN

Palladio's Villa Rotonda uses doorway axes to make a philosophical point about the position and status of human beings in the world.

Enfilade – drawing you forward

In some great houses the rooms are arranged not off corridors but as a long interconnected sequence. This arrangement is called *enfilade*. It is appropriate this is a French word since the device originated in French Baroque palaces in the seventeenth century. The example on the right is a great English house – Petworth – to which major work was done in the eighteenth century.

The rooms along the garden front of the house (to the left in the plan) are arranged *enfilade*. Typically the doorways are aligned, so that when they were all open there would be an impressive vista from one end of the house almost to the other. It is usual that the doorways are not positioned on the axis of the rooms, but to the side nearer the windows. It was probably found inconvenient to create a virtual circulation route down the centres of the rooms; to one side works better, and the window side, away from the fireplaces along the centre wall of the house, leaves the warm side of the rooms clear for occupation.

Such houses are these days usually open to visitors. The doors *enfilade* are left open, and the sequence draws the train of visitors through from room to room.

[You might also recall that in the film *Spellbound* (1945) Alfred Hitchcock used the image of doorways opening *enfilade* to represent the progressive depths of the human psyche.]

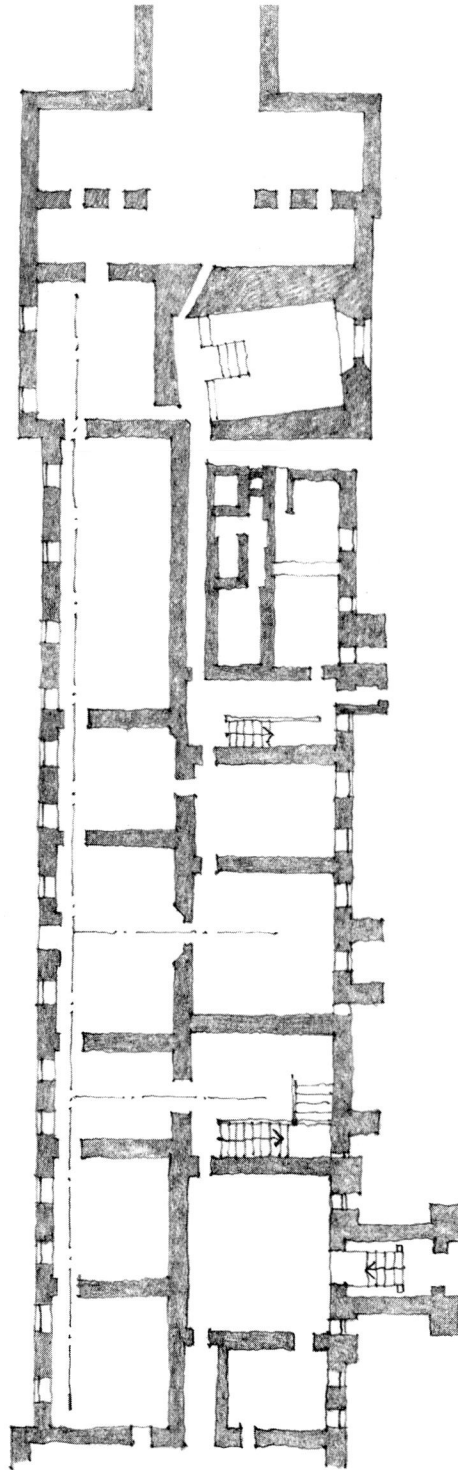

Doorways enfilade *draw the eye, mind and body through from room to room.*

Establishing a datum

Some one and a half thousand years earlier, the House of Pansa belonged to a wealthy citizen of Pompeii. The plan is on the right. Its doorway axis, which stretches from the entrance through the whole house, enhances the status of the house, implying that it is disciplined; it establishes a datum to which everything in the house relates. The street stops the axis projecting further out into the world.

If you entered the house as a guest you would have been impressed by the axial view through the entrance *atrium* and *tablinum* to the columned peristyle garden at the heart of the house and to the *oecus* – the principal entertainment room of the house – beyond that. Entering as the owner or a member of the family you would no doubt have been equally reassured of your own standing by the control exerted by that same axis.

The house is not a temple, and the doorway axis does not generate an axial route of movement through the house. The pathways through the house have to pass around the *impluvium* in the centre of the *atrium*, around the side of the *tablinum*, and around the peristyle to reach the *oecus*. Thus guests would have been tacitly invited to admire the whole house before reaching the place where they would be fed. They would

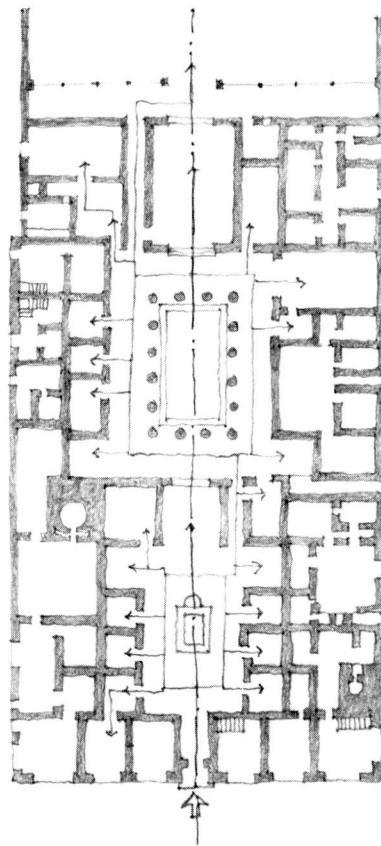

The plan of the House of Pansa in Pompeii. Its doorway axis provides a datum around which movement through the house 'dances' – like a melody around a drone in folk music.

have been led on a genteel 'dance' around the persistent doorway axis, to which they had attached themselves as they entered the house, but which they might occupy again only momentarily until they reached the *oecus*. This doorway axis, though not a route, holds its house together like a skewer.

Doorway axis as an armature

Because of the linkages that doorway axes make they can be used to create an armature that holds a complex of spaces together.

Sissinghurst Castle in Kent (right) dates from at least the fifteenth century but its grounds were laid out by Vita Sackville-West and her husband Harold Nicholson as one of the finest twentieth century gardens in Britain.

The layout of the garden takes up some of the doorway axes created by the existing buildings on the site, especially that of the tower at the centre of the garden, and adds some new ones (some of which are indicated on the plan). Together these are the primary organisational devices of the garden. They provide routes and sight lines that stretch its length and breadth.

In plan these axes give the garden a geometric discipline that helps the disparate group of old buildings work together with the new hedges and flower beds. As you walk around the garden they lead you from place to place, helping you explore the whole. There are points at which intersecting axes create nodes but these are rarely points at which you feel you should stop. The doorway axes at Sissinghurst are about movement, and drawing the visitor forward from one 'room' to the next.

These are not axes that are concerned with religious or political dominion. If anything the dominion they declare is that of human aesthetic sensibility. They are concerned to create a world that derives from and appeals to taste and visual pleasure. They play on the magnetic pull of the doorway and the dramatic potential of its axis.

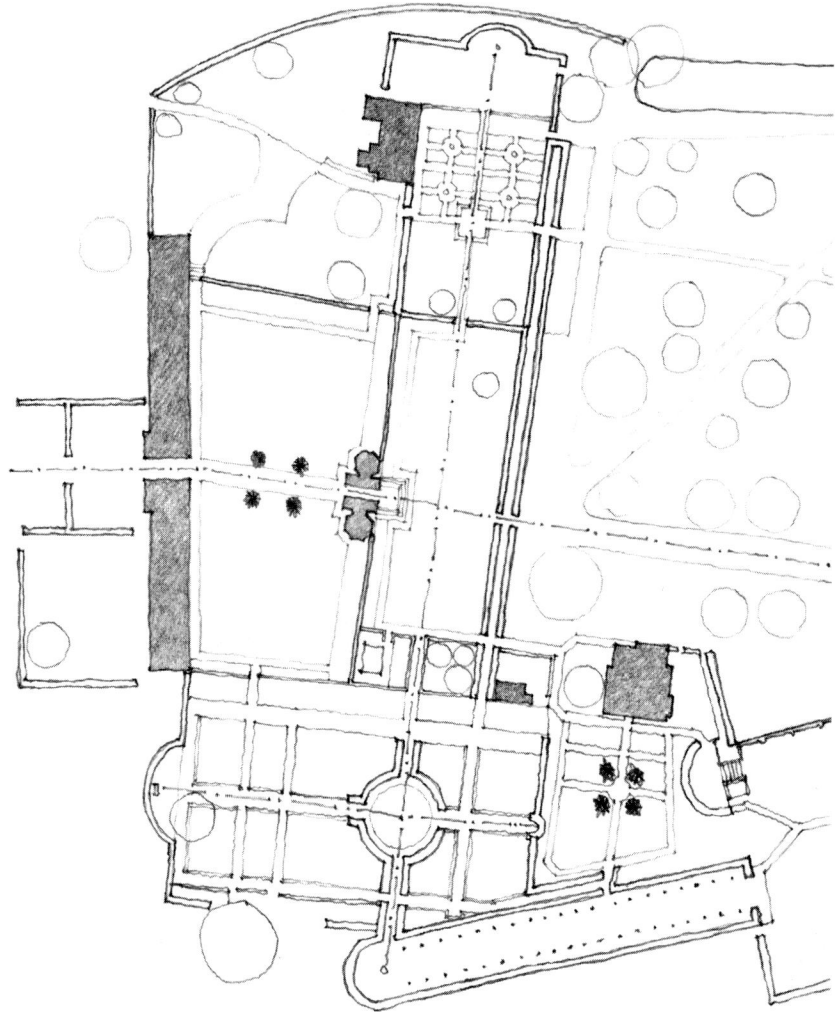

The plan of Sissinghurst Garden showing the principal axes generated by doorways. The photograph at the top left is of the main axis of the gateway in the tower, looking through the double hedge and with the main entrance to the garden in the background.

THE CATHEDRAL, CEFALÙ

When travelling I sometimes make notes describing my experiences of places. Here is a brief description of my approach to the cathedral at the centre of a town on the north coast of Sicily. It says something about the power of architecture to generate a subliminal political/religious message through the use of a doorway axis.

Now I am going to the cathedral. I have not been to this one before, but I can project myself mentally to its doorway even though I do not know how it is exactly. I have seen the great building towering over the town from a distance. But now I must get myself there physically. I am about a mile west of the town, along the coast, so I walk along the promenade with the sea on my left. As I approach the town I can still see the cathedral above the roofs of the houses. The town lies on sloping ground between the sea and a huge rock (La Rocca), at the base of which stands the cathedral. But as I get closer it is hidden by the houses. When I get to the town I enter the narrow streets, and have to consciously remember the rough direction of the cathedral. I don't know the plan of the town and as I enter it I realise that no street leads directly to its doorway. I have to choose a road. Walking deeper into the town I start to feel that I have lost my sense of the direction to the cathedral. I look up the streets as I pass each corner. Eventually I glimpse a space in afternoon sunlight, some distance up a street. Because the streets

are narrow, and the buildings some few storeys high, they all tend to be in shadow. So the space in sunshine must be an open square; and the square in a town like this is usually in front of the cathedral. I walk up the street towards the square. It is a climb, but not very steep. There is a chance that I am approaching the cathedral in its position at the heart of the town. Getting closer I begin to see that I am right. I emerge from the shaded streets into the town square, the space that allows afternoon sunshine to light up the front of the cathedral. It is the Piazza del Duomo – the place of the cathedral. The cathedral dominates the sloping square, apparently filling the higher side, opposite which I have emerged from the maze of streets. The square is cluttered with cafe tables with sunshades, there are a few palm trees and many people talking, watching, sitting, drinking…. Some of this life obscures the cathedral. Behind the cathedral is the huge rocky hill – La Rocca. Through the clutter of sunshades and groups of people, I can see some steps leading up to the cathedral; they are diagonally opposite me, across the square. I can see that the cathedral and the square are not in an axial relationship with each other. The square itself is not regular. Its pavement slopes up towards the cathedral, continuing the slope of the streets of the town, presumably the original slope of the land before the town was built. I walk across the square to the steps up to the cathedral. I cannot walk in a straight

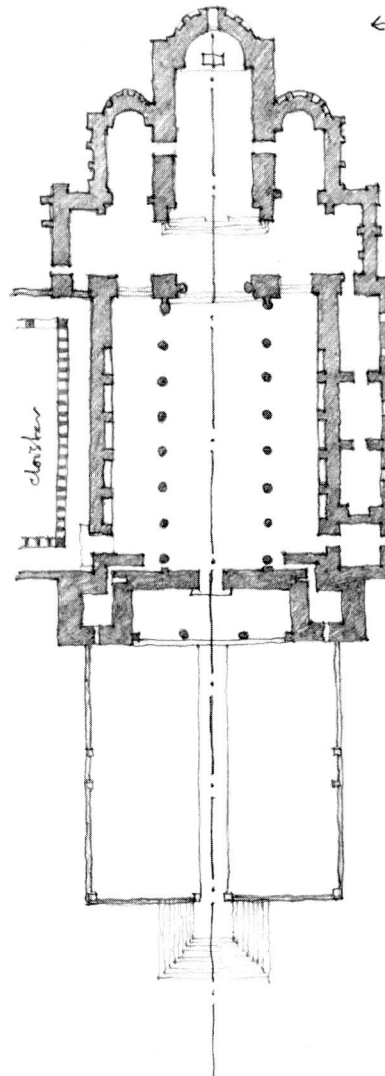

Above: the plan of Cefalù with the cathedral and the Piazza del Duomo in front of it.

Left: the plan of the cathedral is conceptually almost identical to the beach place on p. 41. It has an altar on a doorway axis. Here too the doorway axis projects across the sea to the horizon.

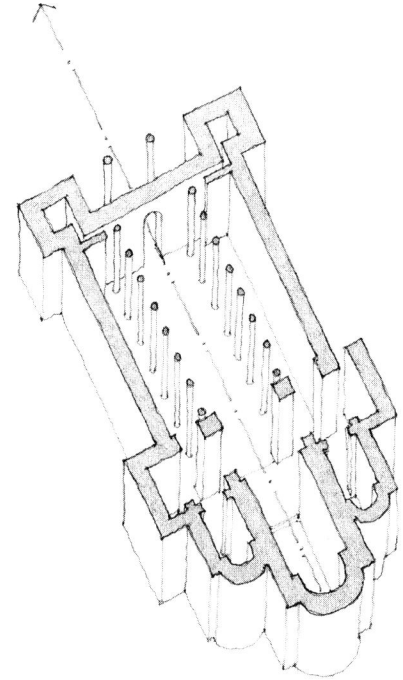

line, but must weave between people and the tables with their sunshades. Now I can feel the heat of the sun. When I reach them, the steps are quite steep; three-quarters of a pyramid, with a flat top where there is the gate into the cathedral forecourt. Because I have approached them diagonally, as most people do, I find that I climb the steps diagonally too, on the right hand side of the pyramid, rather than the front. It has taken me some effort to walk the mile or so to the town, to explore the labyrinth of streets to find the piazza, and to cross the square in the warm sun. But now it takes a little additional burst of effort to climb this pyramid of steep steps. It makes me realise that I am on a pilgrimage, even if only an architectural rather than a religious

one, to somewhere special. The forecourt of the cathedral is a platform, approximately square. Around the edge there are railings. The reward for climbing the steep steps is that the forecourt is flat. It is the first level ground I have encountered since entering the town from the level promenade along the edge of the sea. Along with the flatness of the ground, I now also realise that I have entered a realm ordered by an axis. I have not encountered this axiality either since entering the town. There is an increasing sense of order and geometry as I approach this cathedral. It is as if level ground and the discipline of the axis belong to the church. The gate through which I pass at the top of the steps is on axis with the doorway into the cathedral. This is my first

The clear geometry of the cathedral sits amongst the irregularity of the surrounding houses. The doorway axis projects the presence of the altar out into the world and across the sea.

49

'I am the door: by me if any man enter in, he shall be saved, and shall go in and out, and find pasture.' John 10

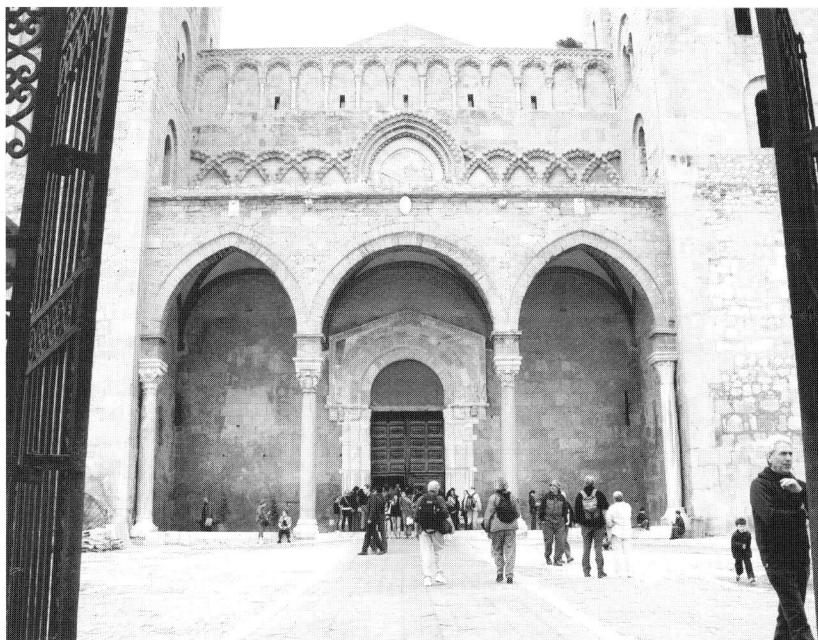

sight of that doorway, which has been the goal of my exploration and journey. Here, my path is clearly laid down for me too. Now I cannot get lost; there is no uncertainty as there was in the maze of the town's narrow streets. Across the forecourt, from the gate to the main door, is a brick path, six feet wide, dead straight. After the uncertainties and wanderings of the town, here is a certain route, which I already understand stretches beyond the church door, into the cathedral, and right to its culmination, the altar in its sanctuary. I have entered the precinct of the church but not yet the church itself, and already I am linked architecturally with the altar that is the goal of my walk. I approach the door of the cathedral along the brick path across the forecourt, still in the sun. The doorway is shaded under a high and wide loggia, with three arches. The doorway itself is quite modest; not small, but not grand either. I step through; I move from the sun of the forecourt, through the shade of the loggia, into the relative darkness of the nave of the church. There is no vestibule, or narthex. At this point the transition seems quite abrupt. The line of the path continues straight into the cathedral, though it is punctuated by the passage through the loggia. Inside, the path becomes the central aisle, and is paved in polished stone rather than brick. The perspective to which it contributes is reinforced by two arcades of arches at either side. All focus on the large cross over the altar. Above this are some

mosaics depicting saints, surmounted by a giant mosaic of Christ Pantocrator with penetrating eyes but also with a hand raised in benediction. Suddenly I am inside the cathedral proper, confronted by that glittering mosaic of Christ; it is framed in another 'doorway', the huge arched opening to the sanctuary, marking a threshold that only the priests (and cleaners) may cross. There is a service going on. I am not part of it. The priest is speaking in Italian; I cannot understand. I stand with other tourists, trying not to disturb the service whilst also looking at the church. My interest is not so much in the organised religion, but in the way in which religion uses architecture subliminally, to reinforce the order and certainty it offers. Here the cathedral sends its axis of certainty out into the irregular surroundings, through a sequence of transitions, to draw one in to its order and

Once you reach the platform on which the cathedral sits you are under the control of the building's geometry. Its doorway axis dictates your path and leads you forward.

discipline. There are doorways in the hierarchy through which all may pass; there are others, further up the hierarchy, through which only the elite priests may pass. The architectural stages one passes through on the way to salvation are clear: from the maze and moral uncertainty of life in the irregular town one finds and is welcomed into the ordered certainty of the cathedral and religion; all under the protective shadow of the rock that dominates the town.'

The architecture of the cathedral in Cefalù exerts a subtle influence over one's experience of the city. Its doorway axis introduces a datum. A similar influence is evident in most cities through history. In the case of the cathedral the datum is offered, through this architectural instrument, by religion. The doorway axis provides the population with a reliable point of reference and invites people into the moral order and discipline of the church. It is the same in a mosque, where the axis from the *mihrab* sets the direction for worship. It was the same in classical Greece when the axis emerging from the doorway of the Parthenon on the acropolis in Athens projected out across the city. It was the same in ancient Egypt when the temple palaces of the pharaohs projected their axes out through their doorways to provide a datum to which their subjects could relate and on which they could depend.

And all these buildings, in their different times and cultures and with their different religious connotations, also do something that Sottsass's simple doorway in the desert does. They evoke the idea of a place beyond, a place to which one might aspire. They draw one towards a place that, ultimately, one is perhaps not allowed to enter.

From the place beyond its own 'doorway' – the sanctuary arch – the line of sight of Christ Pantocrator is projected out into the world by the cathedral's doorway axis.

51

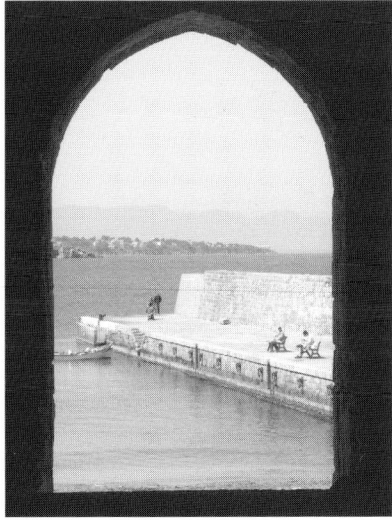

The Porta Pescara

When Cefalù was defended by a town wall around its borders, including along the edge of the sea, the counterpoints to the doorway of the cathedral were the gateways through this wall into the town. Only one remains, the Porta Pescara, which was originally the gateway from the harbour. It would have played its part in the hierarchical sequence of thresholds culminating in the arch over the sanctuary in the cathedral. Fishermen would return from the unpredictable perils of the sea, enter through this fisherman's gate into the town of their homes, at the heart of which stood the cathedral representing protection, stability and security.

If you look at the small city plan of Cefalù on p. 48 you will see that this gateway too, though not directly linked by a road, is on the doorway axis of the cathedral. In this way, though it is not visually apparent, the spatial (and moral) discipline of the church stretches right to the edge of the land and beyond – across the changeful sea to the distant horizon.

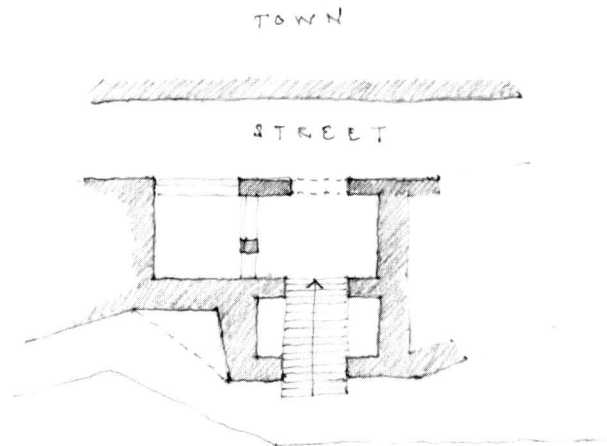

The underlying architecture of the cathedral in Cefalù is surprisingly similar to that of the beach place on p. 41. With the Porta Pescara it is as if the architects of the beach place had marked another doorway down by the water's edge, linked on axis with their first, and thereby asserted their architectural authority over a larger area of territory.

The Porta Pescara picks up the doorway axis of the cathedral as it crosses the margins of the land.

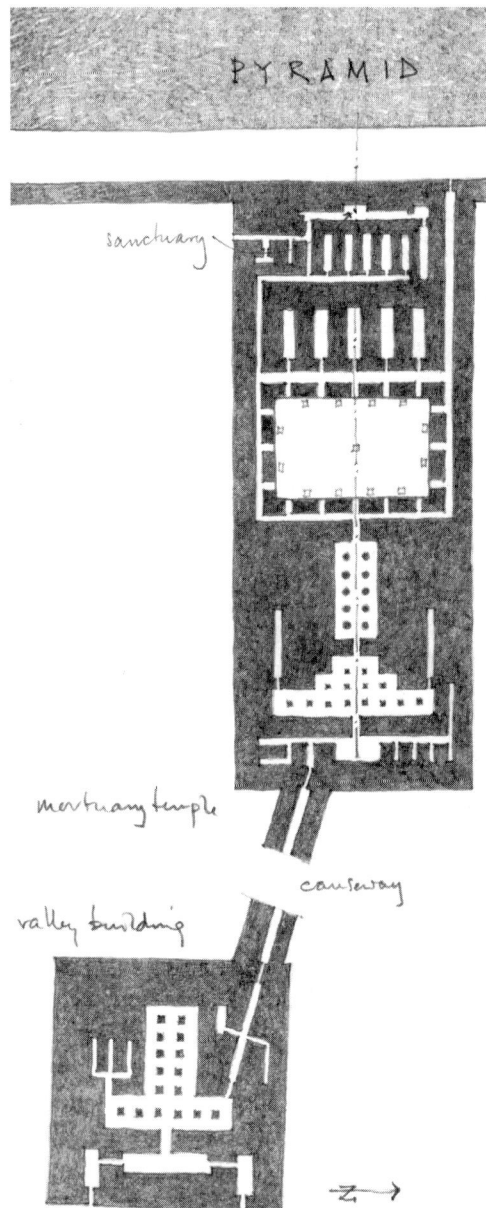

A doorway axis is a powerful weapon; it needs to be handled with care, and sometimes its power has to be curbed, its effects shielded against or deflected.

We have seen that architecture is an instrument for manipulating relationships. In this, the doorway – the point of entry and the generator of an axis – is an especially powerful tool. The buildings we saw in the previous chapter all, through their various doorways, generate axes on which we can position ourselves. When we are on or close to one of these axes we feel that we are in a special relationship, linked to something remote that holds significance: the sea; the sun; a god; Mecca; an altar; maybe some future state of being….

By contrast, this chapter illustrates examples where the doorway axis has been intentionally managed in some way to respect, deflect or curb its power.

Curbing the power of a doorway axis

Ancient Egyptian pyramids were provided with mortuary temples at their bases. They were where priests would tend to the soul of the dead pharaoh whose body was placed at the heart of the pyramid. As part of the funeral ceremony, the body of the pharaoh would be delivered to the pyramid complex by barge on the Nile. A valley building was built for its reception and preparation for burial. The valley building was linked to the mortuary temple by a causeway along which the pharaoh's body would be carried.

The drawing above is the plan of the pyramid complex of Chephren. The mortuary temple is symmetrical about an

The temple complex of the pyramid of Chephren, built around 2570 BC. (The causeway is much longer than shown.)

axis generated principally by two doorways: the doorway near the entrance to the temple; and another, a false doorway, in the sanctuary near the base of the pyramid. The false doorway was provided for the comings and goings of the dead pharaoh's soul. The sanctuary contained an altar on which food was left for the pharaoh. Through the false doorway the axis stretches into the heart of the pyramid, establishing linkage between the temple and the body. But at the entrance end the axis is stopped by a thick wall preventing it from escaping out into the world. The architects of the temple could easily have aligned the entrance with the temple's dominant axis, but did not.

Within the temple one can also see that there is no straight route, on axis, to the sanctuary. The axis indicates the sanctuary's direction but the route is circuitous, making the sanctuary, with its false door and altar, a secluded part of the temple; it is hidden away and private rather than the culmination of an aspirational route.

There seem two possible reasons for these avoidances of the doorway axis. They may have been arranged out of respect for the privacy of the pharaoh's soul and to enhance its seclusion and mystery. They could also be intended to fox the dead spirit, and prevent it escaping to cause havoc in the ordinary world outside.

Avoiding confrontation, or undermining self-importance

Topkapi Palace in Istanbul was built in the fifteenth century. The sultans would receive ambassadors and petitioning subjects in its Hall of Audience (above). The Hall is a rectangular pavilion situated just inside the third courtyard of the palace, adjacent to the Gate of Happiness. Its plan is on the next page. When it was designed there were opportunities for the grand alignment of doorway axes but all were avoided.

The building is geometrically regular with a central axis on which the sultan's

The Hall of Audience in Topkapi Palace, Istanbul.

couch is positioned, but no doorway shares this axis. Nor do any of the three important doorways – the Gate of Happiness, the doorway from the gate into the Hall, and the doorway from the courtyard on the other side of the building – share an axis. In addition, the steps up from the courtyard (shown in the photograph) are arranged oddly, so that their landing aligns neither with the axis of the doorway into the Hall nor with the structural geometry of the columns around its shaded terrace. All is carefully arranged to avoid the alignment of axes.

Here the reasons are different from in the mortuary temple of Chephren's pyramid. In the architecture of the sultans' Hall of Audience the intention seems to have been first to prevent the situation where a petitioner or foreign ambassador would approach the sultan from a confrontational direction, and second to reduce the sense of self-importance felt either by visiting ambassadors or by the sultan himself as they entered the building.

In the Hall of Audience the arrangement of doorway axes is used as an instrument to set an appropriate relationship between the seat of power and supplicants to it, as well as to help to engender appropriate attitudes of mind in the parties involved. But all revolves around the axis of power that the sultan himself generates.

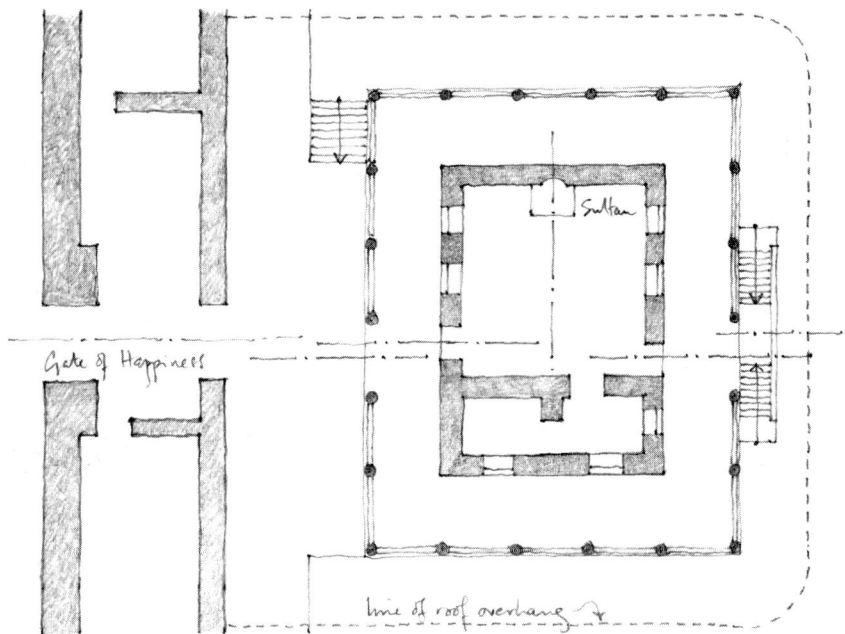

Right-angled approach

The Hall of Audience in Topkapi provides an example of architecture setting up a right-angled approach to an important axis, mainly it seems for reasons that are psychological. Much of these seem to derive from the slight sense of discomfort we can sometimes feel when we occupy an axis.

The Palace at Pylos is mentioned in Homer's *Odyssey* and thus dates from some three thousand years ago. It is where Telemachus, Odysseus's son, went to seek the advice of Nestor, the king of Pylos, regarding his

The doorway axes of the Hall of Audience are arranged to avoid confrontation between visitors and the sultan.

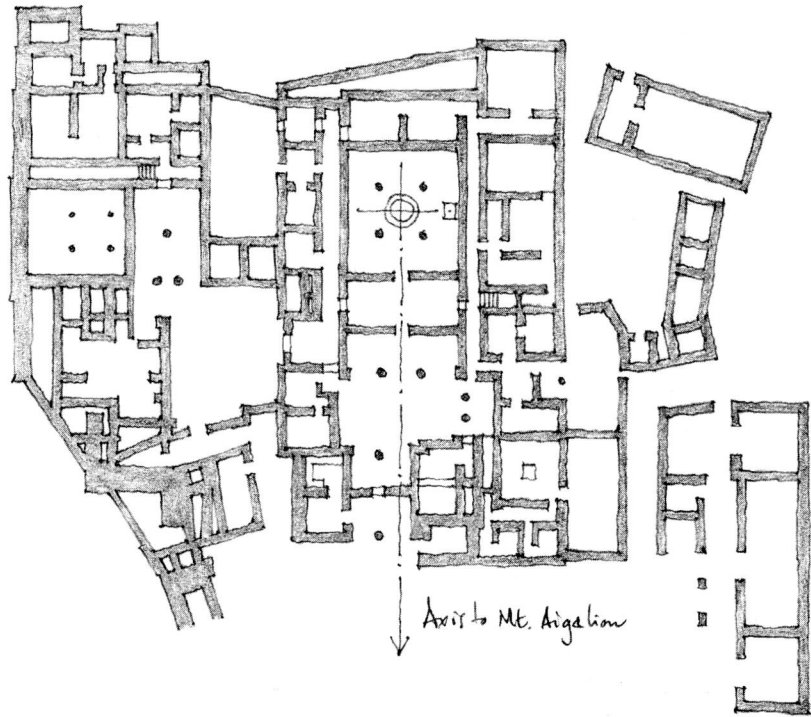

Axis to Mt. Aigalion

search for news of his lost father. The plan of Nestor's palace is on the right. The king's chamber, his *megaron*, is at the core of the complex.

From the plan you can see that, by means of a doorway axis, the architecture of the palace sets up a linkage between the hearth at the centre of the *megaron* and a distant sacred mountain, Mount Aigalion. The doorway is the architectural fulcrum between the hearth and mountain.

But it seems that Nestor himself did not wish to set himself in confrontation with the sacred mountain by positioning his throne opposite the doorway and sharing its axis. His throne is set off to one side, positioned alongside the hearth and with its axis at a right angle to that shared by the hearth, doorway and distant mountain.

In *The Earth, the Temple and the Gods* (1962), Vincent Scully commented on this arrangement:

> *Thus the lord… faced across the short axis of his megaron, here not toward the horns but towards his own fire, which itself burned roughly on axis with them…. The lord's hearth, center of his personal household, is set as the counter-balance to the earth's forms.'*

This arrangement also had a similar effect to the arrangement of doorways in the sultan's Hall of Audience discussed above. It meant that if someone arrived to petition

the king, he or she would approach him in a non-confrontational direction, from the king's left side, and when speaking would not have the advantage of being silhouetted against the rectangle of the doorway. One can imagine Telemachus standing across the hearth from Nestor's throne; both parties to the interview would be lit equally by fire and daylight.

We have seen that doorway axes can be directed both inwards and outwards. The axis of Nestor's *megaron* was directed outwards, establishing a linkage between his hearth and the landscape. In a church or chapel, however, the axis is often directed inwards, towards an altar.

We have already noted that the architecture of the beach place on p. 41 is rather like that of a church. It consists of an altar

Nestor arranged the throne in his megaron *so that it would not share the powerful doorway axis linking his hearth to a distant sacred mountain.*

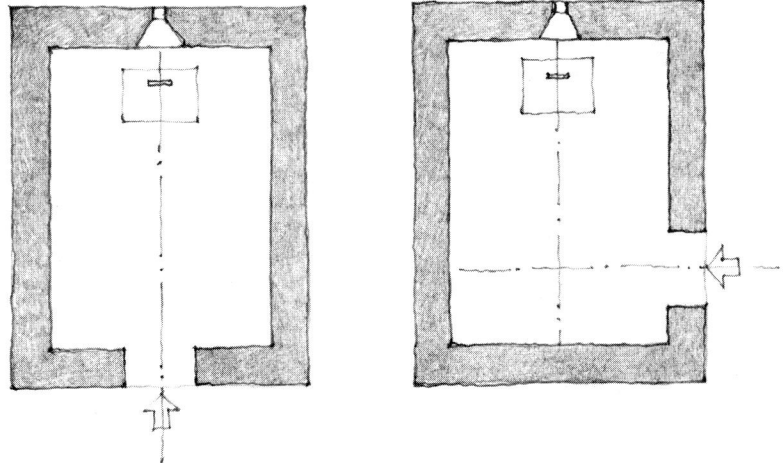

oriented to something remote and significant – the sea and its horizon – by means of a doorway axis. If we built up its walls and gave it a roof its plan would be as in the drawing on the right. (I have moved the altar so that it is fully inside, rather than on the cusp between inside and outside, and added a small window behind it.)

Picture yourself approaching the front of this small chapel; imagine your relationship with the altar as you approach and walk in through the doorway. You could see the altar a little before you reached the doorway, and as you entered you would you find yourself in immediate confrontation with the altar's own axis.

Architects of religious buildings have often accepted that a chief purpose of their building is to establish an axis. Architecturally an axis seems to assert authority and certainty; it offers a security rail onto which people can hold. In both Cefalù cathedral (pp. 47–51) and the temple at Tarxien (p. 40) the entrance doorway is in the broadly equivalent position to that of the beach 'chapel'. As you approach and enter, the doorway locates you on the axis of the altar at the other end of the building.

Imagine now entering a chapel with an identical plan (top right) except that the doorway, though at the far end from the altar, is through one of the side walls. Now the axis

is contained within the building (though the associated symmetry of the building implies its projection into the outside world) and your psychological relationship with the altar as you approach and enter the building is very different. Now as you approach the doorway you cannot see the altar; its mystery is protected; you cannot see it until you are fully inside the building. Also, when you are standing in the doorway, or just inside, you are not immediately confronted by the altar; you have to approach its axis from the side. This arrangement gives you a moment, within the seclusion of the chapel, to prepare for presenting yourself before the altar.

Some churches have two doorways: one on the altar axis, and one to the side. The usual arrangement is for the side door to be on the south elevation (the sunny side), with the altar to the east; but some churches have their side entrance from the north.

The position of the doorway into a small chapel dramatically affects the psychological experience of entering. It changes one's relationship with the altar.

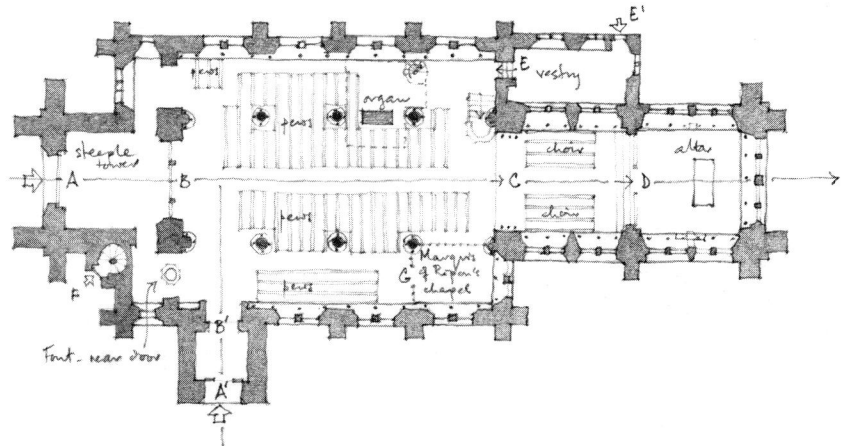

St Mary's Church, Studley Royal in Yorkshire.

The church at Studley Royal was designed in the 1860s by the architect William Burges for the Marquis of Ripon. Its plan is alongside.

Like most churches, St Mary's is oriented with the altar end towards the east. This church is also oriented to its mother church – the cathedral in Ripon some miles to the east. The axis of the church stretches from the eastern horizon, through Ripon cathedral, then the east window of St Mary's, its chancel and choir arches (D and C on the plan, which are doorways to the sanctuary) and the doorways B and A at the west end.

Because of its position on and contribution to the significant axis, doorway A is the one that would be used on ceremonial occasions such as weddings and funerals, when it would be appropriate for a procession to approach along the axis, passing through the congregation before reaching the altar framed by its own doorway – the chancel arch at the east end.

The side entrance into the church is sheltered by a porch and consists of two doorways (A' and B' on the plan). This would be the entrance used on less formal occasions: for the usual Sunday services and personal visits at quiet times. The porch would be where the priest might welcome and say farewell to his congregation before and after services.

In this church, as in most religious buildings across the world, the doorways are used as instruments to manage relationships with the altar.

An office

The line of approach dictated by a doorway has its psychological effects in more mundane situations too.

On the right is a simplified plan of my office. My chair and desk is marked with a dot. The other rectangle is a table. The office has two doorways, one in front of me as I sit at my desk (1, which is shown in a photograph on p. 80) and the other to my left (2). People who visit me say that it feels very different to come in through one doorway rather than the other. Some prefer to come through the more formal, almost axial, approach in front of me. Others prefer to come in by the less formal doorway to my left. Some just come in through one doorway and out of the other.

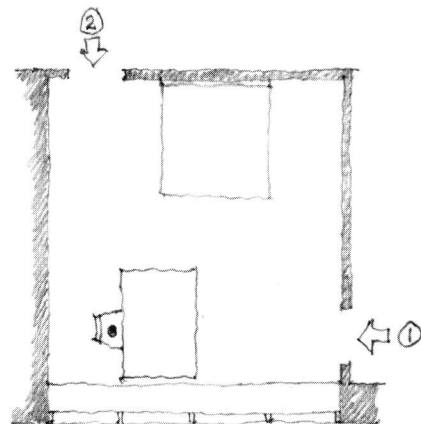

My office has two doorways: one directly in front of me as I sit at my desk; and another to one side.

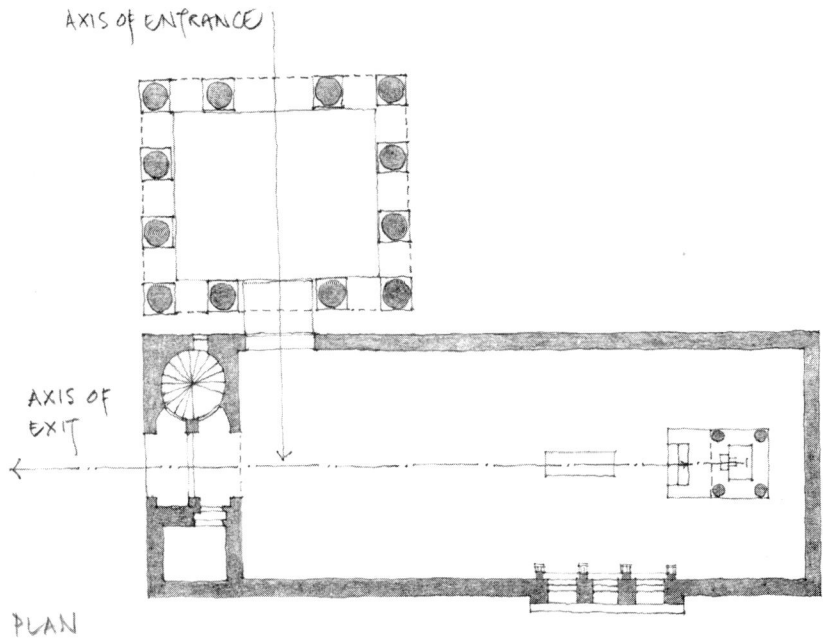

AXIS OF ENTRANCE

AXIS OF EXIT

PLAN

Entrance and departure

The plan on the right is of a crematorium chapel designed around 1918 by the Swedish architect Sigurd Lewerentz. It stands in the grounds of the Woodland Crematorium in the suburbs of Stockholm.

Like previous examples, this chapel has its altar at one end aligned by a doorway axis, in this case, (appropriately, because of the associations with death) to the setting sun in the west. Instead of the towel in the beach place on p. 41, the chapel has a cata-falque on which the coffin is placed during the funeral service. (The body in the coffin would however face in the opposite direction to the sunbathers on their towel.) The altar, catafalque and west door determine the main axis of the chapel.

Like St Mary's Studley Royal (oppo-site) Lewerentz's chapel has a side entrance; but in this instance it is on the north side – the sunless side of the building. This northern entrance is marked by a grand and elaborate neo-classical porch supported on twelve columns (symbolising the twelve disciples of Christ). The porch is detached and not exactly at a right-angle to the main body of the chapel. It stands at the end of a very long, dead straight pathway – a *via dolorosa* (way of tears) – through the woods of the crematorium grounds (right).

It is through this shaded porch that mourners enter the chapel before the service. Apart from the dictates of orientation, this direction of entry means that mourners are not confronted by the axis of the coffin as they come through the doorway.

After the service the mourners leave by the other doorway, along the axis. When the doors are opened, those inside the chapel can see out into the sunlit Elysian Fields of the wooded crematorium landscape. Leaving the coffin behind, for a moment the mourners follow the soul of the dead person on its way to the setting sun.

The doorways are critical to the architecture of the building. In this instance they contribute to the poetic and symbolic messages the building contains. They resonate with and manipulate (in a benevolent way) the senses and the emotions of the people who experience them. They orchestrate relationships: between the mourners and the idea of death; between the mourners and the dead person in the coffin; between the mourners and their return from the realm of death to the landscape outside; between the soul of the dead person and eternity.

The two doorways of the chapel have different characters. The entrance doorway from the north is grand but shaded; it is a doorway into the presence of death. The scale of both the doorway and its portico is larger than life. (And in the pediment is a sculpture of Christ emerging from the doorway of his own tomb – a reminder that the doorway is a time-honoured symbol of death.) By contrast, the west door is small and forbidding; it is no bigger than needed for two people to leave side by side comforting each other. The riveted cross on its surface is like a no-entry sign; and the doors have no external handles. This is a doorway that is meant to be experienced in one direction only, on the way out after the service.

From the left:

The portico of the north entrance, in shade and with the sculpture of Christ emerging from the door of his own tomb.

The axis of the altar, catafalque and west doorway.

The outside of the west door is severe and forbidding. Though a symbol of Christianity, its cross is more like a 'no-entry' sign.

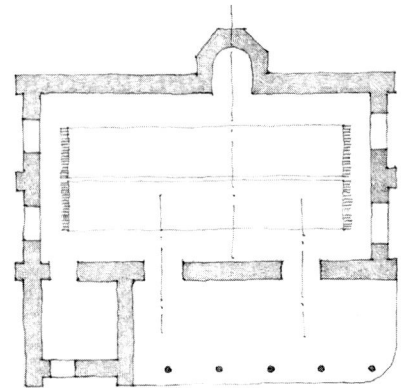

A small mosque with doorways offset from the axis of the mihrab. *(I am grateful to Shabnam Noor for the information on which this plan is based.)*

Chicane

In some cases an alignment of a doorway axis with another significant axis is avoided not by rotation through ninety degrees but by parallel offset.

The plan on the right is of the mosque of a small Moslem community in Bengal, India. Rather than place its entrance on axis with the symbolic doorway of the *mihrab*, its architects/builders chose to offset two doorways, one to either side. Thus the axis to Mecca begins within the prayer hall.

The plan below is of Blackwell, a house on the shores of Lake Windermere in the north of England. It was designed by the

Arts and Crafts architect M.H. Baillie-Scott and built in 1900. The main entrance to the house could easily have been designed as shown in the small drawing below left. But Baillie-Scott was more interested in irregularity and asymmetry and so avoided an axial alignment of doorways. The intention, as through the rest of the house, was to create a variety of experiences; to make a house that did not project authority but which one could explore in a relaxed way. In this instance the chicane prevents one from going straight across the corridor into the Hall; you have to turn for a moment towards the lake, which you can see in the distance through the bay window in the Drawing Room.

Axial alignments of doorways are avoided throughout Blackwell. At the main entrance, the offset doorways deny a straight axis from the courtyard outside to the Hall (left). The route is thus more domestic than ceremonial.

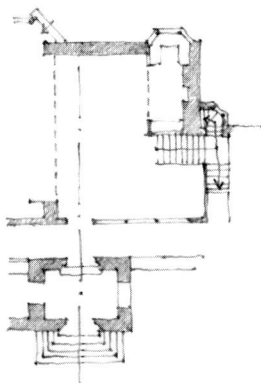

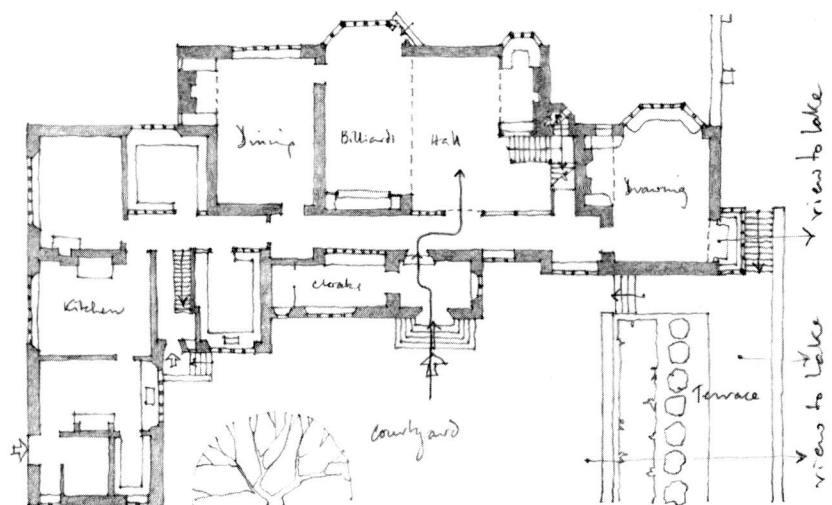

DOORWAYS AND SCALE (pragmatics and symbolism)

When (in a review of student work for example) I look at the plan of a building, and there is no scale provided, I find that I look at the doorways to estimate the size of the rooms. For all intents and purposes the ordinary doorway is a constant. It tends to have a width of between 750mm and 900mm (2' 6" and 3'). In some cases they may be a little narrower and others a little wider but for a single leaf door that tends to be the range.

The reason for the consistency was identified above on p. 31: the geometry, including the dimensions, of doorways responds to the size of people (to allow our passage). For the same reason ordinary doorways have a fairly consistent height too: between 1950mm and 2100mm (6' 6" and 7'). The doorway represents the scale of the human being. So when I use the doorway in a drawing to estimate the sizes of spaces I am not using an abstract scale but one based on the sizes of people. The doorway carries human scale into both plan and section.

When doorways are not for people, or not only for people, their scale may vary. They may be much smaller or much bigger than an ordinary doorway. Leaving a human doorway open to allow the comings and goings of cats would negate the purpose of the door, so cats might be provided with their own doorways to suit their size (right). The doorway of a pigsty tends to be the right size for pigs (pig scale) and that of a jumbo-jet hangar has of course to be big enough for the wing-span of a large aeroplane.

A cat's doorway is smaller than that required for a human being.

Subtleties of scale

But the scale of doorways is not as simple a matter as merely providing an opening suited to the physical size of what will pass through them. Doorways accommodate shadows as well as substance. One abstract dimension of the relationship between doorways and people concerns the affect the scale of a doorway can have on our sense of self, identity and dignity.

You can, for example, imagine what it would be like to live in a pigsty. It might be possible to get through the doorway but, apart from necessary physical contortion and the chill and discomfort of a hard floor, you would probably feel that repeatedly having to crawl in and out through the low opening was an affront to your dignity.

Homeless people often have to live in makeshift shelters made of waste materials, cardboard boxes…. In December 2005 the UK's Channel 4 News reported on the problems facing dispossessed people in Zimbabwe. 'It is not acceptable if I have to crawl into my place as if I was a snake,' one man named Tapuwa said, reminding us of our right as human beings to be able to walk into our houses without having to stoop, let alone crawl.

Humility

Some doorways for human beings are small for pragmatic reasons: one has to crawl into an igloo because otherwise too much heat would be lost from inside; one crawls into an overnight tent because otherwise the tent would have to be too bulky to carry.

But some doorways are designed small to make a point. One can imagine a potentate insisting on a low doorway into his throne room so that visitors would have to bow respectfully as they entered. Some entrances into religious shrines are low for the same reason. Doorways in fortresses have sometimes been made low to slow down attacking forces. Generally speaking, a low doorway makes you pause and think for a moment about passing from one place into the next – or bump your head.

The tea house crawl door

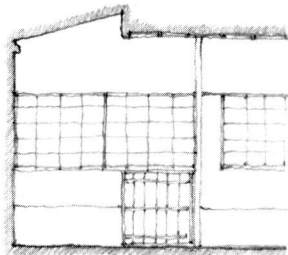

nijiriguchi · crawl·door into tea-house, looking from inside.

The size of the doorway into a traditional Japanese tea house (above) levels all guests to the same status for the duration of the tea ceremony.

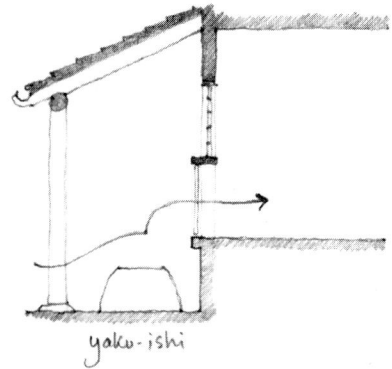

yoku-ishi

The size of the doorway into a grand country house, such as Chiswick Villa in London (below), inflates the status of a particular person – its owner.

The guest entrance into a traditional Japanese tea house (above) is made small to engender humility and equality amongst the participants in the ceremony. The doorway is called *nijiriguchi*. The middle drawing above shows an example in elevation from inside the tea house. Alongside is a section through the same doorway with the inside to the right. To enter, a guest must remove his shoes and using the *yoku-ishi* (a large stone, as a step) crawl into the room. Doing this he cannot retain his dignity. The interaction between the restrictive geometry of the doorway and the geometry of the body have a psychological effect. The architecture tacitly imposes a sociological rule of behaviour and affects the relationship between people.

The scale of dignity

By contrast, the main doorway into Chiswick Villa in London (right) is designed to suggest the opposite of humility. This grand house was built by Richard Boyle, Earl of

Burlington, in the late 1720s. Its entrance is a clear display of social difference. The 'lower' orders – the servants and trades people – would enter the undercroft of the house (the kitchen and store rooms) by the lower doorway in the photograph. It is only just big enough for a normal height person to pass through, stands in a rugged stone wall, and is pinioned on the axis determined by the portico above.

Lord Burlington and his visitors would enter on the upper level. They could reach the portico by way of the steps at either side. The scale of this entrance is more heroic, to suit the assumed status of those who would use it. The finish of the materials is more refined.

The doorway into the central hall of the house is in the dark slot between the central columns. The actual doorway is taller than necessary but its apparent size is exaggerated by the full height slot and the portico.

The main floor of a house like this is called the *piano nobile* or noble floor. The design of Chiswick Villa was influenced directly by Palladio's Villa Rotonda shown on p. 43. The ideas in both houses derive from Roman architecture and evoke associations with human nobility and power.

The grand doorway is a common architectural device to assert power and authority. The photograph above is of one of many possible examples. It is the front of the Sheriff Court in Dundee, Scotland. Like Chiswick Villa this building has a grand portico, in this case to symbolise the authority of the justice system and to impress its authority on all those – criminals, lawyers, witnesses, judges… – who pass through its portal.

The geometry of welcome

We have already seen various examples of the use of scale, in relation to doorways, for symbolic purposes. On p. 43, the Villa

The portico of the Sheriff Court in Dundee symbolises the status and authority of the justice system.

Rotonda, as has just been mentioned, used scale in a similar way to Chiswick Villa, to imply status. On p. 50 we saw that the cathedral at Cefalù has a loggia which exaggerates the size of its doorway and symbolises the authority, status and dignity of the church; here too the arch to the sanctuary of the cathedral is a grand doorway framing the altar and the image of Christ Pantocrator above. And on p. 60 we saw that the north doorway of Lewerentz's Chapel of the Resurrection in Stockholm has a grand portico symbolising the authority, status and dignity of death.

But a doorway's scale can symbolise gentler and more sociable relationships too. The Arts and Crafts architect C.F.A. Voysey, a contemporary of M.H. Baillie Scott (whose Blackwell we saw on p. 61), wrote:

> 'Doors… may partake of the qualities of a good host, hospitable and free in their ample width, yet invested with vertical lines to suggest dignity and grace.'*

The doorway in the photograph on this page was designed by Voysey. It adopts a different attitude to scale and meaning from that displayed in Burlington's Chiswick Villa and Lewerentz's Chapel of the Resurrection. This is the front door of a house called Broad Leys, on the shore of Lake Windermere (not far from Blackwell), and designed in 1898. Here Voysey applies the sentiment expressed in the above quotation and makes a human

scale doorway with a width that is both 'hospitable and free'. If this doorway impresses, it is with its generosity and gentility rather than power and nobility. It is a doorway for the meeting and greeting of equals rather than one by which a superior impresses inferiors with a symbol of status; or by which mourners are reminded of the authority of death. All three buildings – Chiswick, the Chapel of the Resurrection and Broad Leys – have porches and porticoes with columns and triangular pediments; but the intention and effect of the front door of Broad Leys is very different from that of the others. All exaggerate the actual size of the doorway but Voysey exaggerates the width rather than the height. His doorway wraps its arms around visitors rather than standing tall and aloof from them.

The porch and doorway into Broad Leys. The breadth of this entrance is welcoming. Its scale is human. Notice too that the step into the porch is very low, to keep the doorway on the same level as the visitor.

* From C.F.A. Voysey – Individuality (1915)

This statue of St Simon is in the porch of the cathedral at Mosta on the island of Malta.

The symbiotic relationship

We shall see later in this book (p. 154) that the meaning and identity of a doorway may be understood and qualified by the questions: 'What is this doorway allowing in or out?'; and 'Against whom or what might this doorway need defending?'

The relationship between a doorway and what it allows through is more intimate than that between a wall and what it keeps out. At a threshold, at the moment of passage through an opening in a barrier, we find ourselves in a special relationship with the door- or gateway. We are for that moment located in a specific spot – defined precisely by the doorway and its threshold. And at the same moment the doorway's own purpose – its *raison d'être* – is affirmed. This is a moment when the frame and the framed come into a symbiotic relationship, each dependent on the other to achieve a resolution.

The potential moment of congruence between the frame and the framed makes every doorway an invitation. Sottsass's 'Door to enter into darkness' (p. 16) gives the interface between the two worlds of light and shade precise dimensions but it does so in relation to the size of what Sottsass envisaged would pass through it – himself as a representative human being. By its verticality and by its width and height that doorway is clearly a presence waiting specifically for, or an invitation to, a human being to cross its threshold into the grand shadow cast across the landscape. And when a statue of St Simon is framed within a doorway (above) it represents a clear invitation to the saint to return from the realm of shadows, back to the world of light and the living.

THE *PROPYLAEA* OF THE ACROPOLIS IN ATHENS

Many ancient Greek cities have an acropolis. It is the high part of the city, used in the earliest times as a refuge from attack but latterly used as the sacred heart of the city. The most celebrated acropolis is that in Athens. Although it would have been inhabited from much earlier, the ruined buildings that survive date mainly from the fifth century BC. The three principal buildings, which can be seen reconstructed on the model in the photograph alongside, are: the Parthenon – the principal temple which housed a (now lost) statue of the guardian goddess of Athens, Athena; the Erectheion – a more complex but smaller temple to the left of the Parthenon; and the *propylaea* – the gateways into the sacred precinct (the *temenos*), which you can see in the foreground of the model. You can also see on the model a statue standing at what appears to be the centre of gravity of the composition; this was another (also lost) giant statue of Athena.

The lower photograph shows the *propylaea* as they appear in the twenty first century AD. (Major repair work was underway when this and the other site photographs were taken. There is a small temple, to Athena Nike, standing on a bastion to the right of the entrance, which in the photograph is shrouded in scaffolding.) The *propylaea* demonstrate many of the aspects of doorways discussed in the preceding pages.

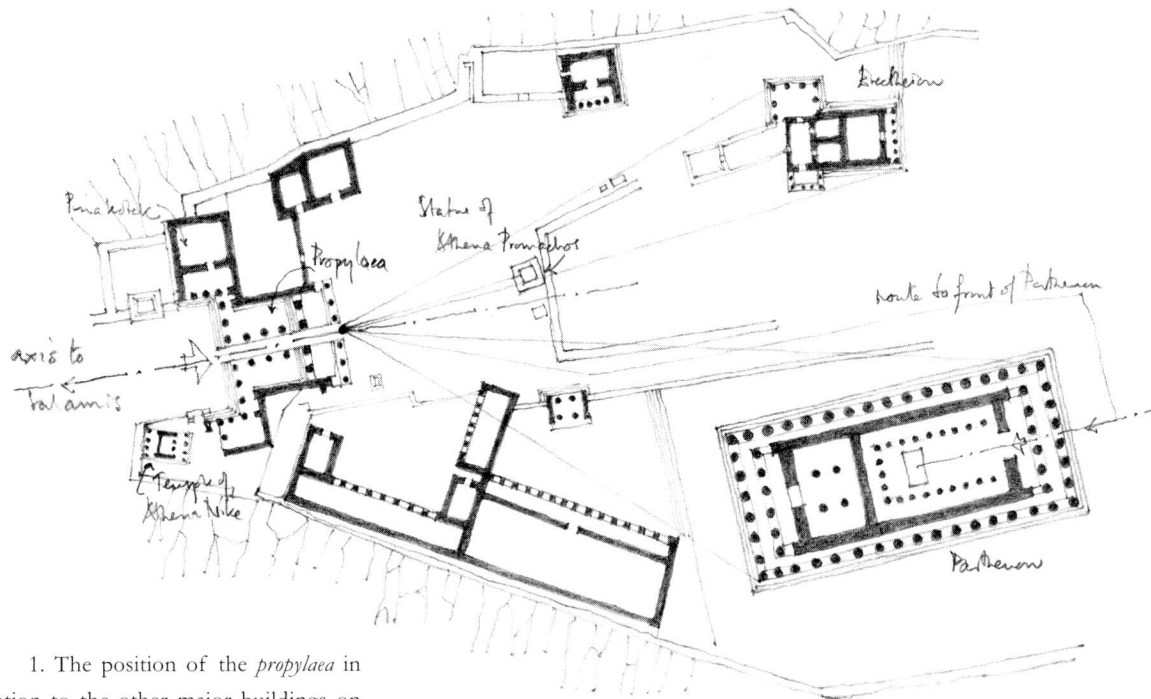

The plan of the acropolis in Athens.

1. The position of the *propylaea* in relation to the other major buildings on the acropolis is shown in the plan above. It stands at the western end of the rocky hill on which the temples are built. This is the only point of access to the heights. So the *propylaea* can be said to mark and formalise what was originally a natural doorway to the defensible refuge on the top of the hill.

2. The *propylaea* create a definite interface between the outside world and the *temenos*. Stepping through it you cross a threshold from the secular to the sacred. When you are outside, in the city around the base of the acropolis, you are aware of this sacred inside. When you are inside, you are aware that you are in the symbolic heart of the city. On special occasions, ceremonial processions would have passed from the *agora* below (the secular core of the city), up to and through the *propylaea*, to the temples above.

3. The *propylaea* establish a definite point of view. As you pass through, you begin to see the Parthenon (right). This is

your first clear view of the sacred precinct, which you cannot see from the city below. As you emerge from the *propylaea* you have a wide view, from the Erectheion on the left (above right) to the Parthenon on the right (below right). The *caryatids* (female statues) in the small porch on the side of the Erectheion look respectfully across to the Parthenon. In the fifth century BC you would also have seen the giant statue of Athena standing in front of you and slightly to the left. Then you would have known that you had arrived in Athena's sacred place. (Nowadays as a traveller, you know that you have arrived in one of the major tourist destinations in the world.)

4. Axes are important in the composition of buildings on the acropolis. The principal entrance into the Parthenon is at the far end of the temple from the *propylaea*. The processional route ran along the left hand side of the temple. As was traditional, the Parthenon faced to the east with the enclosed statue of Athena facing the rising sun along its doorway axis. And just as the doorway axis of the cathedral at Cefalù projects the presence of Christ Pantocrator across the city, so the presence of Athena was projected across the city and the land beyond by the Parthenon's doorway axis.

The *propylaea*'s own axis is important too. It establishes the organisational backbone of the site, with the two main temples balancing each other on either side of it. The giant outdoor statue of Athena stood just to the left of the axis, not terminating it but subtly diverting the eye of the person entering to the major temple to the right, towards the Parthenon.

Looking outwards, the *propylaea*'s axis is important too. But we shall come on to that in a moment, in 6 below.

5. The Parthenon stands as a point of reference for the city as a whole. But the *propylaea* stand as a point of reference with regard to access to and exit from the sacred precinct. When you are in the city below they identify the point of entrance. When you are inside the *temenos* you refer back to them as the point of exit (above right).

6. As you leave the *temenos*, you notice that the actual doorway at the centre of the *propylaea* is oriented directly towards a distant twin-peaked mountain (below right), just like in Nestor's palace (p. 56). This mountain in on the island of Salamis some miles away. And Salamis was, according to Greek mythology, the birthplace of Athena. So the doorway axis of the *propylaea* establishes a direct link between Athena's sacred place at the heart of Athens, and her place of birth.

7. And last, the scale of the doorway is larger than life. It has been made wide enough for the ceremonial processions that

would have passed through it. But more importantly, it is a doorway of a scale suited to the power and authority of a goddess.

We tend to think of architecture in terms of individual buildings, as if they were pieces of sculpture set in the landscape or city. But when one analyses a composition such as the acropolis in Athens, in the terms outlined above focussing in particular on the doorways, then one realises that architecture can also be about the sequence of experiences it offers and the ways in which that sequence is punctuated, managed and orchestrated by thresholds.

EXPERIENCING DOORWAYS

Previous page:

The entrance to the conference centre at the Vitra
Factory in Switzerland. The centre was designed
by the Japanese architect Tadao Ando and built in
1993. The wall accompanies visitors inside.

THRESHOLD

'A threshold is a sacred thing.' **Porphyrus** (*The Nymph's Cave*, AD3rdC).

Recall that *frisson* as you step through an opening. It is as if, in a small sense, you are pushing yourself through a membrane. You half wonder whether you will encounter some strange subtle resistance, whether your passage across the threshold will change you in some way, or expose you to some unforeseen threat.

As I have already suggested, crossing a threshold or entering a place is something we do so often that most of the time we do it without thinking, even though part of our minds is always conscious of where we are and where we are going. We are aware that *entering* takes us from one situation into another, and we are attuned to all sorts of things that are associated with that frequent action – such as whether we have gone into the right place, whether it is safe, whether it is empty or occupied by somebody else, whether we would rather not be there and want to go out again…. But generally we take threshold crossing for granted; (except perhaps when we are thwarted: by a locked door; a 'NO ENTRY' sign; someone pushing a swing-door at the same moment from the other side; or some officious bouncer, doorman or head waiter who will not let us into that club, hotel or restaurant).

Passing through

Imagine the sensation of approaching and passing through the doorway in this photograph. Its dimensions are large enough to accommodate you comfortably; you can walk through easily, without stooping, brushing against the walls or turning sideways. And yet you sense that *frisson* as you go in. You know it is safe to enter but you are not quite sure what you will find inside. It is a sensation we all experience so often that, until reminded of it, we hardly acknowledge it.

Subliminally, you sense the implacability of the wall as you pass through. Its mass is made visible by the separate smooth and chamfered quoins and voussoirs around the doorway. You can empathise with the arch bearing all that weight. You might touch the jamb as you go through, feeling the hardness and texture of the stone with your fingers.

There is a step. You have to make just a little effort to step up. The sill is of a different, white, stone. The floor surface inside the threshold is different from that outside. You cannot see in the black-and-white photograph, but the tiles inside are a rich red, in contrast to the grey stone and sandy-coloured cobbles outside.

As you go through the doorway, the atmosphere changes. The warm sunshine penetrates a little way inside but as you pass through the doorway you pass from light to dark; your eyes have to adjust to the new light level. The air and its movement change. Inside, any slight breeze is stilled. It is cooler. You sense the different quality of that air as

This doorway, like that on the title page of the Introduction, is in the Palazzo Abatellis in Palermo.

you breath it and it touches your skin. There is a slight change in ambient sound: outside noises are muffled; your footsteps reflect off the hard surfaces of the more enclosed space. You feel separated from the world, from other people, from the sky. Inside there is more privacy; a greater sense of security.

The space you enter contains art objects. Almost immediately your mind turns to them. But after a little while you might turn around and see that the opening, which from outside was dark, is now bright with light, with different things framed in it – grass with a loggia beyond. The same doorway is now an entrance in the opposite direction, an entrance into the courtyard. You have experienced two very different environments, linked by an opening through which you can pass, to and fro, in an instant.

Seams in experience

The film editor Walter Murch [*Godfather III* (1990), *Apocalypse Now* (1979), *English Patient* (1996), amongst many others] suggested that a good cut between shots should occur just when the watcher would blink naturally, and thus go unnoticed; the eyes would close for an instant and reopen in a new scene. Unless we make a conscious effort not to, or unexpected circumstances intervene, we tend to treat doorways like this.

Approaching a simple doorway we prepare to enter the inside or outside to which it gives access. Then, as we go through, we mentally blink, ready for the new scene – the new and different set. It is as if the

A threshold offers the opportunity of a seam in one's experience of the world.

The 1748 'Nolli' Plan of Rome, shows the internal layouts of the churches as part of the public realm. But their doorways differentiate their religious space from the profane space of the city streets and squares outside.

transition itself, that passing instant, is empty, without meaning and therefore discounted, disregarded, passed though without a thought. Before entering, your mind projects itself forward in anticipation of the new scene shortly to be encountered. Upon passing through, the new scene and its contents have to be appraised, assimilated, brought into focus and put into some sort of sense. We may not even remember stepping through the doorway, the mind being pre-primed to give its full attention to the new scene.

Doorways are seams in experience. The discovery of the phenomenological transportation they offered (provided) must have seemed, to those of us long ago who experienced them when they were less ubiquitous than they are in the modern world, like a spiritual experience, an epiphany.

In *The Sacred and the Profane* (1957) Mircea Eliade wrote:

'To exemplify the nonhomogeneity of space as experienced by nonreligious man, we may turn to any religion. We will choose an example that is accessible to everyone – a church in a modern city. For a believer, the church shares in a different space from the street in which it stands. The door that opens on the interior of the church actually signifies a solution of continuity.' (Sic; presumably translated from 'solution de continuité' – i.e. a discontinuity or fault

line.) 'The threshold that separates the two spaces also indicates the distance between two modes of being, the profane and the religious. The threshold is the limit, the boundary, the frontier that distinguishes and opposes two worlds – and at the same time the paradoxical place where those worlds communicate, where passage from the profane to the sacred world becomes possible. A similar ritual function falls to the threshold of the human habitation, and it is for this reason that the threshold is an object of great importance. Numerous rites accompany passing the domestic threshold – a bow, a prostration, a pious touch of the hand, and so on. The threshold has its guardians – gods and spirits who forbid entrance both to human enemies and to demons and the powers of pestilence. It is on the threshold that sacrifices to the guardian divinities are offered. Here too certain palaeo-oriental cultures (Babylon, Egypt, Israel) situated the judgement place. The threshold, the door show the solution of continuity...' ('identify the fault-line...') 'in space immediately and concretely; hence their great religious importance, for they are symbols and at the same time vehicles of passage from the one space to the other.'

A threshold separates a place from everywhere else.

(From Experimenting with the Co-experience Environment*, by Marlene Ivey, Centrespace, Visual Research Centre, Dundee Contemporary Arts, December 2005.)*

Threshold

In farming practices of the past, thresholds were timber boards placed across opposing doorways of a barn during threshing.

Threshing involved beating harvested wheat to loosen its protective husk and then tossing the mixture of grain and husks in the natural breeze between the two opposing doorways so that the lighter husks would blow away leaving the grain behind. The thresholds helped keep the valuable grain inside the barn so that it could be collected for grinding into flour. This is the literal meaning of the word. But in this book we have to think of 'threshold' more abstractly. The power of that timber board across the doorway of a barn was not only that it trapped the grain but also that it defined the precise interface between inside the barn and outside. As such it marked a significant junction between places, situations.

But the junction exists whether the board is there or not; the board only draws attention to the interface and provides it with a (slightly tangential) name. When we talk about 'crossing a threshold' we mean moving across a boundary from one situation into another. The threshold is the two-dimensional, invisible, insubstantial but sometimes unnerving screen through which we pass.

Thresholds are points of introduction and control, where separated places meet. They are also points of anticipation and trepidation. They establish the discipline and art of space. They set the starting lines as well as the goals and finishing lines for the journeys we make and the games we play.

Thresholds are fascinating because they punctuate every aspect of our existence; they mark our beginnings and our ends, and many steps and stages in-between. They are instruments of surprise and revelation, mystery and concealment....They can be used as instruments of communication and dramatic emphasis. Metaphorically and physically, thresholds mark the beginnings and ends of everything we do and experience. From time immemorial people have believed that thresholds in space and life possessed some magical association. Because of this, thresholds have been, and are still, seen as places for ritual and ceremony, for encounter and affirmation.

'Odysseus's heart was filled with misgivings as he hesitated before setting foot on the bronze threshold.'

Homer (*The Odyssey*, trans. E.V. Rieu 1946)

The doorway of my office, at which visitors hesitate before entering.

Threshold hesitation

When I am in my office I sit with the door open (right; a sketch plan is on p. 58). Its openness tells people I am in and hopefully makes it easier for them to come in to talk. I can see visitors as they approach and they can see me. They come through a farther door having peeped through the glass to see if I am in. Usually I acknowledge visitors while they are still a few yards outside my doorway and invite them in. But even so, they almost always hesitate, exactly at the threshold of the room, for further permission to enter. It is the same for colleagues and students as it is for strangers. If I ask them about their hesitation they think briefly and then say something along the lines of 'I was recognising that I was entering your personal domain', or 'It's a matter of politeness'. Occasionally people theorise about it, maybe saying something like, 'I think it is a learned response; young children don't do it'.

Threshold uncertainty

I once went to an art exhibition (in Dundee Contemporary Arts) and experienced a powerful and subtle work. In a small room off the main gallery there was a photograph framed on the wall near one corner. As I approached the photograph to see what it was I felt an almost imperceptible physical uncertainty, as if I had stepped onto an access hatch in the floor. Instead of looking at the photograph I looked more closely at the floor. There was no access hatch but I saw that a large square of the floor, tight in the corner of the room,

'We feel giddy at the first step we make on the pavement, for it is of Greek mosaic, waved like the sea, and dyed like a dove's neck.'

John Ruskin (*Stones of Venice*, 1853)

Bernard BAZILE - Brilliance (le coin de billard) 1980

the photograph of the same idea in another place draws you in. You sense crossing the threshold!

a threshold of the clean, or freshly painted.

was very slightly lighter than the rest, as if it had been freshly cleaned or painted. It was the same on the two adjacent walls, so that the three squares of clean or fresh surface implied a cube of space in front of the photograph. (See the drawing on the right.) My uncertainty had struck me just as I crossed the threshold of this cube; my peripheral vision had noticed the tiny change in the floor's tone as I stepped into it and warned me to take care. Eventually, after enjoying the illusion of this cube of space, I went to look at the photograph and found it showed the same work in another, more ornate, gallery; a similar cube of space had been cleaned in front of another framed photograph of the same work in yet another different gallery… producing the effect of a *mise en abŷme*.

Our sense of threshold

These two anecdotes illustrate how keen our sense of threshold is. Our acute sensitivity to thresholds seems part of an innate caution we carry with us as part of our mechanisms for self protection. The visitors who pause at the threshold of my room are not only being polite in waiting for permission to enter but might also be concerned that I may be jealous of my domain. They could also be taking advantage of a first chance to survey the whole room to see if anyone else

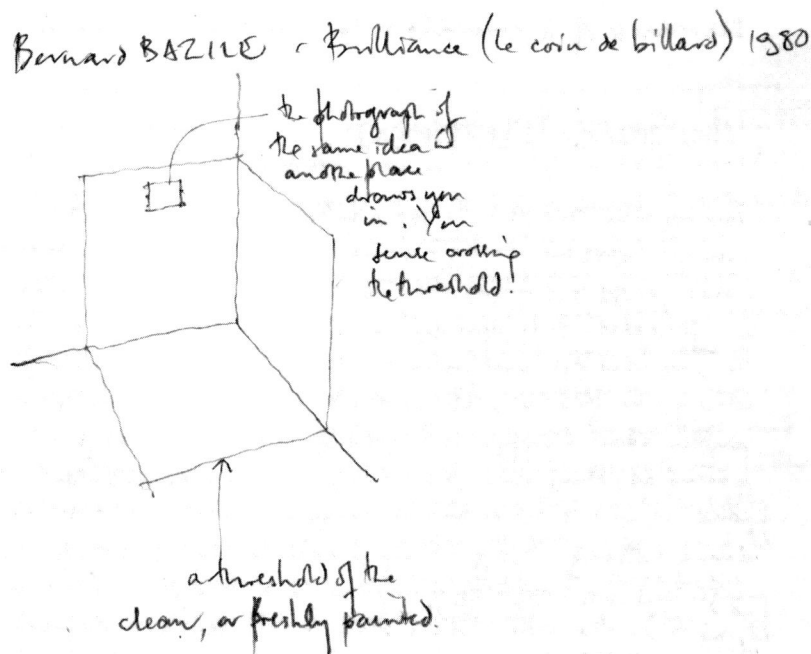

is there who might, by their presence, change the nature of our conversation. And when I stepped onto the area of clean fresh floor in the art gallery I was concerned that I had maybe stepped onto something that did not have the same solid firmness as the proper floor. I was, just for an instant, worried that I had put my safety in jeopardy, that I might fall through the floor or had stepped on something I should not have.

Research with small children suggests that the wariness of thresholds develops sometime between the ages of five and nine months. An experiment was set up using a glass table top with a visually solid surface beneath part of it, producing the appearance of a precipice. At five months babies would happily crawl across the apparent chasm to reach their mothers. But at nine

The drawing is a poor diagram of the work – 'Brilliance (le coin du billard)' by Bernard Bazile (1980). The lines that I have had to use to clarify the edges of the 'clean' areas were not there in the real work.

81

months they stopped at the 'edge' and cried, no matter how much their mothers coaxed them forward.*

Our sense of threshold is powerful. It seems bound up with human morality. In 1894 H. Clay Trumbull published a book called *The Threshold Covenant* in which he collected many examples of rites and ceremonies performed at thresholds in different cultures across the world. Amongst these he reported a brief conversation he had had with a Syrian woman:

'I asked (her), "If a thief wanted to get into your home to steal from you, would he come in at the door, if he saw that open?" "Oh, no!" she answered, "he would come in at the window, or would dig in from behind." "Why wouldn't he come in at the door?" I asked. "Because his reverence would keep him from that," she said, in evident reference to the superstitious dread of crossing a threshold with evil intent.'

Trumbull reported similar reverence for the threshold amongst contemporary Scandinavian immigrants in Wisconsin and Minnesota.

Our sense of threshold seems innate, or at least it is a profound faculty by which we learn, even as very young children, to make sense of the world in our minds. Sometimes children as they get older assert their developing independence by standing in places that are clearly separate from their parents: on top of a rock; inside a cave; in a tide pool on the beach; on the other side of a bush… and then taunt their parents with calls of 'can't catch me', or 'I'm the king of the castle'. To do so a child crosses a threshold that it senses, leaving the place it sees as being occupied by its parents and entering another apparently distinct place, to occupy it alone… and with (mock?) defiance. Throughout growing up, many further thresholds are crossed, some with their own manifestations in place and architecture: the adolescent bedroom that parents must not clean or even enter; the giving of a key to the door of the house; moving out to a house or flat….

Lines of discontinuity

The primary manifestation of the seam is of course the doorway in its wall. But often there are subtle nuances associated with the opening that reinforce its role as a fairly precise though insubstantial interface between places. There is a step and a change in floor surfaces between the jambs of the doorway in the photograph on p. 76; and some of the more mundane occurrences are shown in the drawing on the next page. There might be a step or a strip of wood; it might be the metal bar that a carpet-layer uses to join two carpets; it might be the frame a door closes

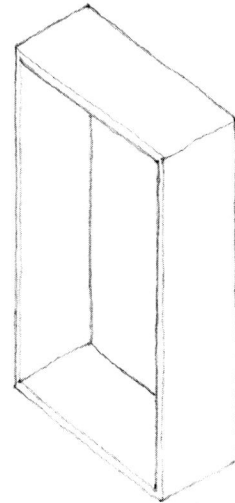

One of the strongest experiences of 'threshold uncertainty' is when we pass through the magnetic gateway of airport security. At the moment of transition we know we are under scrutiny.

* *This research was reported in Walk R.D. & Gibson, E.J. – 'A comparative and analytical study of visual depth perception', in* Psychological Monographs *75, 519, 1961.*

against, or just a change in the material or texture of the floor. A line of stones, a step or the frame of a door may be there for functional reasons – to stop rain water flowing inside or to hold a door in place – but they also make the threshold between inside and out, which is framed by the doorway in the wall, more precise, more like the line in the sand. The line of stones and the step also make you acknowledge the threshold by stepping over or up. If you were asked to point to the junction between inside and out it is likely you would point to the line of stones, the step or the frame.

Some more poetic examples

Sometimes architects make more of this seam in experience, and draw our attention to it in subtle and poetic ways.

The gap between these two stepping stones (right) is in a traditional Japanese garden, forming the approach to the entrance of a shelter. As well as allowing the water of the small stream to flow freely, the gap affects how you approach the doorway. It accentuates the seam in experience involved in entering the realm of the building. In making you step carefully and deliberately, it makes you aware that you are passing from one world into another, from the garden to the interior.

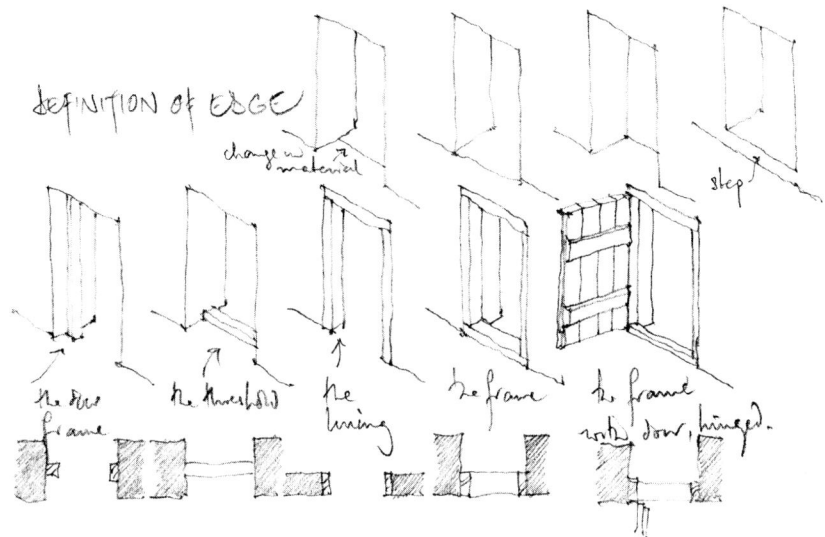

The line of threshold is marked in various ways, even in mundane doorways (above).

Sometimes attention is drawn to the seam in more poetic ways, as in this example from a traditional Japanese garden.

The Swiss architect Peter Zumthor has designed entrances that draw particular attention to the 'solution de continuité' that occurs at the entrance to a building. Here are two examples from his work in the 1990s. Both are in Switzerland.

In Chur, Zumthor designed a shelter for some Roman archaeological remains. Its doorway is formed in a steel box that projects out of the slatted timber walls of the shelter. (The remains need the ventilation the open slats provide.) The steel box incorporates four steps up to the doorway, but it does not touch the ground. You have to step up, crossing the vertical gap, and into the blinkered enclosure of the box before entering the building to see the remains. This entrance is like a bridge between the present and the historic past inside; it detaches you from the everyday world around before it allows you into the special world of the archaeology, which you view from a raised gantry. Of course the metal box *gives* very slightly as you step onto it, and that slight insecurity resonates with the natural uncertainty you experience as you step through any entrance.

The second example is on a remote hillside at Song Benedikt. Here Zumthor built a small chapel with a plan like a tear drop (right). This entrance projects into the outside world too, but not in the same way

as at Chur. The projection of this doorway allows you, when you have climbed the steps and opened the door, to see the interior without being quite inside. There is a small buffer zone between outside and inside.

The seam in experience at the doorway is subtly underlined, literally, by the fact that the concrete steps do not quite touch the sill of the door. Here too there is a discontinuity, a vertical gap between the steps and the building. This gap is narrow; but it is enough to reinforce one's sense of stepping from a grounded surface (the concrete steps) onto a floating one (the floor of the church). The experience of entering is similar to stepping onto a boat. (There is, of course, a long established symbolic association between churches and boats.)

Above left: the entrance to the shelter for the Roman archaeological remains in Chur.

Above: the entrance to the small chapel at Song Benedikt. The plan of the chapel is shown below.

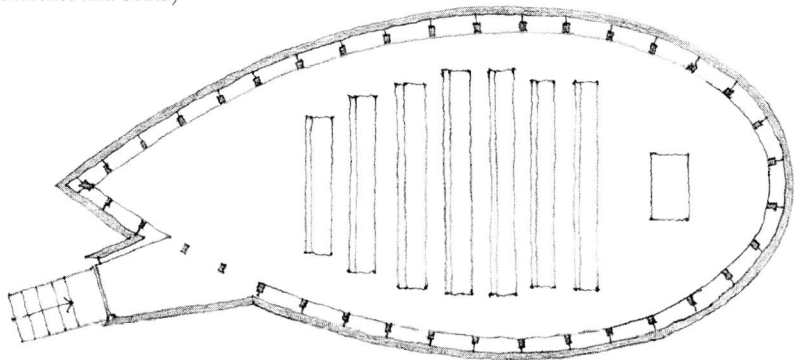

TRANSGRESSION (illicit doorways)

'Flopsy, Mopsy and Cottontail, who were good little bunnies, went down the lane to gather blackberries. But Peter, who was very naughty, ran straight away to Mr McGregor's garden, and squeezed under the gate.'

Beatrix Potter *(The Tale of Peter Rabbit, 1902)*

The Syrian woman reported by Trumbull (p. 82) suggested that a thief's 'reverence' for a threshold would keep him from entering the house of his victim through an open doorway. Both the recluse (p. 18) and the man on the beach (p. 15) used physically inadequate means to exert psychological influence on strangers to keep out of their territory. These examples allude to rules of behaviour associated with the powers of lines of demarcation.

Building walls and fitting doors reinforces the psychological power of seams in experience by physical means. And if a wall is the physical manifestation of a spatial rule, then climbing over it, breaking through it, tunnelling under it... – i.e. breaching it in any way other than entering through a doorway open as a sign of permission – is a transgression of that rule. The moral point is made in the Bible:

'Verily, verily, I say unto you, He that entereth not by the door into the sheepfold, but climbeth up in some other way, the same is a thief and a robber.' (John 10:1-3)

But lines of demarcation, rules, invite transgression. We know there are thieves that do not revere thresholds; and that there are some for whom the recluse's truck or the man on the beach's line in the sand would be more a challenge than a barrier.

The doorway is the right and proper way to enter, to pass through a wall; to enter by any other way would be false and subversive. But children must climb over orchard walls to steal apples; to go in through the gate would spoil the excitement. Remus had to challenge Romulus's furrow (p. 14) even though it resulted in his death.

It is essential to the Steve McQueen character in *The Great Escape* (John Sturges, 1963) that he transgresses boundaries. It is

There is a place on the line of Hadrian's Wall, which stretched from coast to coast across the north of England, called 'Busy Gap'. As a lasting barrier, the wall defined a physical boundary between land to the north and land to the south even after the imperial Roman legions had left Britain. In medieval times, the 'Busy Gap' was a broad opening in the wall through which there was much illicit movement of livestock between Scotland and England.

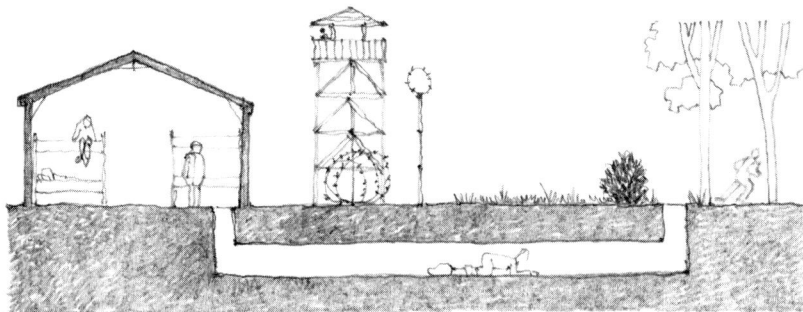

An escape tunnel from a prison camp is a doorway to freedom that breaks the rule established by the fence. To one side in the war, the escapers are villains, to the other, heroes.

an aspect of his heroism; and he does it in different ways: being cheeky to the guards; escaping from the prison camp through a tunnel; jumping a barbed wire fence on his motorbike…. A rebellious American youth of the 1950s would not be seen opening the door of his convertible; he would rather leap over it directly into the driving seat. That womanizing agent of government espionage and power, James Bond, would always rather arrive at the boundary of his adversary's territory underwater in a wet suit over a cream dinner jacket, or by crashing through a wall in a speedboat, than by any conventional route. And those East Berliners who previously could not have passed through Checkpoint Charlie, and who managed to create ruptures in the Berlin Wall in 1989 so that the barrier between East and West was broken, were considered heroes and agents of liberation.

We have an equivocating relationship with rules. Some of the most intriguing doorways are those through which we ought not to pass, or those that are not proper doorways at all but breaks in fences or gaps in walls. Metaphorically and actually, we may think of these as doorways of escape and creativity, of covert desire and unexpected discovery, of secret incursion and the subversion of authority. Illicit doorways may be the points of access for thieves intent on robbing our houses, or conduits to freedom for psychotic murderers escaping from prison, but they are also the routes taken by geniuses and heroes, artists and spies, adventurers and liberating armies.

A break in a fence is an illicit entrance, open for those the fence was made to keep out.

The stitching of a break in a fence is reassertion of the rule the fence establishes.

A crack in the wall

In the story of Pyramus and Thisbe as told by the Roman poet Ovid, it is through a crack in the wall between them that two lovers communicate. This extract is from Ted Hughes's version of the story:

> 'In the shared wall that divided their houses, Earth-tremors had opened a fissure. For years, neither household had noticed. But these lovers noticed. Love is not blind. And where love cannot peer Pure clairvoyance whispers in its ear. This crack, this dusty crawl-space for a spider, Became the highway of their love-murmurs. Brows to the plaster, lips to the leak of air And cooking smells from the other interior, The lovers kneeled, confessing their passion, Sealing their two fates with a fracture. Sometimes they slapped the wall, in frustration: "How can a wall be so jealous! So deaf to us, so grudging with permission! If you can open this far for our voices Why not fall wide open, let us kiss, Let us join bodies as well as voices." "No, that would be too much. That would mean The wall repaired to part us utterly." "O wall, we are grateful. Nowhere in the world But in this tiny crack may our great loves, Invisibly to us, meet and mingle." '

The crack symbolises the precarious and seemingly illicit threshold of intimacy and empathy that exists between the lovers. It makes an unregulated break in the wall of individuality that separates the two people. Though this is one that they may not pass through to kiss, like any threshold it represents the point at which people meet.

Summer of 27 Missing Kisses

In the film *Summer of 27 Missing Kisses* (Nana Dzhordzhadze, 2000), it is part of the mood of the film that its characters often transgress physical boundaries in the same unconventional ways they transgress social boundaries. Often the heroine, the fourteen year old Sybilla, and her co-characters, disdain to use doorways and prefer to enter or leave rooms by any other available opening, such as a window or a broken wire fence.

In one scene, when she is spying on the middle-aged man she loves (unrequitedly), who is meeting his lover in an empty house, Sybilla swims across a river, climbs a wall, and clambers in through a window to hide under the table on which the man and woman have sex. In other scenes, she climbs through rifts in broken fences, or through the cleft in a tree to find honey, or precariously crosses fragile single plank bridges. With the boy who loves her (also unrequitedly – the son of the man she loves), she breaks in to the back of the cinema where the grown-ups are watching the sex film *Emmanuelle*, and they both sit behind the screen watching both

'Since I had shut the gate
And locked the door
Whence did you, dear one, enter
To appear in my dream?

Though you had shut the gate
And locked the door,
I must have come to you in your dream
Through the hole cut by a thief.'

Anonymous (*Man'yōshū*, AD8thC, trans. Hodgson *et al*)

the film and the audience. Testing boundaries, and orthodox moral compartments, is essential to the film. It is expressed in the characters' behaviour and in the ways they navigate architectural space.

Artificial rupture

Some architects have tried to exploit the poetic rebellious and creative aspects of a rupture as a threshold. For example, in the 1970s the American architects called SITE designed a store for Best supermarkets (top right). At the beginning of each day the store was opened by pulling a section of brick wall away from one corner. Shoppers entered the store through this artificial rupture in the wall.

When, in August 2005, the guerilla artist Banksy made a series of stencil pictures on the Palestinian side of the Israeli wall around the West Bank, he chose images that implied escape (a ladder, and a girl hanging from a bunch of balloons; the cut-out goal on p. 21) and of imagined breaches in the wall. One is an image of a small boy with a bucket and spade standing on a rock in front of a blue sky, peering inquisitively as if through a hole in the wall (bottom right).

Ruptures that are illicit doorways are like wounds in the skin of a body. A gap in a fence or crack in a wall is like a wound in

the fabric that controls space. Science fiction uses the idea of 'warps' between one time and another. One of the heroes of Philip Pullman's *His Dark Materials* trilogy obtains a 'subtle knife' with which he is able to cut through the fabric of space between parallel worlds. A wound is an entrance that should not be there. A wound disrupts the integrity of a body and threatens its well-being. A wound is made better when it heals. A break in the security fence of a police station in Northern Ireland, a military base in Iraq or of an airport anywhere, threatens its security. A break in the wall of your garden lets in the sheep to eat your cabbages. A wound in the wall of a house can kill it by destroying the shelter and privacy it provides.

St Bride's, East Kilbride

Perhaps it is because architects are essentially agents of control, and certainly they would worry if their walls developed cracks (lovers or no lovers), that their attempts to create entrances as rifts in the fabric of a barrier often seem contrived. The real breaks that the East Germans made in the Berlin Wall in 1989 to enter the West seem more powerful than any contrived by the design of architects. More poetic than most is the entrance to this church in Scotland. St Bride's, East Kilbride (opposite), has an entrance that is

SITE architects designed a supermarket with an entrance like a crack in the wall.

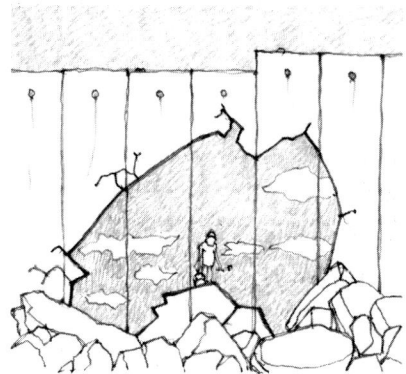

The artisit Banksy subversively suggested broken openings in the wall between Israel and the West Bank.

unusual; it is like a warp in the severe high brick wall that encloses the main body of the church.

The approach to the church (above) is from the everyday world of a rather ordinary and quite busy road, up some steps onto a forecourt which is like the piazza in front of an Italian church. The actual entrance is however very different from an orthodox doorway through a wall. Whereas the entrance in many Italian churches is on axis with the altar, and as you enter you are confronted with the sanctuary, as in the cathedral at Cefalù (pp. 47–51), here you seem to insinuate yourself through a fissure in the church's brick wall.

Italian churches often assert an order that confidently asserts the presence of religion in the landscape or at the heart of a town. Here at St Bride's the entrance suggests a secret, more mysterious and primal religion. The church interior, echoing some of the work of Le Corbusier and of Sigurd Lewerentz (whose church at Klippan is described later in this book), is something more like a cave. Here there is the sense of a religion needing protection behind its curtain wall. As you enter you feel complicit in the concealment of the rites that are practised inside. It is not so much going through a doorway, but pushing through the overlap of a pair of grand brick curtains, either to reach the sacred stage within, or to leave the secular stage behind to present oneself to the audience of a judge. The curtain has not been opened for you. Entering, you feel a little like Sybilla and her friend in *27*

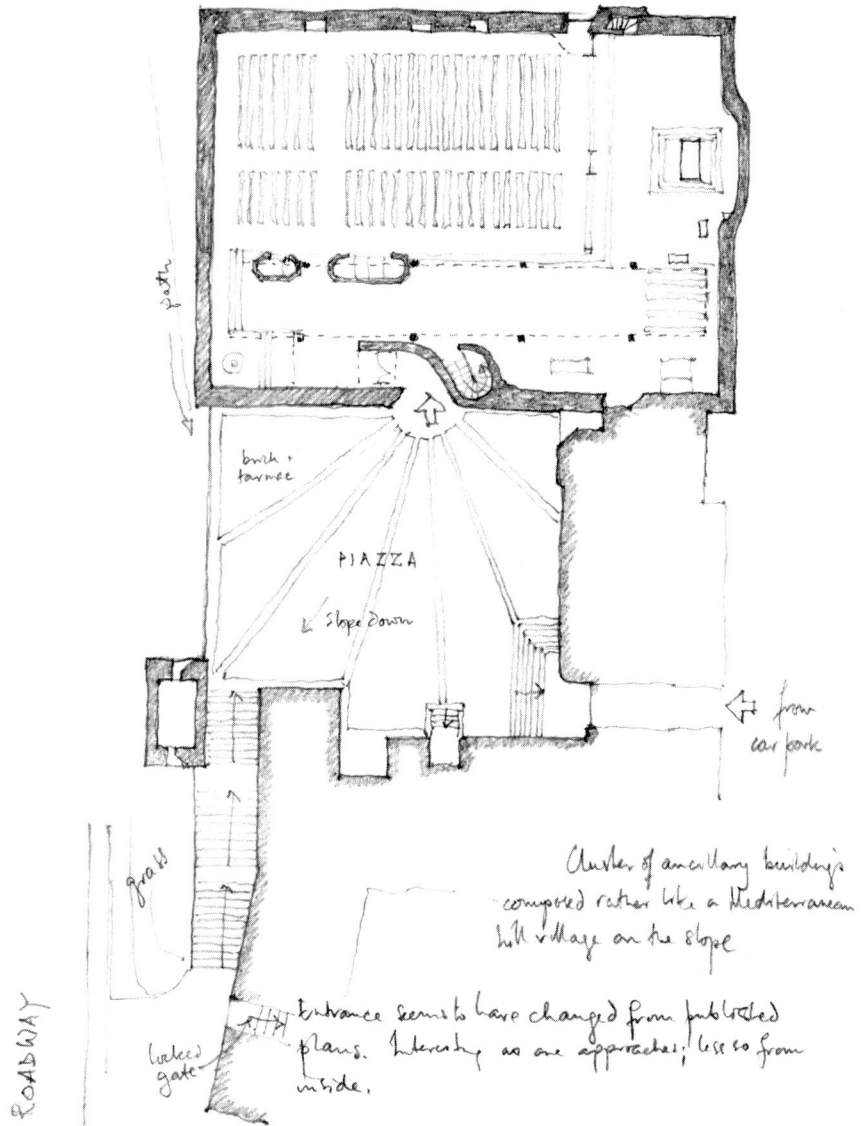

Entering this church in East Kilbride is like pushing through between two huge brick curtains to find the secret audience behind.

89

PLAN

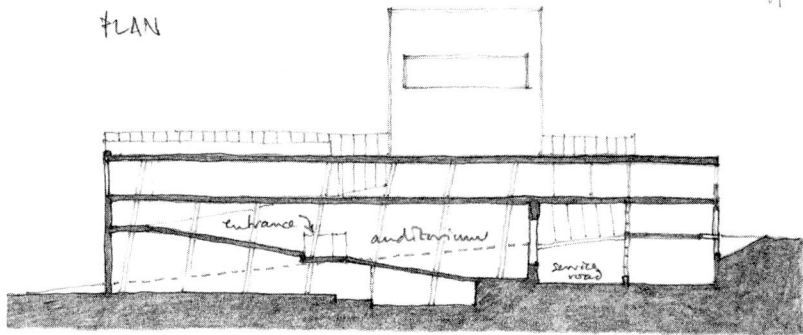

SECTION through auditorium with line of ramp ('street') dashed, and entrance at point of crossing

Missing Kisses sneaking behind the curtains in the cinema. The rift in the wall that forms the entrance makes entrance into the church feel like intrusion.

Kunsthal, Rotterdam

If you were to visit the Kunsthal in Rotterdam, designed by Rem Koolhaas and built in 1993 (right), it is likely you would first try to enter in the wrong place and hit up against an impenetrable glass wall. The actual entrance is hidden away down a sloping 'street' that runs through the building, and feels subversive. Andrew MacNair (in *Architecture and Urbanism*, August 1994) described Koolhaas's entrance (with some hyperbole) like this:

> *'At the point of shear, Bang! – a rupture occurs between these two concrete planes; the tiny ticket booth and small, almost obscure entrance door and miniature vestibule form a crunched entrance – a compressed doorway off the main street. Point of rupture equals entrance/exit: jammed into the most sensitive and critical fault line breaking the two slopes and marking the only safe leap from one shifting broken land plane to the next. Entrance is a leap of faith. While impossible for the handicapped, this tiny but monumental moment celebrates notions of aberrant structure, a fundamental of De-constructivist architecture, an architecture of anxiety. The entrance is the post-disaster episode*

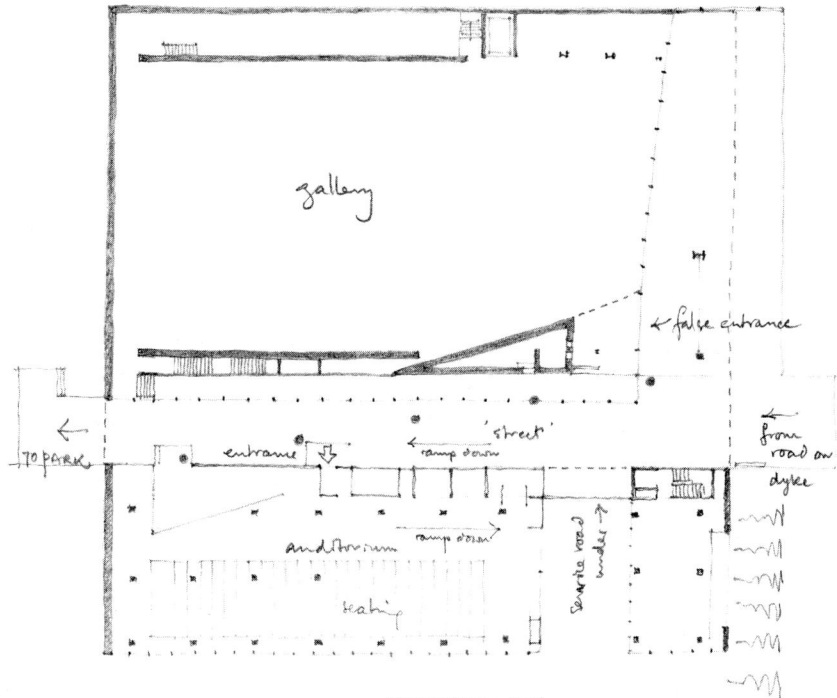

before the disaster hits, a post-earthquake model made into theory and simultaneously built into pre-earthquake practice. There is no retro-active manifesto, only hard-core evidence.'

The actual entrance to the Kunsthal could hardly live up to MacNair's prose; but the poetic idea of the doorway situated at a rupture, and which feels in some way illicit or subversive, remains a possibility.

Koolhaas's Kunsthal in Rotterdam has an entrance that is hidden away, and feels subversive. It contrasts with the celebratory entrances of most art galleries and public buildings.

REFUGE

In her novel *Eva Luna* (1987), Isabel Allende describes Eva finding refuge in a church:

> *'Soldiers came and fought their way through with clubs and gunfire. I started to run, looking for a place where I could wait until both the tumult in the plaza and the rhythm of my breathing died down. I saw that the side door of the church was half-open, and I ran straight to it and slipped inside. I could still hear the noise outside, but it was muted, as if happening in some distant time. I sat down in the nearest pew, suddenly weak from the accumulated exhaustion of the last days. I put my feet on the kneeler and rested my head on the back of the pew. Little by little I began to feel calm; it was peaceful in that dark refuge, surrounded by columns and immutable saints, cloaked in silence and coolness.'*

In this example the doorway through which Eva slips is the threshold between danger and safety. On one side of it she is running for her life amidst chaos in the street. On the other she can catch her breath. The doorway is the interface. Her passage through it changes her state of being. Her refuge might not be completely safe from violation by the rampaging soldiers but it feels like an escape.

This is an intuitive response to the world. We need respite and rest. When a mouse senses danger it runs for its hole in the skirting board. A bullied child hides in a lavatory cubicle. When we have been out or away we come back through our front door and are home, where we can relax.

Where they are needed we make doorways that offer refuge. The first prehistoric doorway was probably a doorway into safety; into a cave or shelter. A doorway transports us from one world into another and crossing the threshold affects our state of being and state of mind.

Cells

Remember what it feels like to go into a garden shed (above). It is like going inside

A shed in the countryside offers a refuge from the agoraphobia of the landscape.

your own head. It is dark and calm; probably distinctly warmer or cooler than outside. As in Eva's refuge, the sound inside is muffled. There is no breeze. Outside, we are under the bright light of the sky and under the scrutiny of other people. Inside, we find calm to gather our thoughts and reflect; to commune with the gods that live in small cells.

We tend to think of a doorway as serving the space into which it leads but it can be the other way around, with the space serving the doorway.

The chapel in the photograph alongside is a built doorway into peace and dark. The inside serves the experience expected of going through the doorway. It is the doorway that is the verb of the architectural sentence that the chapel represents. You are the object and the space inside the subject. The walls and roof provide the refuge that the doorway offers.

This is a timeless effect. It is as powerful today as it has always been.

In Switzerland there is a tradition of building small single-cell chapels in the countryside, often at the base of great mountains. They are always open so climbers may pray in them before their ascent. The spiritual refuge they provide is similar to the physical refuge mountain rescue huts provide in remote places, where climbers might need to escape from the storm. The example alongside is

the chapel at Oberrealta, designed by Rudolf Fontana and built in 1994. It is simply built of one material, concrete. Like the chapel above, it provides a simple doorway into a place of seclusion, an enclosed cell.

These doorways are like the mouse's hole in the skirting board. They take you out of the world. They offer refuge, and something else – sense and order.

Above: a tiny chapel on the island of Corsica.

Below: the front elevation and plan of the small chapel at Oberrealta, designed by Rudolf Fontana.

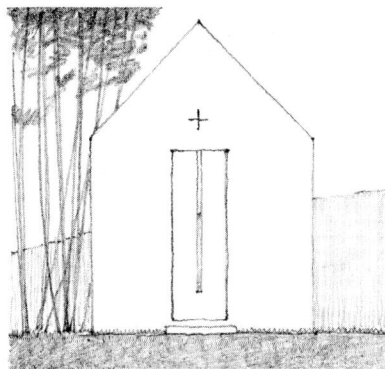

'We can imagine a time when, in the infancy of the human race, some enterprising mortal crept into a hollow in a rock for shelter.'
        Henry David Thoreau (*Walden*, 1854)

Thoreau's cabin

When the American philosopher Henry David Thoreau decided, in the 1840s, to withdraw from the world and live a simple life by Walden Pond, he built himself a cabin. It was tiny – ten feet by fifteen (3 metres by 4.5) – and, according to its modern reconstruction, looked like nothing more than a garden shed (right).

But Thoreau's dwelling, with its simple form and arrangement, was just as much as his writings a product of his philosophy – the world he imagined for himself. It tells of the way he wanted to live and of the places he gave himself to sleep, cook, pile his logs for fuel, and write. Its simple, direct and purposeful construction was a physical manifestation of his simple, direct and self-reliant attitude to life.

Within the rectangle of its plan are contained a hearth for warmth, a bed for sleep, a table by the window at which to sit and write, and a chest for storage.

In his book *Walden* (1854), Thoreau described his life by the pond. He told how he built his cabin. He even gave a detailed list of the materials he used. On his motives for building himself a cabin he commented:

'There is some of the same fitness in a man's building his own house that there is in a bird's building its own nest. Who knows but if men constructed their dwellings with their own hands… the poetic faculty would be universally developed, as birds universally sing when they are so engaged?'

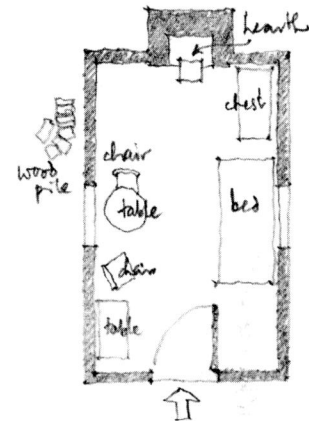

He might have added to the first sentence of the above quotation: '… or in a man's developing his own philosophy of life'. Thoreau's ideas were framed by the form of his cabin as much as by his framing of them in words. Perhaps his cabin is an even more direct and eloquent expression of his philosophy than his words.

The reconstruction of Thoreau's cabin once featured in a radio talk on the B.B.C. Standing inside the cabin the speaker, Geoff Ward, commented:

'It hardly seems big enough to contain Thoreau's mind… and anyway, can a house ever be just a house? Isn't a house this size, as the door closes around its single inhabitant, more like a brain; some kind of containment which is barely bigger than the human being who sleeps and works inside it?'

The front elevation and plan of Thoreau's cabin at Walden Pond near Concord, Massachusetts.

'The set is the geometry of the eventual play, so that the wrong set makes many scenes impossible to play, and even destroys many possibilities for the actors.'

Peter Brook (*The Empty Space*, 1968)

This comment seems to put a finger on the intimate relationship that can exist between a place and the life it accommodates. Even a simple cabin is the product as well as the container of a mind. As architect/philosopher, Thoreau used his hearth, roof, walls, a doorway, windows and furniture to give sense and order to the space in which he was to live. Its walls and roof protected him from the wind, rain and snow; the hearth gave it warmth and he gave it life. Thoreau did this practically, poetically and as a manifesto on how people might live in the world.

Thoreau's cabin, like his philosophy, made a virtue of simplicity. Its floor, walls and roof mediated between him and the landscape and weather; its interior gave a centre to his world, an inside juxtaposed with the great outside. He lived in his cabin and in the landscape but his single-roomed cell provided him with a datum, a point of reference he could call home.

When Thoreau lived there, there were many links between his inside living space and his outside world. He took his mind and senses out with him into the woods and onto the pond. He brought his thoughts and observations back inside with him in his memory and noted them down.

Thoreau passed through his doorway many times. Although the threads linking inside and outside were many and subtle, they gathered at the cabin's door – the threshold: the point where he instantly changed from being a 'person inside' to a 'person out in the world'; where he could close the door and shut himself in his own solitude; where he might welcome a visitor, or just sit musing:

'There were times when I could not sacrifice the bloom of the present moment to any work, whether of the head or hands. I love a broad margin to my life. Sometimes, in a summer morning, having taken my accustomed bath, I sat in my sunny doorway from sunrise until noon, rapt in revery, amidst the pines and hickories and sumachs, in undisturbed solitude and stillness, while the birds sang around or flitted noiseless through the house, until by the sun falling in at my west window, or the noise of some traveller's wagon on the distant highway, I was reminded of the lapse of time. I grew in those seasons like corn in the night, and they were far better than any work of the hands would have been. They were not time subtracted from my life, but so much over and above my usual allowance.'

The framing of Thoreau's deep meditation sitting in the sun by the doorway of his cabin – the point between the interior world (of the mind) and the external world (of nature and other people) – evokes an image with which it is easy to identify. Everyone of us will at some time have paused for a moment of thought at a threshold.

CHANGING HOW ONE SEES THE WORLD

Architecture is the medium through which the world is changed. Destruction and building are twin activities by which we alter our surroundings physically. As a consequence of the architectural impetus to make places to accommodate our lives and possessions, ground is levelled, forests are cleared, existing buildings demolished, boundaries defined, pathways struck, walls erected and roofs raised.

But the powers of architecture are not confined within the material forms of buildings. Elements of architecture project their influence around them into space. A wall may support a roof but it also divides or encloses space. We have seen how a doorway, through its axis, can establish linkage between people and places that may be as remote as a distant star. They can also change how the world appears to us, and the meanings we invest in it.

For the imagination, two trees growing close together in the woods suggest a doorway into another world where strange creatures live and magical things happen. One can get a glimpse of that other world through the gap between the trees.

Doorways can always stimulate our imaginations. They suggest to us that what lies through them is a world that is in some way different from the one we are in. Doorways can be frightening because we do not know what is through them. But they may alternatively make the place on the other side seem more sacred or more comfortable, more exclusive or privileged, more culturally refined or just sunnier than ours. They can make us imbue that other place with special virtues, yearn to go there, and respect or envy those who are lucky enough to be there.

Shinto gate

A doorway in open countryside, like the doorway 'to enter into darkness' erected by Sottsass in the desert (p. 16), transforms the landscape. In a similar way a Shinto gateway (above) changes the whole landscape, not only by its own sculptural presence, nor the scene it frames like a picture, but by its suggestion of a different world beyond. It provokes the idea that you might undergo some spiritual change if you were to pass through it. Because of it the world looks different. It offers the promise of another, presumably, better world. It divides a sacred world from the profane. It projects sacredness from one into the other.

In Japan a Shinto gate defines a sacred place.

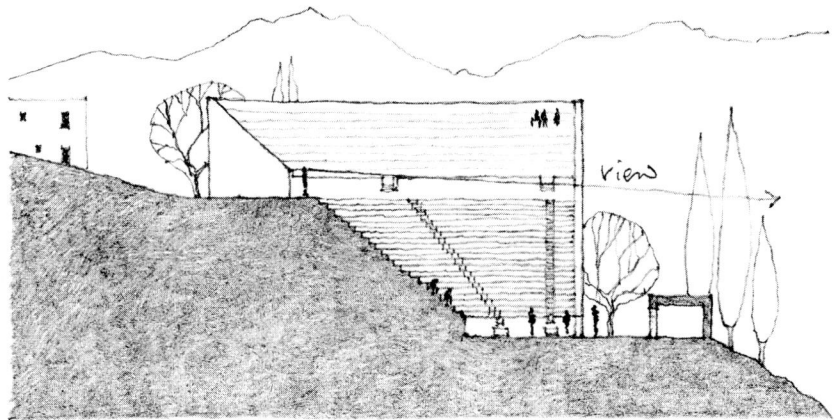

SECTION

Theatre, Segesta

There is a small ancient theatre near the top of a hill at Segesta in Sicily. It is set amongst the broad and dramatic island landscape. The theatre was built by the Greeks some two thousand years ago. Its plan and section are on this page.

To approach the theatre you must climb a substantial hill from the valley below (where there is a great unfinished temple in a sacred landscape). You have to cross the top of the hill where the ancient town of Segesta once stood, to reach the curved back wall of the theatre.

When you get there you see an opening in the wall, which invites you to enter the theatre. (See the top photograph on the opposite page.) You walk between the topmost ranks of seating (see the section above) and emerge into the theatre about two-thirds the way up. You are enclosed by its curve. You look down the steps of seating to the magic circle of the theatre's *orkestra* (performance area). Most impressively, you see the landscape framed by the theatre. (See the lower photograph on the opposite page.)

The theatre transforms the landscape. There are the same mountains that you were amongst before as you crossed the top of the hill, but when you enter the theatre they become special, imbued with

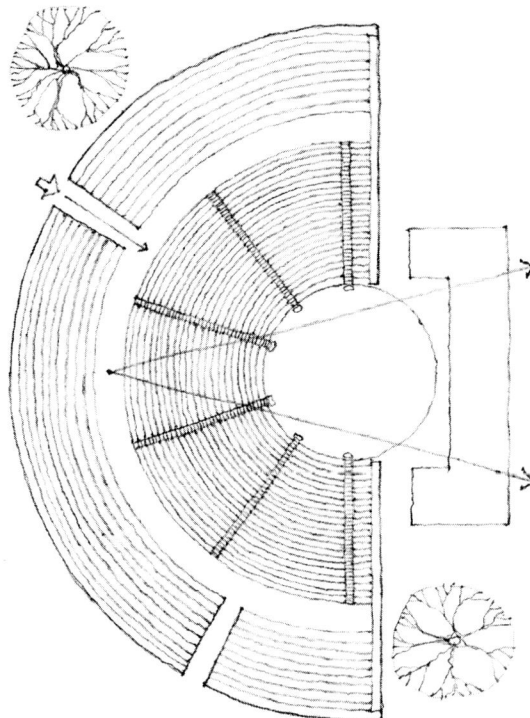

PLAN

dramatic presence. The effect is compelling. Because the steps in front of you are steep you feel a slight vertigo, as if you are floating above the real ground. The landscape in the distance is separate and ominous. The theatre's inverted half-cone of seating points directly towards the peak of one particular mountain – the sanctuary of a god who will watch and intervene in the play.

The theatre faces north; the sun is behind you, to light the actors. As clouds make moving shadows across the land, the whole scene changes in the sunlight like a motion picture projected on a screen before you. The screen is not there but stands between you and the distance – a threshold beyond a threshold, dividing the special realm of the drama from that of the god-inhabited landscape.

The physical form of the theatre is the architectural instrument that produces these effects – the disposition of zones for you, for the actors and for the gods. It is a subtle frame and displacement device, like that of a painting, movie screen, television or computer. The screen, the frame, the displacement, conjure up the in-between realm where the drama takes place. It was the doorway of the theatre that propelled you into this situation where you see the world differently, where the gods are unseen actors in the narrative of the play.

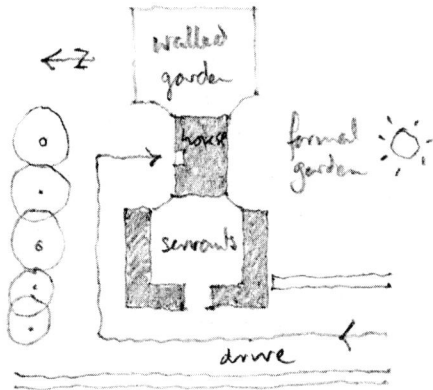

House of Dun

The ancient Greeks were sensitive to the ways in which they could change perceptions of the landscape by their insertions into it. Wealthy gentlemen in eighteenth century Britain were conscious of the ways in which they could enhance people's perceptions of their nobility, culture and status by the architecture of the grand houses within which they wrapped and structured their domestic lives.

The House of Dun, near Montrose in Scotland, was designed by William Adam and built in the 1730s for David Erskine, 13th Lord of Dun. The house stands some distance on the north side of a public road and, as one might expect, is oriented so that the principal rooms face the sun in the south. (The plan and section are on this page.)

The approach to the house is also from the south, but rather than take the visitor directly to the front of the house facing the approach, Adam takes the approach drive around to the north elevation which, when the sun shines, is in shadow. (See the small plan above.) The drive rises up a gentle slope, past fields and hedges that screen the gardens from view, and past the grandly arched entrance into the servants yard. In itself, this extended approach impresses the visitor with the lord's extensive estate.

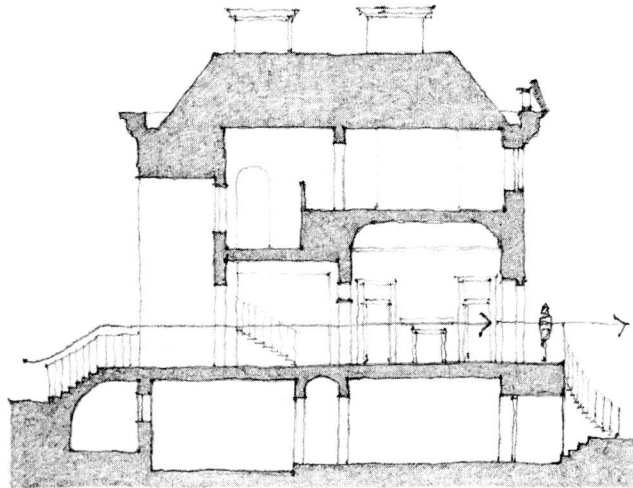

SECTION

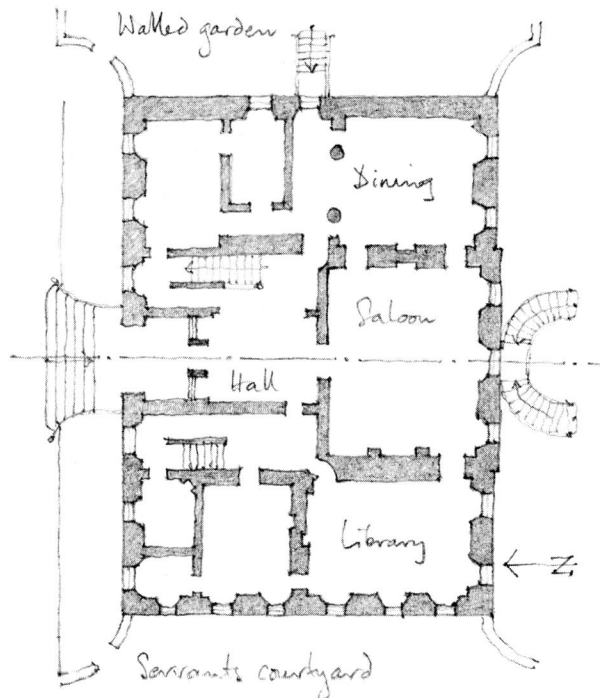

PLAN

The main door of the house, which is on the central axis of the north elevation, is set within a deep arched recess shown in the photographs on the right. To reach the door you ascend a short and wide flight of steps, which bridges over a servants passageway beneath. As you approach the half-glazed front door you see a window, on axis, at the opposite side of the house, through the Saloon. In contrast to the shaded elevation you have approached, the window is bright with sunshine. As you walk through the doorway you enter a world of sunshine. This is the world in which the owners of the house live.

Having been granted entry, you cross the house, with it rising ceilings, to stand by the windows of the Saloon and look out into a world that appears different from the one through which you arrived. Now you find yourself on the superior level inhabited by the lord and his family, raised a storey above ground level. Beneath, as in the slightly earlier Chiswick Villa (p. 64) and the much earlier Villa Rotonda (p. 43), is the world of the servants.

The sunny world you see from this privileged vantage point is of a neat and well-ordered formal garden with a distant view of fertile farm land (and the Montrose Basin, a sea-water lake, in the distance). The axis you joined at the front door can now be seen to

99

extend into the formal garden and through a sun dial in the middle distance, suggesting that it projects across the land to the distant horizon (right).

A panel under the central Saloon window opens so that it becomes a doorway. When you have descended the elegant steps into the garden you can look back and see the neatly ordered house brightly lit against a dark backdrop of large Wellingtonia trees.

The House of Dun is an example of the surreptitious manipulation of experience and emotion that architecture can achieve. The effect depends partly on the Classical character of the building and its devotion to the discipline and projection of the doorway axis. More, it comes from the architect's sensitivity to route management, orientation and the timelessly dramatic potential of entrance through a doorway.

The view from the south front of the House of Dun.

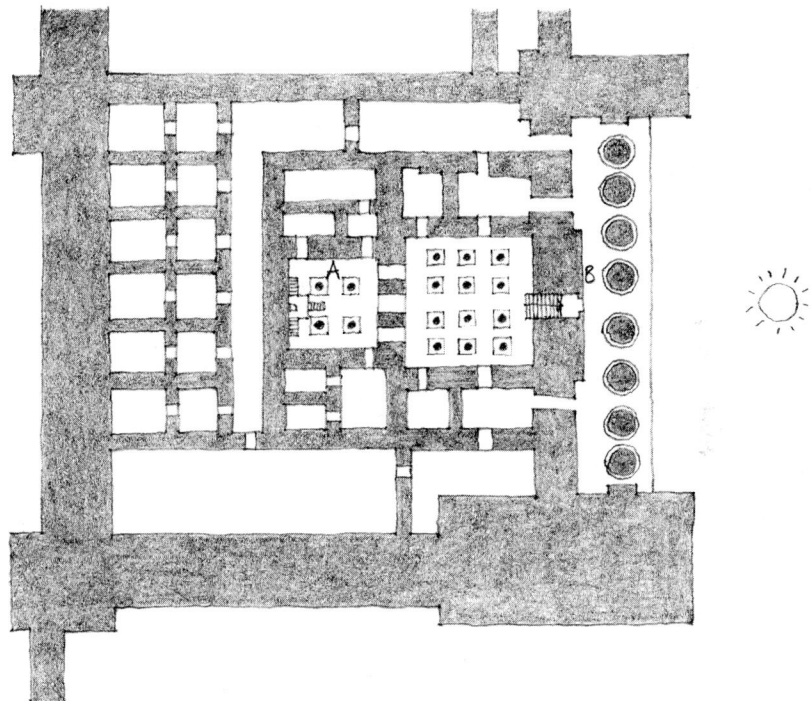

Because they are frames and may be operated like switches, doorways and doors can be used to orchestrate the drama of appearance. Sometimes a doorway is made specifically for this purpose. On television chat shows for example, guests arrive on the set usually through a doorway. The doorway manages their appearance: one moment the host's introduction is filling the audience with anticipation; the next, the guest appears and the audience applaud and cheer wildly. On programmes such as the *Jerry Springer Show* (which make an entertainment out of people's deepest traumas and insecurities) unfaithful husbands, illicit sexual partners, angry children... are kept backstage before being brought through a doorway to confront the person they have damaged or who has in some way damaged them. The spring is coiled and suddenly released. The doorway is used as an instrument of confrontation: it holds the tension until the host gauges that the moment is right. Sometimes its release triggers mayhem.

Doorways of appearance

The dramatic potential of the doorway's sudden transition – from concealment into exposure, from privacy into the public gaze, from shadow into bright light – has been recognised for a long time.

About three thousand years ago in Egypt the pharaoh Rameses III had a temple palace built. Part of it was specifically made to create a 'doorway of appearance' (above and right). At dawn, as the sun was rising, the pharaoh would rise from his throne (A on the plan) as if awoken by the sunlight entering through the doorway (B). He would walk to the opening along its axis. As he climbed the steps, it would seem to the crowds outside that he too, like the sun, was rising to illuminate their world.

Something similar happens when a new pope appears on the central balcony of the basilica of St Peter in Rome to be greeted by crowds of Roman Catholics and tourists.

The Temple Palace of Rameses III at Medinet Habu, 1175 BC. A brief animation of Rameses appearing before his subjects can be seen on the website at:

http://archpropplan.auckland.ac.nz/virtualtour/rameses/

101

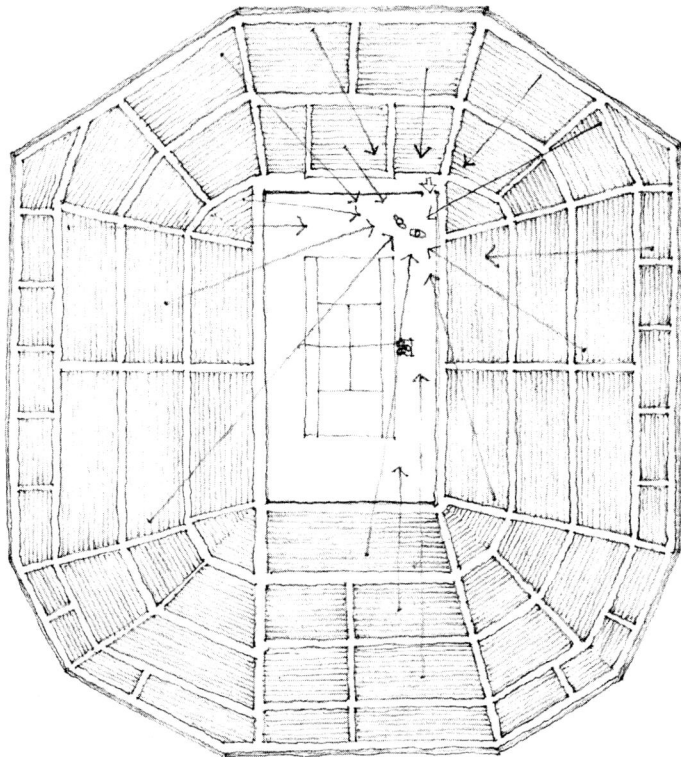

On other occasions the pope appears at a window of his apartment high up in the Vatican palace. The window he uses was not designed specifically for his appearances and is far away from the great doorway axis of St Peter's Basilica (which stretches, like that of the cathedral in Cefalù, across the city). This window has acquired its significance as a 'doorway of appearance' through use. The pope, as did Rameses, appears at an opening from his private realm (like an eye from the brain) where he enjoys the privileges of his office and deals with the demands of leadership. He comes to the verge of this private realm to appear to the outside world. While he does so he is suspended in interaction with the crowds, between his elite world and that of his subjects.

Dramatic entrance

The essence of transcendence and of drama is distilled into the doorway. Remember the effect on Wimbledon Centre Court (above) when a great tennis player appears through that unassuming corner entrance in front of a huge crowd. Remember the stage-managed appearance of the band at a rock concert, and the effect on the audience. Remember the appearance of the President of the United States into the press conference room of the White House, or that of the Queen of England into the House of Lords to open the British parliament…. Remember President Ceaucescu of Romania, in the last fatal days in 1989 of his presidency, appearing on the balcony of a government building in Bucharest to face the jeers and heckling of an angry crowd who would, a few days later, kill him. In all cases the architecture provides the crux of the relationship between actor and audience.

Remember too, how in those reality television shows – such as *Big Brother* – the doorway between the inside of the house (in which a group of people is closeted for weeks under the voyeuristic gaze of

The doorway is the point at which the contestants in a tennis final become visible to the cheering crowd.

'As I rode in through the rainbow door, there were cheering voices from all over the universe.' **Black Elk** (*Black Elk Speaks*, 1932)

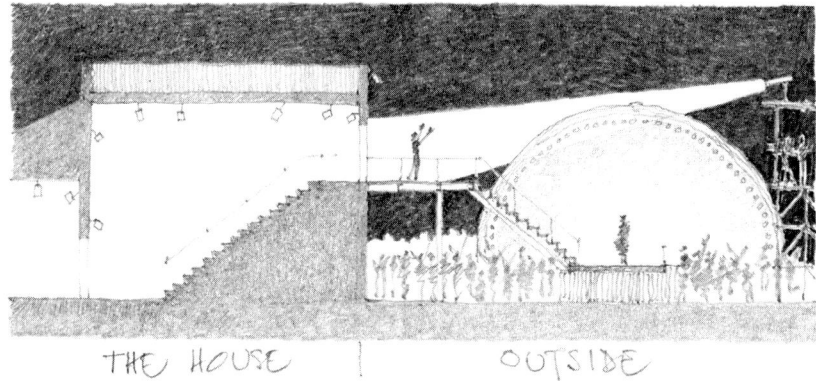

THE HOUSE | OUTSIDE

television cameras) and the everyday world outside, is raised high on a platform. Evicted housemates must climb stairs to emerge, exposed at this high level to meet the boos or cheers of the crowd (right). Usually they do so with trepidation. The architecture of the exit from the *Big Brother* house is almost identical to that of the 'doorway of appearance' of the temple palace of Rameses III (even the rising sun is represented by a spotlight), except that the pharaoh perhaps did not anticipate eviction; nor did he emerge and descend into the ordinary world.

As in the case of Rameses's temple palace, the doorway of the *Big Brother* house stands between a place apart and the outside world, between the cocooned world in which the housemates are imprisoned for weeks, and the everyday world from which they have been isolated. As an evicted housemate prepares to leave the house the audience outside watches on a large television screen. But immediately before a housemate is evicted it is the doorway that is the focus of the crowd's attention. When the time comes, the doorway dramatises the moment of appearance by making it precise. In the moment of passing through, the evictee is both celebrated as a freed prisoner and mocked as a failure. After the eviction the doorway returns to its latent state, like a guillotine, waiting for the next eviction.

Exposure to ridicule

Once I was at a rugby football match between Scotland and Wales in Edinburgh. After the game a crowd was gathered outside the doorway from the V.I.P. suite, anticipating the emergence of Princess Anne (daughter of the Queen of England), who often supports the Scottish rugby team. Her limousine was waiting. People were standing on stairs and gantries watching the door. Special Branch police officers were surveying the crowd for potential terrorists. For a long time no one came out. The crowd was full of anticipation…. And then the doors twitched. After the suspense, everyone was on the verge of applause, or at least curious to see this special person. But when the doors opened, instead of the Princess, two Welsh rugby fans decked with scarves, large plastic leeks and huge hats with dragons on them emerged instead. They looked silly and slightly drunk. The tension was broken. The crowd cheered and the two

In a television show like Big Brother, *the doorway between the isolated inside of the house and the outside world is carefully staged to exhibit those who are evicted to the crowds.*

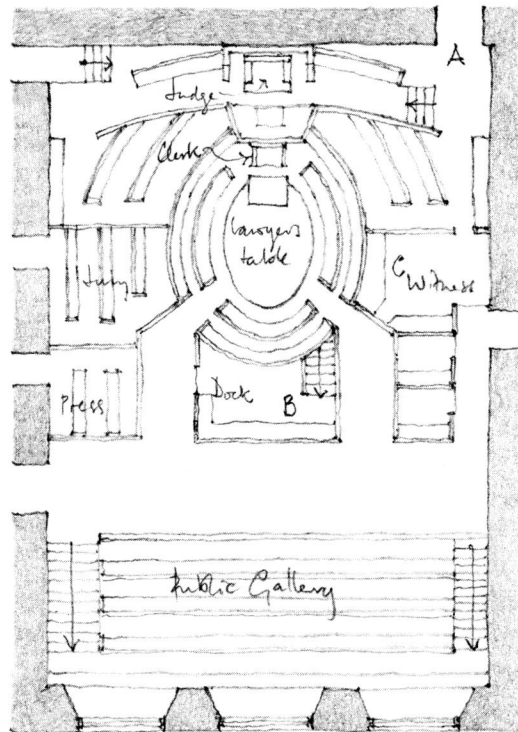

lady fans, realising that everyone was looking at them, felt bemused and embarrassed. The doorway they had approached from inside thinking it was just an ordinary exit from the stadium had delivered them onto a stage in front of an audience. After a brief attempt to act the part by punching the air, they disappeared quickly into the crowd. Everyone had to wait a little longer to see the Princess, who was neither bemused nor embarrassed when she emerged.

Exposure to scrutiny

The drama of appearance is strong too in a court of law. The drawing on the right shows the layout of a nineteenth century courtroom. Like the processes that must be gone through in a trial, it is a highly structured space. All the different players in the drama have their own clearly defined compartments: the judge on his bench presiding over proceedings; the jury to one side; a box for witnesses; and compartments for the press and the public. The lawyers and the clerk to the court sit around the table at the centre.

When the judge enters through the doorway from his chambers (A on the plan) everyone stands in respect. Then the court is in session and the trial begins. The defendant is called to face the charges against him. If he has been kept overnight in the cells underneath the court then he must enter (in this case) up steep steps directly into the dock (B on the plan). One can imagine what it must feel like to emerge through the floor into a crowded court with everyone's eyes fixed on you. Albert Camus, in *The Outsider* (1942, trans. Laredo 1983) gives an idea of how it might feel to be a defendant being led into the dock (though in this case not up through the floor):

> 'After a short while a little bell rang in the room. They then took off my handcuffs. They opened the door and led me into the dock. The room was full to bursting. In spite of the blinds, the sun was filtering through in places and the air was

In a court of law, entrance is part of the drama. It marks the beginning of the trial, and all the stages that lead to the final verdict and sentencing that decides the fate of the defendant. The drawing above is based on the courtroom at Presteigne in Wales.

'When the Bishops were first presented to the Queen, she received them with all possible dignity, and then retired. She passed through a glass door, and, forgetting its transparency, was seen to run off like a girl, as she is.'

Henry Crabb Robinson (*Diary*, 1837)

already stifling. They'd left the windows shut. I sat down with the policemen on either side of me. It was at that point that I noticed a row of faces in front of me. They were all looking at me: I realized that they were the jury. But I couldn't make any distinctions between them. I just had one impression: I was in a tram and all these anonymous passengers on the opposite seat were scrutinizing the new arrival to find his peculiarities. I know it was a silly idea since it wasn't peculiarities they were looking for, but criminality.'

Theatre

One might describe all the above instances – the chat show guest, Rameses, the pope, the *Big Brother* contestants, the rugby fans, the judge and defendant entering the court… – as theatrical in one way or another. The doorways that frame their presentation to a particular world, prompt not only change in their situation and circumstances but also alter who they are. At the doorway, each of them becomes an actor.

In *The Presentation of Self in Everyday Life* (1959) Erving Goffman, the sociologist, explored this particular effect of doorways, suggesting that they affect many more aspects of our lives than we might think. He borrowed examples from George Orwell and from Monica Dickens to make the point:

'One of the most interesting times to observe impression management is the moment when a performer leaves the back region and enters the place where the audience is to be found, or when he returns therefrom, for at these moments one can detect a wonderful putting on and taking off of character. Orwell, speaking of waiters, and speaking from the backstage point of view of dishwashers, provides us with an example:

"It is an instructive sight to see a waiter going into a hotel dining room. As he passes the door a sudden change comes over him. The set of his shoulders alters; all the dirt and hurry and irritation have dropped off in an instant. He glides over the carpet, with a solemn priest-like air. I remember our assistant maître d'hôtel*, a fiery Italian, pausing at the dining-room door to address his apprentice who had broken a bottle of wine. Shaking his fist above his head he yelled (luckily the door was more or less soundproof).' 'Tu me fais – Do you call yourself a waiter, you young bastard? You a waiter! You're not fit to scrub floors in the brothel your mother came from.* Maquereau!' *'Words failing him, he turned to the door; and as he opened it he delivered a final insult in the same manner as Squire Western in* Tom Jones. *'Then he entered the dining-room and sailed across it dish in hand, graceful as a swan. Ten seconds later he was bowing reverently to a*

customer. And you could not help thinking, as you saw him bow and smile, with that benign smile of the trained waiter, that the customer was put to shame by having such an aristocrat to serve him."

'Another illustration is provided by another English downwardly-participating observer:

"The said maid – her name was Addie, I discovered – and the two witnesses were behaving like people acting in a play. They would sweep into the kitchen as if coming off stage into the wings, with trays held high and a tense expression of hauteur still on their faces; relax for a moment in the frenzy of getting the new dishes loaded, and glide off again with faces prepared to make their next entrance. The cook and I were left like stagehands among the debris, as if having seen a glimpse of another world, we almost listened for the applause of the unseen audience." '

The implication of Goffman's examples is that such effects occur in all sorts of different circumstances in our lives: when we arrive at a party; when we emerge from our private offices into the general community of our workplace; when we enter a conference room for a meeting with important clients; when we enter an interview room hoping for a new job; when we enter a hotel and approach the reception desk; when we go into a doctor's consultation room with an unexplained pain; even when we step into a corner shop to buy a newspaper. In each instance we change, we become actors.

The power of entrance is well-recognised in professional theatre. In an interview in 2002, Elizabeth LeCompte (the New York based exponent of experimental theatre) remarked:

'Entrances and exits are extremely important, That's the defining thing, isn't it? In theatre. That's essential. It's the deepest, deepest place for me.'

And in a television interview in 1984 John Gielgud, the British actor, commented wistfully on what had motivated him throughout his career; it was, he said, the opportunity 'to shut myself up in a dressing room and come out as someone else'.

[It is a stimulating, and daunting, challenge to architects to realise that they are responsible for those instruments of personal change, the doorways through which people pass and alter who they are.]

When the priest steps from the vestry into the church to conduct a service he takes on a special role.

'The dynamic in all transitions – social as well as metaphysical – is essentially the same. It involves dying in one state or status and being reborn in another.'

Herbert Hoffmann (*Sotades*, 1997)

In street theatre (which includes when we meet a friend) the point of transition onto the stage may not be clear; the actors involved have to go through a doorway in their minds to step into character. In the formal setting of an ancient Greek theatre set in the landscape (right), the drama begins when an actor steps into the magic circle of the *orkestra*. Sometimes in plays, opera, ballet… actors enter through curtains at the side of the stage, called the wings.

Sometimes too actors enter through an actual doorway, maybe into a stage-set room or street that provides the narrative setting for the drama. All are essential conduits between the real world outside and the make-believe world of the stage, from the place where actors prepare, mentally and by changing their clothes, to enter the arena of the stage. All play a key part in generating what would in science fiction be called the force field that maintains and supports the arena of the drama. If you explore any of these theatres, even when they are dormant, as you step across one of these thresholds, you feel the power of that force field.

The Globe

In *As You Like It*, Shakespeare famously included the lines:

'All the world's a stage, And all the men and women merely players. They have their exits and their entrances, And one man in his time plays many parts.'

Shakespeare's theatre, The Globe, has been reconstructed on the banks of the Thames in London (the plan and section are on the next page). When we look at the plan we see it as a great circle (the 'wooden O' Shakespeare called it in *Henry V*) which separates the space of the theatre from everywhere else and encloses the audience together with the play. As they troop in before the performance the audience feel that sense of entering a special place, a lens that will focus their attention on the action that will be played out on the stage.

When an actor steps into the magic circle of a Greek theatre he also steps into character.

'The moment of performance, when it comes, is reached through two passageways — the foyer and the stage door. Are these, in symbolic terms, links or are they to be seen as symbols of separation?'
Peter Brook (*The Empty Space*, 1968)

But at the heart of The Globe theatre is the most powerful element of its composition, a doorway.

It is a doorway of appearance. It is the doorway through which actors arrive on the stage. It is the doorway that leads from the 'tiring room' where they change into their costumes and into their personas as characters in the play. It is a doorway that, in different circumstances, is called upon to act the part of different sorts of thresholds and entrances: the gateway of a city or castle; the doorway into a ballroom or lover's house; the verge of a battlefield or heath.

This doorway is an interface between the concealed world of backstage and the world of the stage on which the performers present themselves as pretend characters to the audience. The doorway is an interface at which those who pass through it change who they are. It prompts changes in personality, character, behaviour…; this doorway, like all doorways (though perhaps more powerful than most), is an instrument of change of identity.

This is what we expect in the theatre, where we go to witness and be entertained by people pretending to be other than their ordinary selves. But even in our everyday lives doorways can prompt changes in the personalities, characters and the behaviours of people who pass through them.

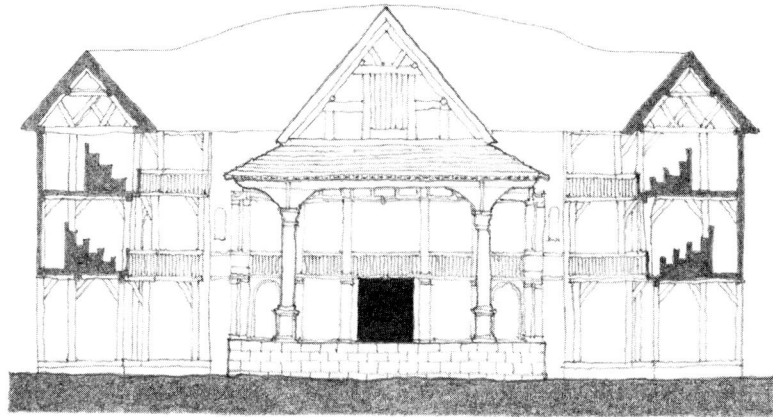

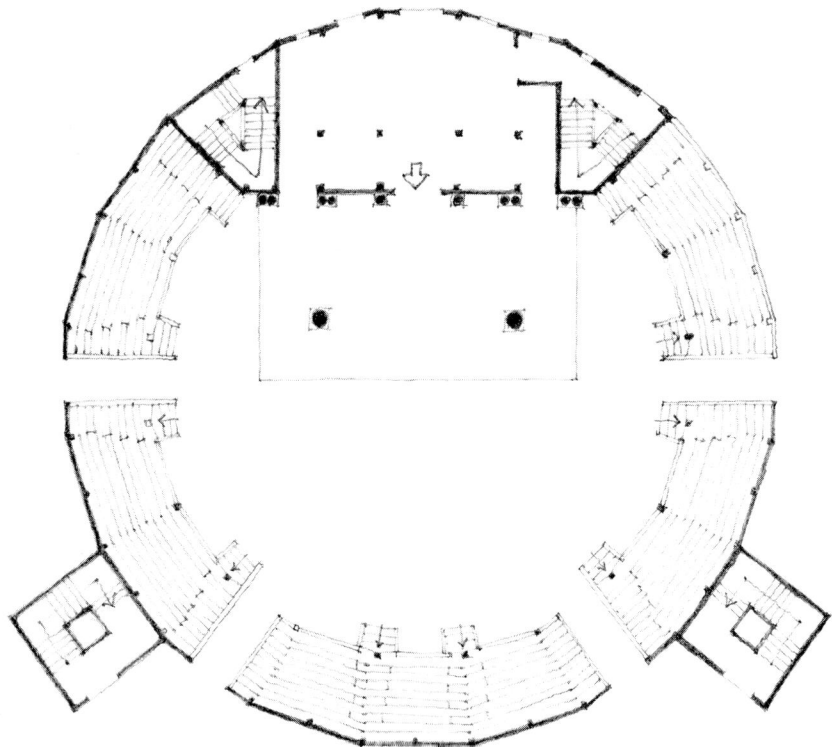

Affirmation

Passing through a doorway can define, in a spatial way, a change in persona. This is apparent particularly in the role doorways often play in ceremonies associated with transitions in life.

When a bride arrives at the church she walks in through the doorway, on the arm of her father, as a single woman (right). After the service she re-emerges with her husband. The moment of transition occurs within the church, but the doorway defines its relationship with the outside world, the community for whom the person changes. Later, when the couple go to the house they will share, the husband might carry the bride across the threshold to symbolise their dwelling there, joined together as a single family unit.

There are many examples of the affirmative role of doorways in ceremonies of transition.

When a Roman general was victorious in a great battle, his status as a hero was affirmed by his riding through an arch of triumph. Through the history of the Roman Empire such triumphal gateways became grander and grander, standing as lasting symbols of military success.

Generally speaking Australian Aborigines, living in their traditional ways on the land, live in a world without doorways. But

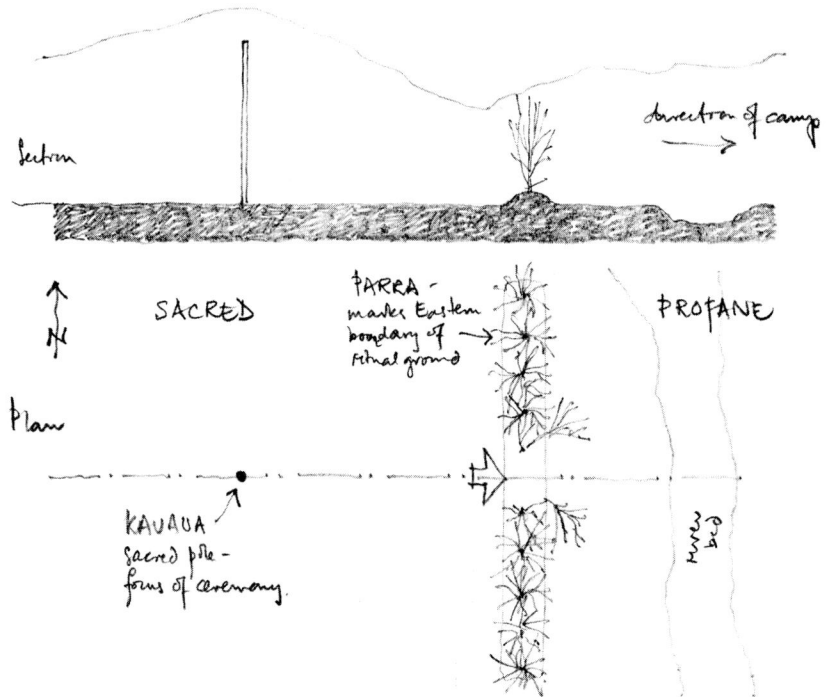

sometimes, especially for initiation ceremonies, they make them. The drawings on the right show the ceremonial ground of the *Engwura* sub-incision initiation ceremony, performed on boys by Aboriginal tribes in central Australia. The ceremony takes place at the *Kauaua* – a sacred pole – screened from the rest of the tribe by the *Parra* – a low earth bank topped with branches – which marks the eastern boundary of the ritual area. After the ceremony the *Parra* is broken open on the axis of the sacred pole to make a gateway through which the boy, now transformed by the ceremony into an adult, returns to the tribe.

The use of doorways for affirmation of rites of passage is common to many cultures across the world.

When university students have completed their studies, they attend a special ceremony where they are awarded their degrees (right). This is their initiation ceremony. The students emerge from the doorway of the building in which the ceremony is held, affirmed in their new status as graduates.

In these ways, and many others, doorways punctuate our experience of life, giving a spatial frame to changes in our states of being. The liminality of the doorway represents and affirms liminal moments in our lives.

Doorways offer passage from one place into another. When the threshold is no more than a line on the ground the transition, if you step over it without hesitation, is more or less instantaneous. But there is a split second when you are neither in one place nor the other, neither inside nor outside; when you are in-between.

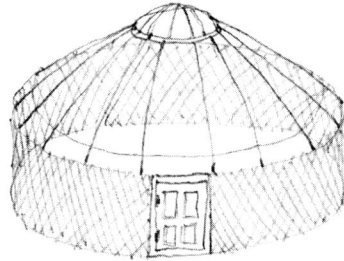

Mongolian superstition

The walls of a Mongolian *gher* (a transportable house similar to a *yurt*) are made of felt attached to a slight framework of timber slats; they are therefore quite thin. A sketch of the framework and a typical *gher* plan are on the right. The door is set in its own rectangular frame complete with a threshold bar for structural rigidity. When it is fitted into the walls, stepping through this door is an immediate transition from the open landscape of the Mongolian desert into the refuge of the *gher* – a world centred on the stove which provides warmth and a place to cook food.

You should not step, and certainly not stand, on the threshold of a *gher*. Some of the reasons behind this tradition may be practical: the frame of the door is attached to the slight framework of the walls, so standing on the threshold could weaken the structure; and, in a cold windswept landscape, a door should

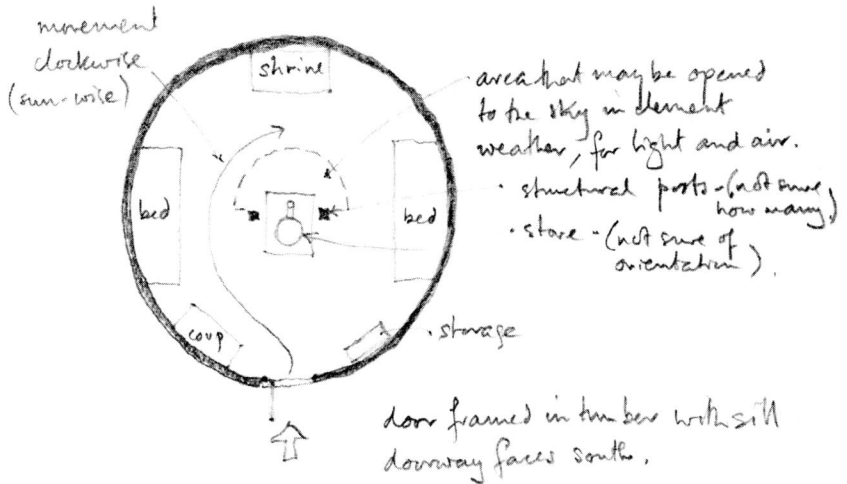

be open no longer than necessary, to keep warmth in and dust out. But Mongolian proscription of standing on a threshold derives from superstition too. The in-between is considered not a good place to be.

Neither here nor there

Our superstitions about the in-between range from the playful to the gruesome. Every child at some time plays the game of avoiding the cracks between paving stones. And gruesomely, the 'bog bodies' that have been found in parts of northern Europe are thought to have been buried in that way as a punishment for unforgivable crimes such as cowardice or homosexual behaviour. Victims were taken to the point of death and then submerged

Notice how similar the layout of the gher *is to that of the Skara Brae houses on p. 36. There is a central stove, with a doorway axis that determines the position of a dresser shrine, and beds to either side. It seems very unlikely that there might be any cultural linkage between present day Mongolia and the ancient Orkneys. It is as if the layout derives from an innate way that human beings relate to their enclosed place of habitation.*

in the bog, held down by a hurdle; they were thus left, for eternity, neither in this world nor the next, but on the threshold of the doorway in-between (above). Ghost stories too, such as Edgar Allan Poe's story 'The Black Cat', play on the dread of the in-between.

The idea of things or people being 'in their place' is an important one psychologically and in architecture. At its root, the task of architecture is to make places for things and people: a place to park the car; a place to judge criminals; a place to learn mathematics; a place for the king… and so on through the myriad aspects and activities of human life. The doorway, necessary for access between places, introduces the notion of a different sort of place; one that is dynamic and transient rather than static and settled. The doorway suggests aspiration, and a sense of the uncertain moment.

Neither past nor future

Over fifty years ago, Jorge Luis Borges wrote a timeless short story called 'The Man on the Threshold' (included in *The Aleph and Other Stories*, 1952). The narrator of the story encounters a man sitting on the threshold of a house. Through the doorway he can see a receding series of courtyards:

The sun had gone down when I got there. The quarter was poor but not rowdy; the house was quite low; from the street I caught a glimpse of a succession of unpaved minor courtyards, and somewhere at the far end an opening. There, some kind of Muslim ceremony was being held; a blind man entered with a lute made of reddish wood. At my feet, motionless as an object, an old, old man squatted on the threshold. I'll tell

A doorway suggests aspiration and a sense of the moment it takes to pass from here to there.

'To stand on the meeting of two eternities, the past and future, which is precisely the present moment; to toe that line.'

Henry David Thoreau (*Walden*, 1854)

you what he was like, for he is an essential part of the story. His many years had worn him down and polished him as smooth as water polishes stone, or as the generations of men polish a sentence. Long rags covered him, or so it seemed to me, and the cloth he wore around his head was one rag more. In the dusk, he lifted a dark face and a white beard. I began speaking to him without preamble.... I felt, on speaking these words, the pointlessness of questioning this old man for whom the present was hardly more than a dim rumor.'

The old man tells the narrator a story about a foreigner who was killed by a crowd of people. He tells the story as if it happened long ago. But when the story is over the narrator enters the house, goes through the courtyards, and finds in the last that the murder has just happened. It was happening as the old man was telling the story.

The story-teller is poised not only on a spatial threshold between outside and inside, but also on the threshold of the moment, and he holds the narrator with him. The tale he recounts lives in the eternal present. The threshold at which the story is told is a spatial metaphor of the moment the narrator of Borges's story heard it, the moment Borges wrote it, and the moment we read it. The unfolding story, word leading to word, moment to moment, is the threshold on which we all stand.

Borges's story uses the doorway as a metaphor for the moment. It works because the doorway is not only a metaphor; it is an *embodiment* of the moment we pass through it. Before we reach a doorway it stands there as a prediction of the moment we shall pass through it; and afterwards it is a lingering reminder of the moment when we entered or left the room. A doorway is a persistent representation of our passage through. It crystalises that moment in time.

A doorway is a place of escape, where we can remind ourselves that there is a world outside.

In India however it is thought inadvisable to sit at a threshold either at dawn or dusk. To do so would be to incite the jeopardy of too many thresholds – in time and space – simultaneously.

'Behold this gateway… it has two aspects. Two paths come together here: no one has ever reached their end…. They are in opposition to one another, these paths; they abut one another: and it is here at this gateway that they come together. The name of the gateway is written above it: "Moment".' **Nietzsche** (*Thus Spoke Zarathustra*, 1883. trans. Hollingdale)

Informal occupation of doorways

Like the old man in Borges's story, and notwithstanding Mongolian superstitions, we all find ourselves at one time or another occupying a doorway, on the step between one place and another. When we do it is as if the doorway is our own personal temple, framing us as we stand or sit on the threshold. (Some ancient grave stones depict a person standing in a doorway.)

A doorway is where we can take a break from whatever is occupying us inside and remind ourselves that there is a world outside full of other people doing other things.

In countries where smoking inside shops, restaurants and office buildings is not allowed, the doorway becomes a gathering place for smokers. It is the first opportunity, on emerging from the building, where they are allowed to smoke; they need go no further. They change the nature of the doorway for people going in and out.

For some people a doorway is a place to spend the night (right); more a cave than a temple. It becomes a bed, sheltered from the wind and rain and maybe borrowing a little warmth from inside the building.

For Gabriel García Márquez doorways have been where various informal things happened. In his autobiography, *Living to Tell the Tale* (2003), he remembers one of his relatives:

> *'She would wash her hair with perfumed water once a week and sit to comb it in the doorway of her bedroom in a sacred ritual that took several hours, consuming without pause cigarettes made of harsh tobacco that she smoked backwards, with the lit end inside her mouth.'*

A doorway is a place for a quiet smoke…

… or a bed for the night.

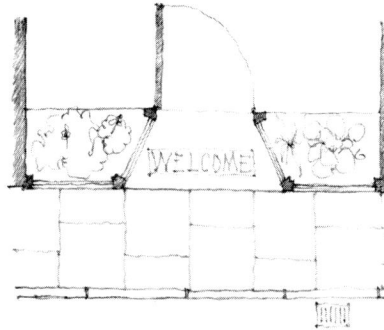

And in his novel *In Evil Hour* (1962), the doorway is the place for illicit liaisons:

'With a dreamy anxiety he was talking about his past without privations, with long Sundays of sea and insatiable mulatto women who made love standing up behind the doors of entranceways.'

Doorways are where we stand and wait for a friend or hide to surprise them. In some cases the fronts of shops (above) are designed so that the doorway provides an escape from the pavement. It is intended as a place where, on entering, you can stop to open the door or, on coming out, pause before rejoining the passing crowds on the pavement. But it also provides a place where you can shelter for a moment from the rain.

Doorways are where we gossip with neighbours (right). When we pass their door or gateway it is where we meet and greet each other. So it is the natural place to stop and talk. In doing so we are poised on the threshold between their domain and the common pavement. It is as if they remain part of their abode; like the head of a snail emerging from its shell. We, the free and wandering agents, engage with this attached person, held into their domicile by an invisible rope that stretches through their doorway. When we move on, they are pulled back into their private world.

Entrances are where things are delivered or left for collection. The postman delivers mail, the milkman leaves a bottle of milk on the doorstep. The waste-disposal officers of the local authority collect the garbage and black rubbish bags from our front gates. Entrances, doorways, gates represent that interface between the private realm of the individual or family, and the public services that help support them. When we put something outside of our gate or doorway it is no longer ours.

A doorway can be where we might stop for a moment just to take stock, watch the world go by, and decide where we might go next. Doorways present themselves to us as specific, definite, non-arbitrary places. We appropriate them as impromptu shelters and frames for intercourse. They seem to put us in our place.

Entrances are where we argue with political canvassers or religious evangelists. The threshold of the door represents the interface between our views and theirs. Our control of the door is often the decisive terminal punctuation of such conversations; though the salesman's foot sometimes usurps that control.

Entrances are places of preparation, mental and physical. Public lavatories years ago would have small signs on the way out asking gentlemen to 'adjust their clothing before leaving' rather than upsetting people by doing up their flies on the pavement or station platform. Many religions require proper reverence and preparation before a church, mosque or temple may be entered. Some cross themselves as they enter a chapel. It is at the door that women will arrange a shawl around their shoulders before entering a Roman Catholic church. There are provisions for worshippers to wash themselves in the courtyards of mosques before prayer.

A doorway is a good place for a busker: out of the way of pedestrians; framed by the rectangular opening; and with the sound projected out into the street.

'When Caesar came to the river Rubicon... he checked his course and ordered a halt... computing how many calamaties his passing that river would bring upon mankind.'

Plutarch (*Caesar*, AD75)

When we kiss our love goodbye, the doorway is like an electrical device through which the magnetic field of attachment is concentrated.

When Christmas carol singers call, the doorway is the proscenium arch between us and their performance. For a busker a doorway is an ideal place to perform; it frames him and projects his sound forwards, out into the street.

Sometimes unwanted babies are left swaddled in doorways, as if they are the sanctuaries of churches.

For a drunk, a doorway might be a public convenience or a place to vomit.

For a king or despot it is a place of self-display to the adulation of the crowd. For the man shot on his doorstep by a jealous husband, the threshold is a place of execution, an altar of retribution.

Aldo van Eyck

Aldo van Eyck was an architect in Holland in the second half of the twentieth century. His mission was to humanise architecture. He was a leading member of a group of architects called Team 10. He was particularly interested in the importance of the entrance. He felt it was undervalued in much architecture and that it should be given more thought and attention, as a significant place in everyone's experience and relationships. This is a passage from one of his talks which was published in *The Team 10 Primer* (1968, ed. Smithson):

'Take an example: the world of the house with me inside and you outside, or vice versa. There's also the world of the street – the city – with you inside and me outside or vice versa. Get what I mean? Two worlds clashing, no transition. The individual on one side, the collective on the other. It's terrifying. Between the two, society in general throws up lots of barriers, whilst architects in particular are so poor in spirit that they provide doors 2in thick and 6ft high; flat surfaces in a flat surface – of glass as often as not. Just think of it: 2in – or ¼in if it is glass – between such fantastic phenomena – hair-raising, brutal – like a guillotine. Every time we pass through a door like that we're split in two – but we don't take notice anymore, and simply walk on, halved. Is that the reality of a door? What then, I ask, is the greater reality? Well, perhaps the greater reality of a door is the localized setting for a wonderful human gesture: conscious entry and departure. That's what a door is, something that frames your coming and going, for it's a vital experience not only for those that do so, but also for those encountered or left behind. A door is a place made for an occasion. A door is a place made for an act that is repeated millions of times in a lifetime between the first entry and the last exit.'

Kafka

If you read Franz Kafka's novel *The Trial* (1925) you will see described many ways in which the doorway may be used informally. It is as if Kafka wanted to use the doorway as a narrative device to accentuate the labyrinthine nature of the world in which his existential, anti-church story is set. He also alluded to the way in which the church presents itself as the doorway to salvation, guarded by priests. In *The Trial* doorways are places where people spy on each other and conduits for secret communication. They are offered as places of escape or barred as assertions of imprisonment or exclusion. They are instruments of oppression and expose one to judgement. There is a moment where a man is seen standing in a doorway with his hands on the top of the frame, as if the doorway is a contraption for torture, or crucifixion. There is another instance where K, the main character in the book, is reprimanded by his uncle by being thrown forcibly against a door. But perhaps above all, for Kafka, doorways are places at which we wait. Towards the end of the book there is the 'parable of the door' at which a man waits in vain for years for admission through the doorway to 'the Law'. And at the end of the book K sits by a doorway waiting to be taken out into the countryside to meet his end.

A slate worker's cottage

A doorway is the quintessential stage of the in-between. Take the simple example in this photograph. This slate-worker's cottage from north Wales has very thick walls made of boulders. The plan and section are on the next page. As you go into the cottage, there is a moment when you are within the thickness of the wall. It is possible to stand there, as a place in itself.

Llainfadyn, a slate-worker's cottage from north Wales re-erected at the Museum of Welsh Life in St Fagans near Cardiff.

118

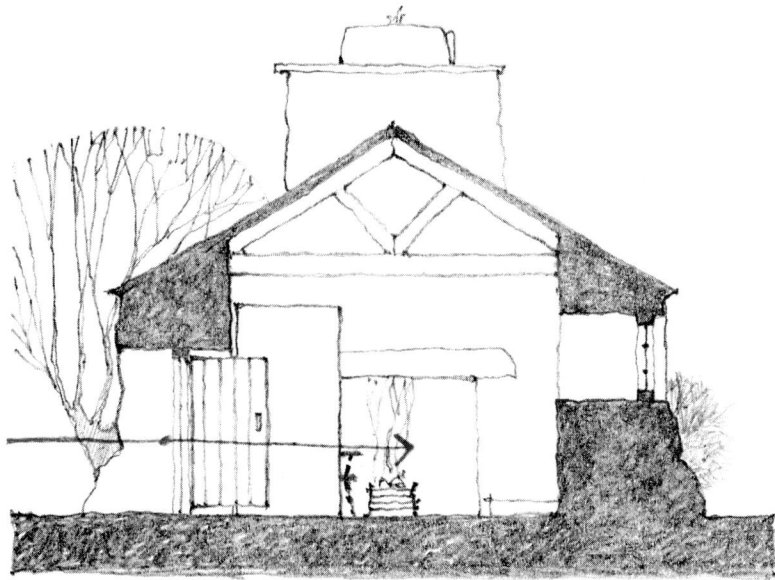

SECTION

The experience of going in is further extended by the slate draught-screen which delays the moment when you feel that you are fully inside until you reach the middle of the plan. Then you can see the fire. As well as extending the experience of entrance, this screen, together with the thickness of the walls, makes the feeling of being inside a cave-like place, stronger.

We can imagine how this simple yet subtle transition zone is used and affects behaviour and relationships between visitors and someone inside the cottage. First, the wall is thick enough that even with the door closed a visitor might be able to shelter from the rain whilst waiting for the door to be answered. Second, on the way out from the cottage one would be able to pause within the thickness of the wall to assess the weather. Third, it is within the thickness of the wall that greetings and farewells would be made. Fourth, as a friend entering without waiting to be allowed in, one would have time to call 'hello' as a warning before intruding.

Porch

The attenuation of the moment of entrance and exit in the slateworker's cottage is inwards from the outer face of the building. It is a consequence of the thick walls and draught-screen. Often, however, transition

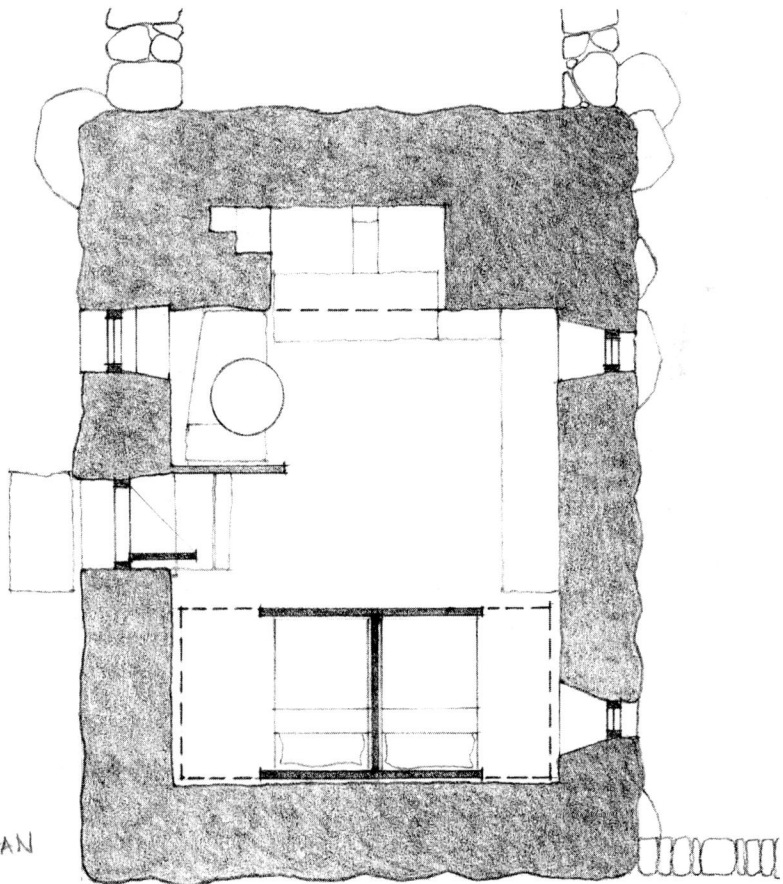

PLAN

is architecturally stretched outwards, by the addition of a porch.

Herman Muthesius, a German diplomat stationed in Britain, wrote a survey of contemporary English house architecture – *Das Englische Haus* (1904). His observations included the following:

> *'There is invariably an open porch… in front of the front-door of an English house. It is a survival of the ancient antechamber that precedes the main chamber in both the ecclesiastical and the secular architecture of all countries and at all periods. There was always a porch before the entrance to the hall of the house in the medieval manor, where it sheltered the caller from wind and weather as he waited for the door to open…. The porch is as much part of the English house as the nose is of the face.'*

Some porches are no more than a small roof, such as that at Kelmscott Manor (illustrated on the right). Others have two doors, making a sort of 'air lock' to prevent warm air being lost when someone enters or leaves. Some are provided with bench seats along one or both sides; some are cluttered with all sorts of paraphernalia not wanted in the house proper, including logs, toys, cricket bats, hats, croquet sets, plants, walking sticks….

A porch extends or adds to the experience of entering or leaving a building. It can significantly modify a simple door in a blank wall. It can make a building reach out to protect (to embrace) a visitor even before he or she is properly inside. A porch offers a welcome before the visitor has even knocked on the door. It is a gesture of comfort and shelter projected into the world outside. A porch is gentle and decorous, kindly and well-mannered, even when there is no one at home.

The porch at Kelmscott Manor, which was once lived in by William Morris, the nineteenth century craftsman and social reformer.

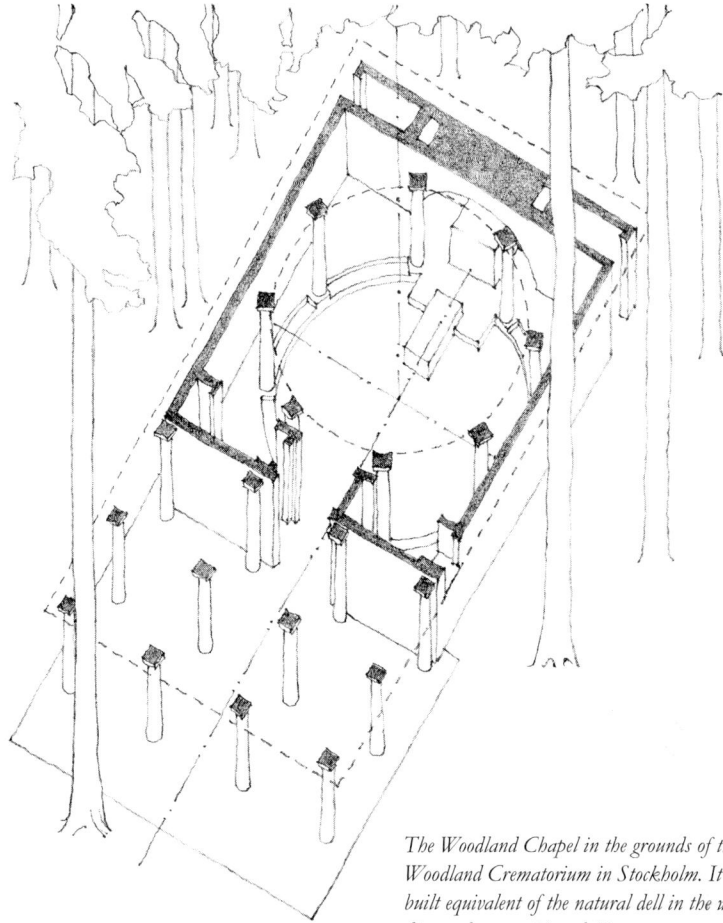

The Woodland Chapel

The Woodland Chapel, designed by Gunnar Asplund around 1918, was discussed as a case study in *Analysing Architecture*. It provides a good example of the 'in-between'.

The whole building can be considered an in-between place in that it is a place for saying goodbye. It is a place of transition. People arrive with the body of a dead friend or relative. They leave without it. The building itself is a doorway through which one person goes alone.

The chapel has subsidiary in-between places too. The walls at the doorway are turned inwards to make them seem much thicker than they are. This makes a transition space similar to that in the slateworker's cottage looked at above. But before the doorway is a large roof overhang supported by twelve equally spaced columns. The whole composition is reminiscent of the dell we looked at on p. 11. The clutch of columns supporting the roof is equivalent to the group of trees forming the portico of the dell, except that here they are geometrically arranged.

The space under this roof is an in-between place where in-between things happen. This is where mourners meet and gather before going inside for the service. This is where friends comfort the bereaved after the service.

The Woodland Chapel in the grounds of the Woodland Crematorium in Stockholm. It is a built equivalent of the natural dell in the woods discussed on pp. 11 and 12.

Gates and gatehouses

Another way in which the in-between can be identified as a place in its own right is with a gatehouse. We have already seen a prime example on pp. 68–71 – the propylaea of the acropolis in Athens. The gateway is an important device in making a place seem special and apart from the everyday world. It is used by all major religions of the world to set a place apart from the profane.

Often the gateways into sacred precincts were provided with their own buildings, maybe as lodges for porters or precinct guards, or maybe as a place to pause and reflect for a moment before entering the sacred area. As with porches, there are too many types of gatehouse to be able to give even a representative selection here. The lychgate of an English churchyard is a particular example.

The lychgate is a poetic as well as practical instance of a building as a doorway. It marks the entrance into the graveyard of a Christian church. It was where, when there was a funeral, the coffin would be set down by the bearers waiting for the appropriate time to carry it into the church. As well as having this practical purpose of providing temporary shelter for the coffin and its bearers, the lychgate has the symbolic role of separating the sanctified ground of the

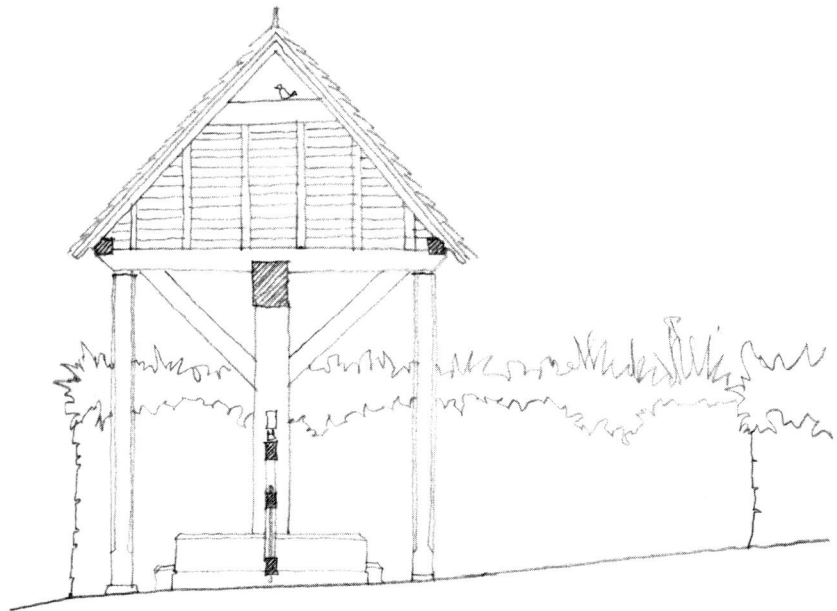

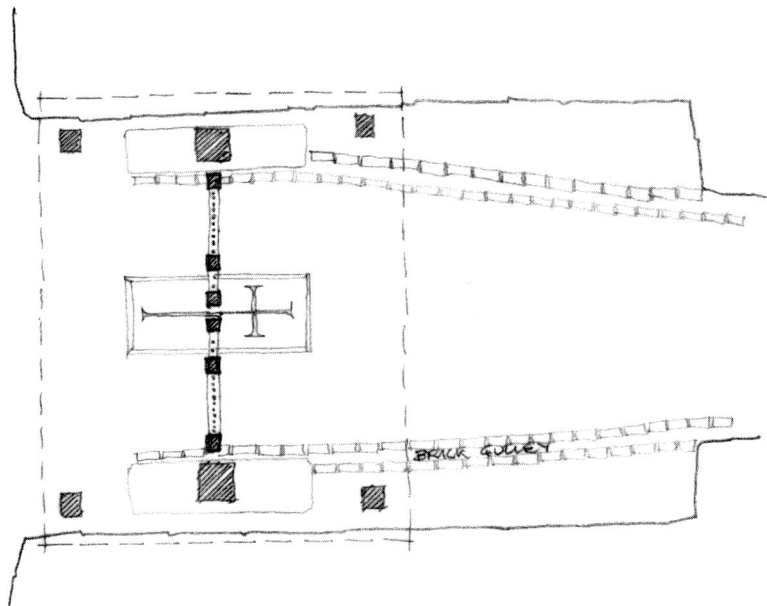

churchyard from the profane world outside. The particular example illustrated above is the lychgate at Rame Church near Plymouth. It has a platform set under the roof canopy, over which the gates close. The place where the coffin briefly rests is located exactly on the threshold. For the moment it stops in the lychgate the coffin is poised symbolically between this world and the next, on the threshold of eternity.

[For these drawings and photograph of Rame lychgate I am grateful to Anthony Aldrich of the School of Architecture at the University of Plymouth. The copyright remains his.]

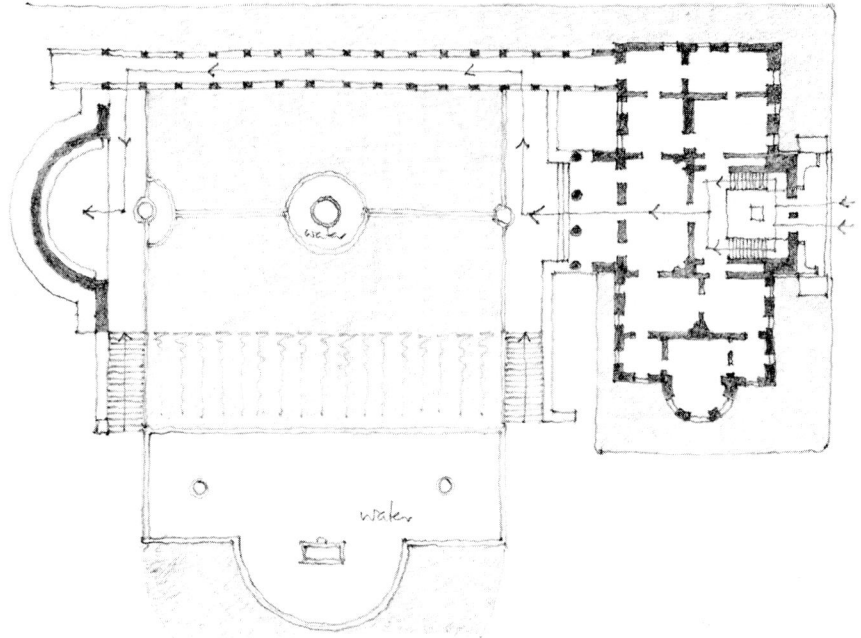

Living in the in-between

The architecture of the in-between is a rich and subtle subject, worthy of a book of its own. Schloss Charlottenhof is a house designed by Karl Friedrich Schinkel in the grounds of Sansoucci Palace near Potsdam. It was built by 1829. The house is a doorway into its own garden, which is raised a few metres above the surrounding park. The plan is a neo-Classical, axial composition (see the plan alongside). The change in level is achieved by the stairs in the entrance hall.

Thinking of a house as a route rather than a resting place poses a question, framed in architecture, about what it means to live in the in-between. Where Schloss Charlottenhof makes a house of the threshold between landscape and formal garden, the Villa Savoye (right, 1929), by Le Corbusier, makes a house of the in-between, between earth and sky.

The entrance through the glass wall at ground floor level is set so well back from the edge of the overhanging floor above, that there is purposefully room for a motor car to pull up in front of the door for people to get out under shelter; the overhang above provides shelter for those entering. But this is only the first in a series of transition zones that take you from the outside ground level up to the upper roof terrace. As soon as

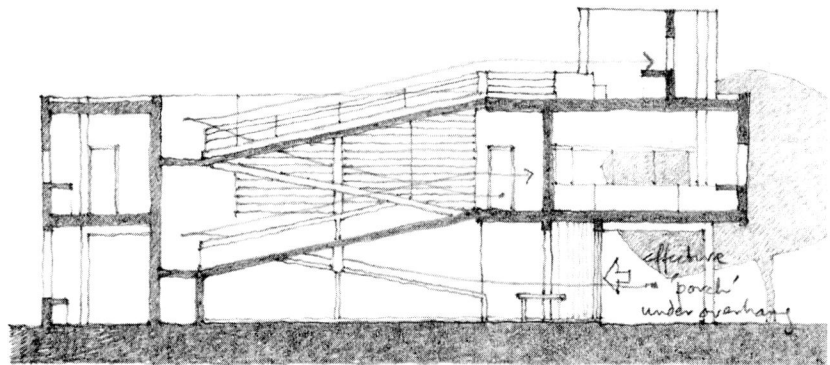

you step inside you are faced by a ramp that takes you up to the first floor and to the main living space, the *salon*. This too feels like a transition zone because its large glass wall opens to let you out onto the first floor roof terrace, which is an outdoor room. From here you take a further ramp, above the first ramp, up to the solarium (sun-bathing place) on the upper roof level. At this level there is a glass-less window over the entrance (taking you back to where you started) but your only ceiling is the sky. The house, like a poem, has transported you from the ground to the sky.

Above: the ground plan of Schloss Charlottenhof.

Below: the cross section through the Villa Savoye.

(The two drawings are not to the same scale.)

123

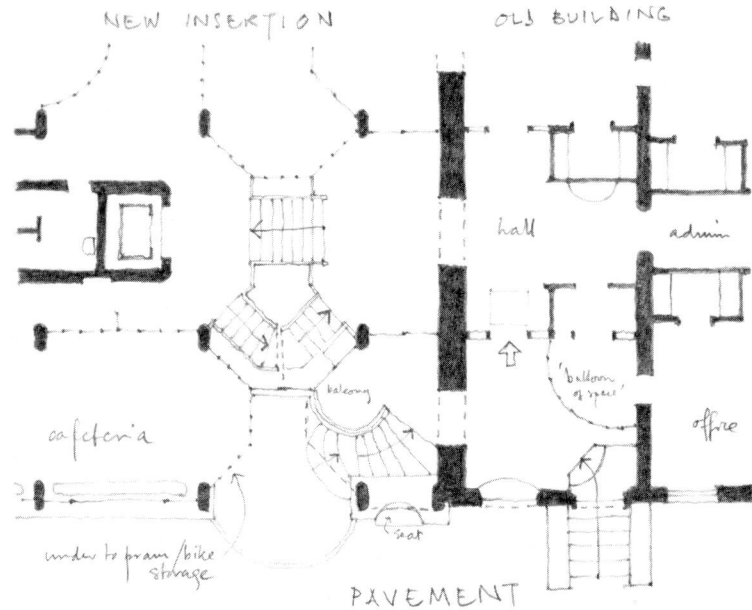

NEW INSERTION   OLD BUILDING

hall   admin

cafeteria   'balloon of space'

balcony   office

under to pram/bike storage

seat

PAVEMENT

Time stands still

You can pause within the thickness of the slate-worker's cottage wall but it is not intended as a place to stop and spend time. You can walk through the Schloss Charlottenhof and climb the ramps in the Villa Savoye but these imply a restless definition of existence. Sometimes however an in-between space can be an enjoyable place to rest and do things. It can be a place where you find (like Thoreau on p. 94) that time stands still or passes without you realising it.

Van Eyck found the in-between a satisfying place where differences are reconciled.

> 'Take off your shoes and walk along a beach through the ocean's last thin sheet of water gliding landwards and seawards. You feel reconciled in a way you would not feel if there were a forced dialogue between you and either one or the other of these great phenomena. For here, in between land and ocean   in this in-between realm, something happens to you that is quite different from the seaman's alternating nostalgia. No landward yearning from the sea, no seaward yearning from the land.' *

Others find the in-between to be the situation with the most creative potential, as if all creativity is a state of being neither here nor there but in a state of becoming. The feeling of being in a place in-between is

a fascinating one. In the quotation below the performance artist Marina Abramovic draws attention to the element of time which is essential to any drawn out transitional space. She was speaking about transitional experiences on quite a large scale, as being essential to creative thinking. She twins the idea of the 'in-between' with the idea of 'waiting':

> 'And my main concept is the "space in-between". You know, the time when you leave one country — you've called everywhere, you take a plane, you go to the train station, to wherever. And then you go somewhere else. But before you arrive, that space in-between — that's the space where it is most intense. It's the space where you're open, where you're sensitive, vulnerable — and anything can happen. And another space I propose is the waiting space. We always consider waiting as losing time, but waiting is extremely important. It is where we used to put emphasis, because to wait is to deal with doing nothing. Doing nothing is exactly what's it's all about. Cage says, we have to go to boredom, only through

In his design for The Mothers' House in Amsterdam (mid 1970s) van Eyck paid special attention to the design of the entrances, to make them 'wonderful human gestures.' Part of the accommodation was housed in an old building (the part of the plan above with the thick walls). The original doorway of this building was at the top of the steps you can see in the plan. Van Eyck did not accept this as the doorway into the refurbished building, but instead extended the entrance by creating a terraced, raised above the level of the pavement, within the walls of the old building. The actual doorway to the interior was then pushed back a few metres, with a place for the porter alongside. These entrance places were not intended as somewhere to sit and pass time, but as 'something that frames your coming and going.'

* Aldo van Eyck in The Team Ten Primer, 1968, ed. Smithson.

boredom can we come to another side. So the space in-between and the waiting space – that's where it happens.' **

The observations of Abramovic and van Eyck remind us that in-between places and times, far from being non-places or non-times, are significant in our experience of the world. They may be the places where the most interesting things happen. Established places – insides – seem settled in their identities, static and clear. In-between places, because of their uncertainty and sense of dynamic, are edgy, more stimulating to the nerves and intellect; more in tune with our existence as creatures of space-time.

The Japanese concept of 'EN'

One example is the veranda of a traditional Japanese house – the *en* or *engawa*. Such a house may have a veranda to the garden as well as to the street. Its roles in the workings of the house are subtle and different at different times and in different conditions. Its use and the materials from which it is made, as well as its situation, speak of its being an intermediate zone where the threshold between inside and outside is expanded to make a place for things to happen. In his book *Japanese Houses: Patterns for Living* (1967, trans. Gage), Kiyoyuki Nishihara has described the *engawa*:

'The space that connects the garden with the interior of the house is the engawa…. *A highly multi-purpose space, the veranda, because it opens on the garden and is a long narrow wooden-floor space, is used as a corridor, though this is not its original function. In its role as a link between inside and outside it is not exterior space, but it is also not an independent room, and whether it is part of some room or a completely different kind of space remains a vague point. Since its floor is wooden, it does not matter too much should it be wet in heavy rainfall. On more sunny days, it is counted as no discourtesy to receive guests whom you know well on the veranda. On sunny winter days, it is a bright warm sunroom where children play and housewives fold and sort their laundry or do their sewing. Sometimes in case of a sudden downpour, the veranda is a good place to put all the laundry till it can be hung out again. Just as the nature of the room is midway between exterior and interior spaces, so the materials used*

It is at doorways that we wait and queue. This is the queue waiting to enter one of the monasteries in the Greek region of Meteora, where they are perched on the tops of dramatic rock formations.

** *Marina Abramovic: interview in* The Twentieth Century Performance Reader, *1996, eds. Huxley and Witts)*

'I have spoken of place... of the in-between realm as man's home realm.'   **Aldo van Eyck** (*Team 10 Primer*, 1962, ed. Smithson)

in its construction are a little coarser than those found in other rooms. Round logs are favored for columns and rafters as is wood with a large grain, and round thin logs, branches, or even bamboo in the ceiling.'

Here then is a threshold which is not crossed in a moment but one on which to linger. The *engawa* is a zone which is part of the street or garden as well as being part of the house. It is considered a suitable area in which to do things, and to entertain guests. It is a place in itself.

The idea of the intermediate zone that is neither outside nor inside is not exclusive to Japan. Many other cultures, especially in warm climates, have similar spaces. Often, for convenience, they are situated alongside or in front of the main doorway into the house. The example in the photograph is from a Saxon village in Transylvania (Romania). This roofed but open area has an oven and is where many of the daily activities of the house take place.

This open but sheltered space is an in-between place – neither inside nor outside.

Because doorways are transitions between situations where conditions differ they challenge our senses as well as psyches. As well as being interfaces between private and public, being hidden away and being on show…, doorways are interfaces between dark and light, warm and cold, wet and dry, calm and turbulent, noisy and quiet, smelly and fresh….

Dark and light

In our dreams and in reality the doorways we encounter are often ways from light into darkness or from darkness into light. The doorway is a frame for both, and an interface between them. Light leaks into darkness; and a dark doorway can infect a light space. Light and dark have associations with understanding and superstition.

Our association of doorways with transitions between light and dark is one of the most profound. At birth, in our own personal prehistories, we emerged from darkness into light. People who return from near-death experiences describe a tunnel leading to a bright light. When we lived in caves, we went from the light back into a dark 'womb'. When we built artificial caves, they created a volume of artificial and protective darkness within the daylight of the sky, and a capsule of firelight under the night. During the day, the light would glare in through the doorway, a reminder of the outside world of exploration and adventure. At night that same doorway would be a portal to the dark world of ghosts or, from outside, a lantern leading back to security of the fire.

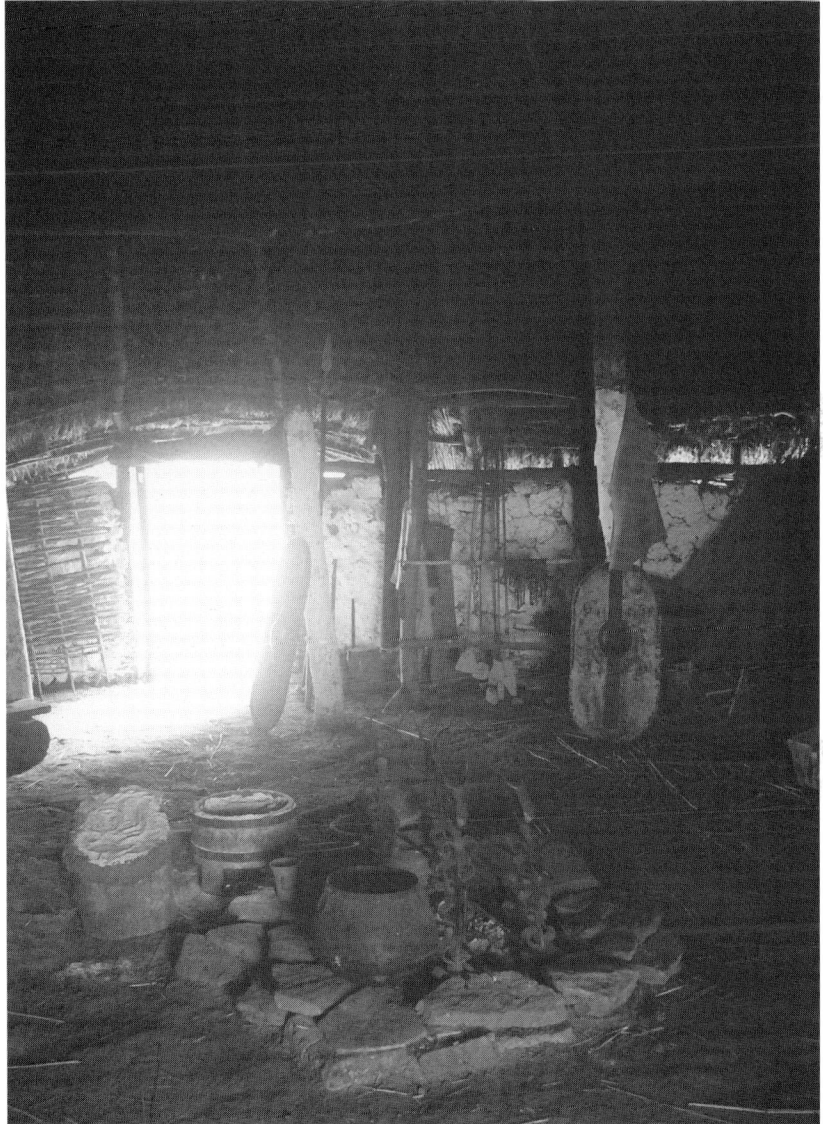

Before there were windows – in iron-age conical houses for example – crossing a threshold was a passage into darkness. If a fire was lit, there would be the glow of the embers; otherwise the only light inside would be that from the doorway.

127

'Should it be asked, What becomes of Darkness, when Light enters into it? We reply that Darkness doth not make its escape.'

Joseph Unwin (*Materialism Refuted*, 1829)

Edzell Castle walled garden

Just as I used La Congiunta (the small concrete art gallery in Switzerland, pp. 32–35) to illustrate doorways as 'frames of reference' I shall use a specific example to illustrate some aspects of the relationships between doorways and light – Edzell Castle in Scotland. The plan is on p. 130. Not a real fortification, Edzell has one of the finest walled gardens in Britain, built in 1604.

In the corner of the walled garden is a small summerhouse. The photographs on this and the previous page show its doorway looking in from and out into the garden. The experience of first looking in through a doorway and then, shortly afterwards, looking back out through the same doorway is a common one.

Light, or its absence, is an ingredient in the mystery of and revelation provided by doorways. Imagine you are inside looking out through the doorway into the bright garden. Inside, you are concealed in the darkness, watching the landscape and anyone who might be wandering outside (as if they were a film projected on a screen – the screen of the threshold). It is as if you are inside an extra skull looking out through the eye of the doorway.

Now imagine the opposite. You are outside, looking in. You approach the doorway, maybe a little cautiously. You are now the one that may be being watched by someone concealed by the darkness inside. You peer in to check if you can enter without intruding on or being challenged by

From outside, a dark interior is mysterious.

someone already inside. You wait for your eyes to adjust to the darkness before you commit yourself.

In this instance, as in many similar situations, light projects from the outside to the inside, but sight projects in the other direction, from inside to out. This is part of the drama of a doorway. It is a daytime characteristic of any house. It is critical to the drama of the 'doorways' at the heart of a theatre – that from the backstage, and the proscenium arch – which separate the special world of the stage from the preparation zone behind, and from the audience in front, who sit in darkness watching the performance illuminated by bright lights.

At night in Edzell the dramatic inter-action between inside and outside would be reversed. Lights inside the summerhouse would turn it into a stage. From outside, you could spy like a voyeur hidden by the night.

As we saw in the case of the House of Dun (pp. 98–100), light plays a part in how we interpret the world, and how we give different places value. The drama of door-ways and light does not necessarily depend on an interior and an exterior. A wall in the landscape has one side in shade while the other is in sunlight. Passing through a door in such a wall is to pass from shade into sun, or *vice versa*. In the case of the walled garden at Edzell Castle, the passage from shade into light (see the photograph on p. 131) accompanies the passage from the exterior landscape into the carefully tended and geo-metrically organised garden inside the walls. The instrument of transition is the 'nothing' of the doorway.

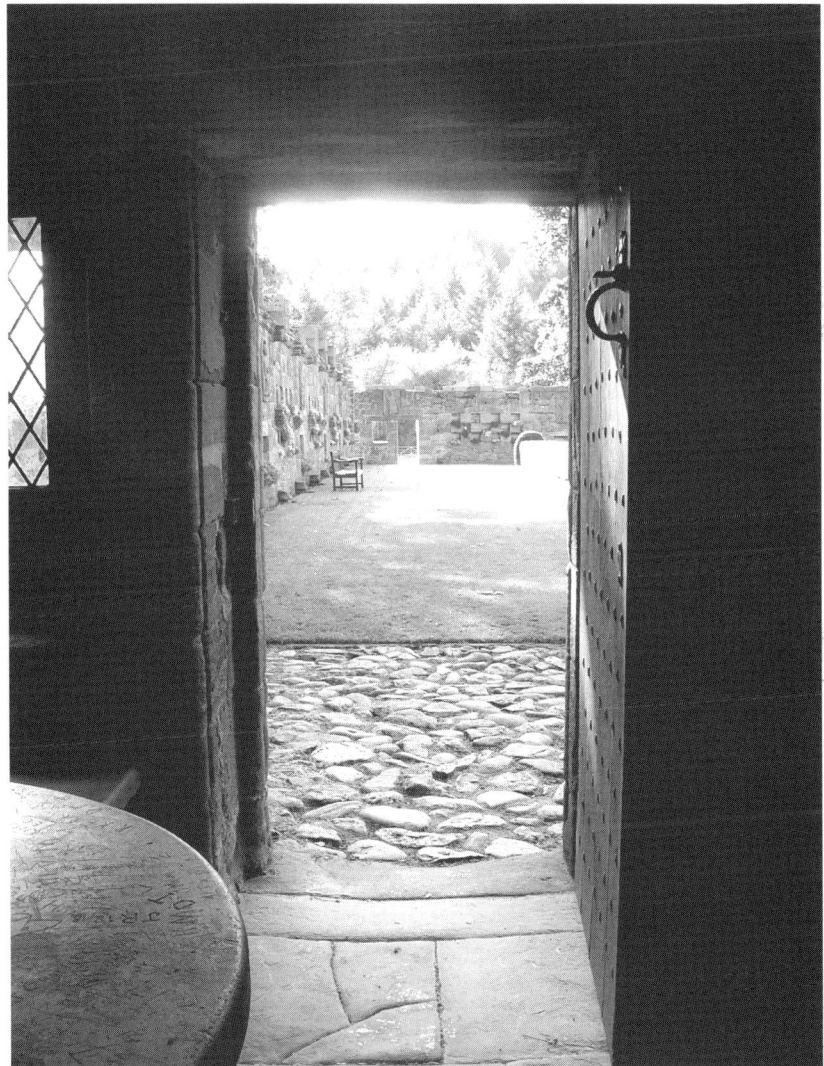

Sitting inside you can look out into the world.

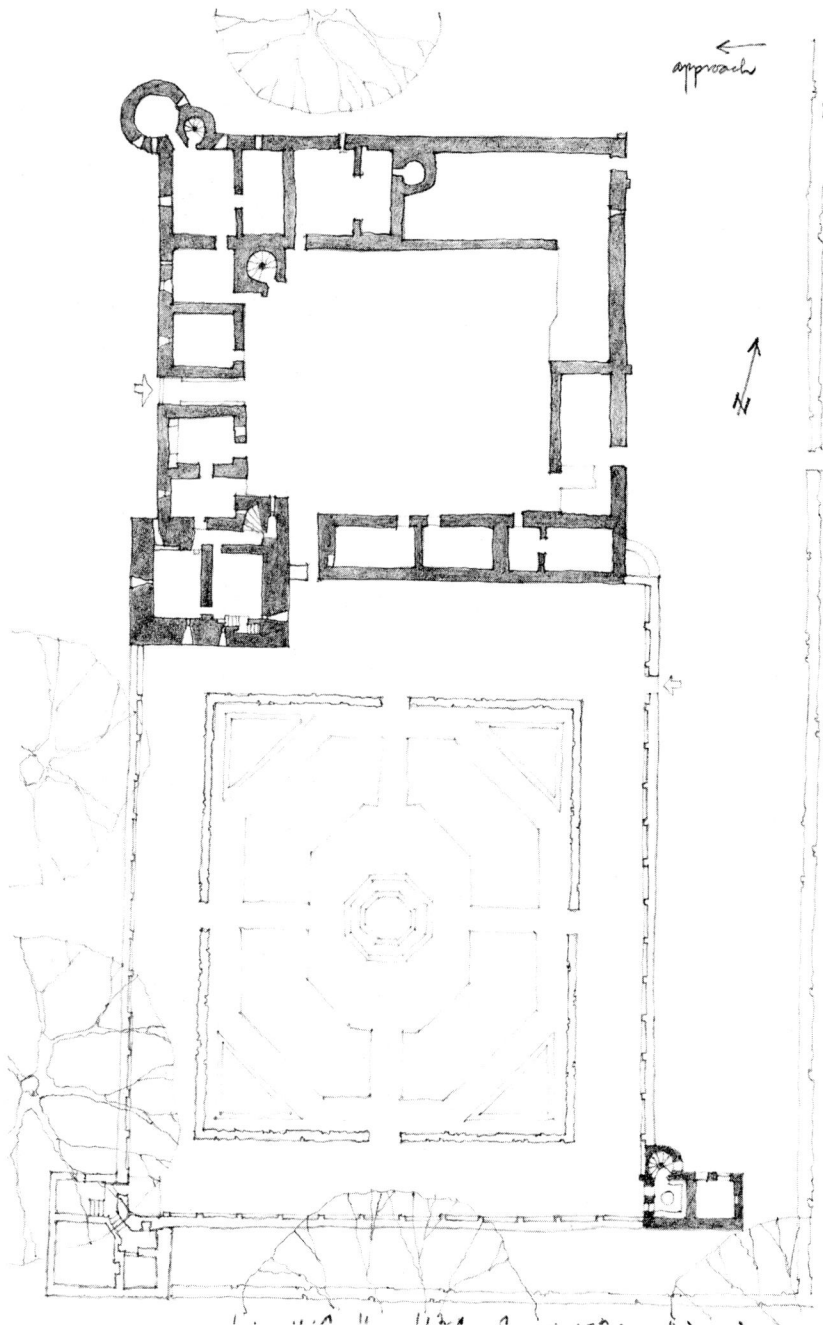

Doorways and senses other than sight

Light is essential, and evocative; it is a consistent element in elegance and refinement. We speak of the 'light' coming from a beautiful face; or of the 'beaming' smile of a child; or from a perceptive observation.

Light is a threshold in itself, and it makes its own thresholds. You can step into the light coming through a doorway before you actually step across the threshold of the doorway itself. And with light comes other things: colour, warmth, perfume, even a sense of euphoria.

Aldous Huxley, in *Crome Yellow* (1921), described the contrast entering a garden:

'It was a landscape of black and white. For colour there was the flower-garden; it lay to one side of the pool, separated from it by a huge Babylonian wall of yews. You passed through a tunnel in the hedge, you opened a wicket in a wall, and you found yourself, startlingly and suddenly, in the world of colour.... With its high brick walls the garden was like a great tank of warmth and perfume and colour.'

And in the thirteenth century tale *The Romance of the Rose*, the hero encounters a walled garden:

The wall, which was as high and formed a square, served instead of a hedge to enclose and fence off a garden where no shepherd had ever been.... When I heard the birds singing, I strove

with great distress to discover by what device or trick I might enter the garden. But I could find no place to get in.... I was tormented by anguish, until at last I remembered that it was completely unheard of for so beautiful a garden to have no door or ladder or opening of any sort. Then I set off in great haste, skirting the enclosure and

The plan of Edzell Castle. The summerhouse is in the bottom right hand corner. The doorway on the opposite page enters the garden from the east, and is indicated by an arrow in the above plan.

the wall that surrounded it on all sides until I found a very cramped, small, and narrow little door. No one could enter any other way. I began to knock at the door, for I did not know where to look for any other entrance.... Then the gate, which was made of hornbeam, was opened by a most lovely and beautiful maiden.... I thanked her most heartily, and asked her her name, and who she was. She was not too proud or too haughty to reply. "Those who know me call me Idleness." Then without another word, I entered the garden by the door that Idleness had opened for me, and once inside, I grew happy, gay, and joyful; indeed I assure you that I truly believed myself to be in the earthly paradise, for the place was so delightful that it seemed quite ethereal.'
(trans. Horgan)

The sensual and emotional changes elicited by passing through doorways are the stuff of story telling. Many senses contribute to the sensations felt crossing a threshold or opening a door. Threshold crossings stimulate all our senses; we experience them with our ears and noses, even sometimes with our tongues and the saliva glands in our mouths; we experience them with our skin and with the muscles of our limbs.

When we go into a library or cathedral the quiet quietens us. When we go into an unclean public lavatory the stink catches at our throats, making us screw up our faces. But when we go into a fish and chip shop, our mouths water (or cough at the smell of salty vinegar). With the skin of our faces, and of our arms and legs, we sense the changes in temperature and humidity that occur at doorways: from an air-conditioned store into tropical heat. And not always, but very often, passing through a doorway involves physical effort: we have to climb a step, manipulate a key, turn a handle, push the door.... And the material of the step, the stiffness of the key,

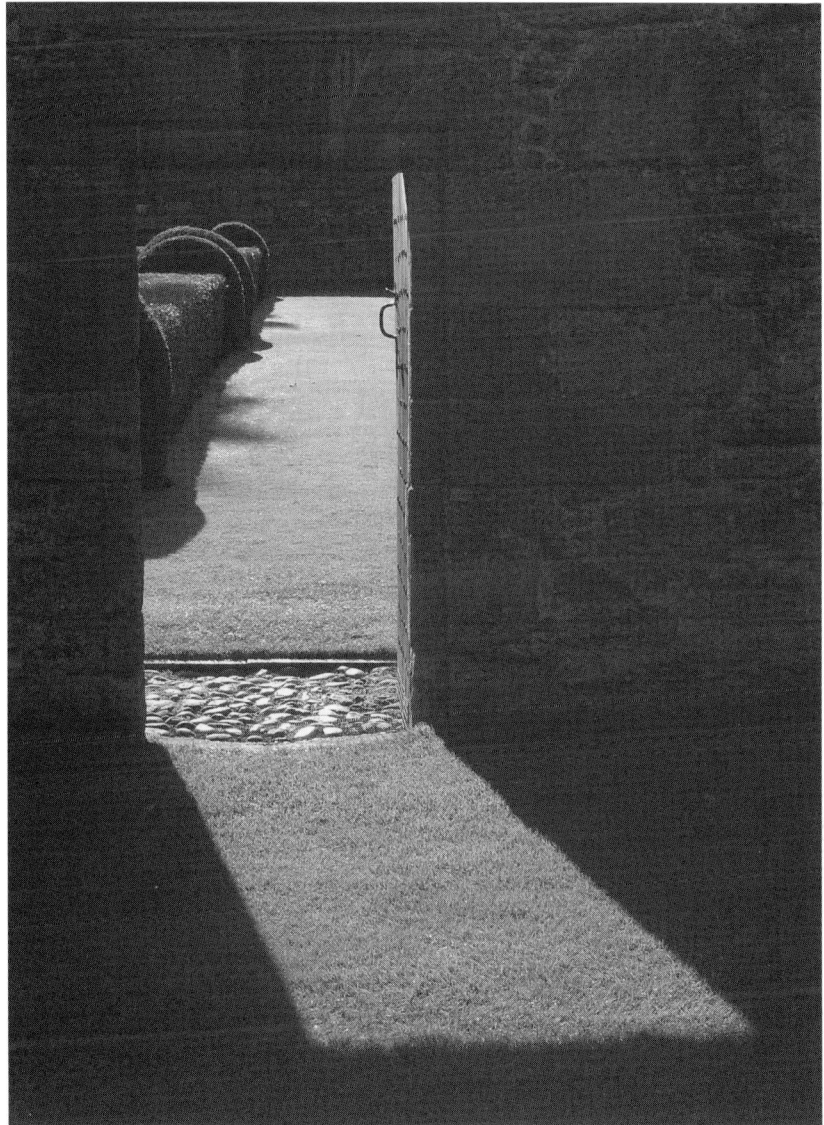

One of the gates into the walled garden at Edzell Castle.

'He opened the heavy door which led straight into the airy upper salon. At my age I could, can, take any amount of light and heat, and both these properties of the South roared in, like a Rossini finale in stereophony, from the open and unshuttered casements.'

Anthony Burgess (*Earthly Powers*, 1980)

the smoothness of the handle, the weight of the door or the strength of the spring that keeps it closed…, all these things affect our experience of going through a doorway.

Some descriptions of entrance

The power of entrance can be affected by many things that are beyond the control of architects. There are social situations that can invert the ways in which we experience doorways – such as when a surprise party turns a room thought of as a refuge into a stage on which the embarrassed entrant becomes the focus of excited celebration; where expected quiet is replaced by clamour.

There are the effects of neglect too, such as those experienced by Kim Woodburn and Aggie MacKenzie, who present the television programme *How Clean is Your House?*:

> *'We knew we were in trouble as soon as we crossed the threshold of the homes we had the dubious joy of visiting. First there was the terrible stale stink that rushed out and punched us on the hooter with all the force of a bunch of fives.'*

The smells encountered as one passes through a doorway are not always unpleasant; they might come from the materials used – leather, scented wood – from perfumed plants or warm grass, as well as from the smells of inhabitation – cooking, polish, flowers, disinfectant, sweat, stale urine…. Gabriel García Márquez gives us an idea of the possibilities when, in *Living to Tell the Tale* (2003), he recalls childhood memories of his blind aunt Petra (who turns out to have been a ghost):

> *'She lived in the room next to the office, where the workshop was later, and she developed a magical skill for moving around in her darkness without anyone's help. I still remember her as if it were yesterday, walking without a stick as if she had both eyes, slow but without hesitation, guided only by different smells. She recognized her room by the vapor of muriatic acid in the workshop next door, the hallway by the perfume of jasmines in the garden, my grandparents' bedroom by the smell of wood alcohol they both would rub on their bodies before they went to sleep, Aunt Mama's room by the odor of oil in the lamps on the altar, and, at the end of the hallway, the succulent smell of the kitchen.'* (trans. Grossman)

The Finnish architect and writer, Juhani Pallasmaa, wrote in his book *Eyes of the Skin* (1996) about his powerful tactile as well as olfactory memory of going through the doorway of his grandfather's house as a child:

> *'I cannot remember the appearance of the door to my grandfather's farmhouse in my early childhood, but I do remember the resistance of*

its weight and the patina of its wood surface scarred by decades of use, and I recall especially vividly the scent of home that hit my face as an invisible wall behind the door.'

Similarly, Gaston Bachelard, in *The Poetics of Space* (1958) reflects on a particular experience of opening a door:

'I alone in my memories of another century, can open the deep cupboard that still retains for me alone that unique odour, the odour of raisins drying on a wicker tray. The odour of raisins! It is an odour that is beyond description, one that takes a lot of imagination to smell.'

It is not clear from this passage, one suspects intentionally, whether the 'deep cupboard' was an actual cupboard where raisins were kept drying, or is being used by Bachelard as a metaphor for his memory. This confusion serves only to accentuate the sensual possibilities of opening a door.

With regard to the door itself, Pallasmaa's description introduces senses other than that of smell: the sense of touch – 'the patina of its wood' – and that of effort – 'the resistance of its weight'. It also implies a sense of moving into warmth.

In *The Big Sleep* (1939), Raymond Chandler vividly reminds us what it is like to go into a warm and humid greenhouse:

'We went out at the French doors and along a smooth red-flagged path that skirted the far side of the lawn from the garage.... The path took us

along to the side of the greenhouse and the butler opened the door and stood aside. It opened into a sort of vestibule that was about as warm as a slow oven. He came in after me, shut the outer door, opened an inner door and we went through that. Then it was really hot. The air was thick, wet, steamy and larded with the cloying smell of tropical orchids in bloom. The glass walls and roof were heavily misted and big drops of moisture splashed down on the plants. The light had an unreal greenish colour, like light filtered through an aquarium tank. The plants filled the place, a forest of them, with nasty meaty leaves and stalks like the newly washed fingers of a dead man. They smelled as overpowering as boiling alcohol under a blanket.'

Isabel Allende, in *Eva Luna* (1987), associates the simple entrance from the jungle into a nun's cloister with many sensations: shade, geometry, movement, sound, colour, the taste of cool water... and even imprisonment and suffocation:

'A nun with a jailer's key opened an iron door and led them into a large shady patio with cloistered corridors on four sides; in the center, doves, thrushes, and hummingbirds were drinking from a fountain of coloured tiles.... Consuelo... was too exhausted and too assailed by claustrophobia. She had never before been inside a walled enclosure, and when she looked up and saw the sky reduced to a rectangle, she felt she was suffocating.'

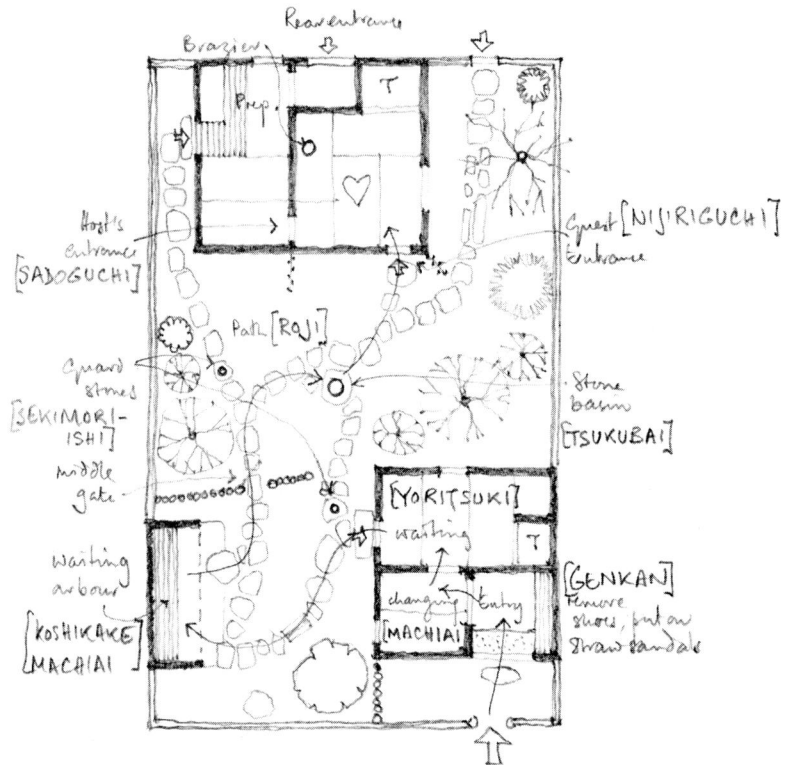

Going through doorways can also provoke feelings of excitement, trepidation and adventure. This passage, describing an interloper illicitly exploring someone else's house, is from Aleksandr Pushkin's short story 'The Queen of Spades':

'At exactly half past eleven, Hermann walked up the steps to the Countess's porch and entered the brightly lit lobby. There was no hall porter. Hermann ran up the stairs, opened the door into the ante-room and found a servant asleep under a lamp in an ancient, stained armchair. With a light resolute step Hermann walked past him. The hall and drawing room were dark, lit only dimly from the ante-room. Hermann entered the bedroom.... Hermann went behind the screen. There he found a small iron bedstead. To the right was the door to the study; to the left – the other door, into the passage. Hermann opened this door and saw the narrow spiral staircase that led to the bedroom of the poor young ward. But he turned back and entered the dark study.'

In this passage Pushkin uses various dramatic effects of lighting and the presence of a sleeping servant to ratchet up the tension, but the strongest impression is of the sense of uncertainty and trepidation that Hermann, his heart beating faster than normal, would have felt each time he quietly opened door after door.

At the other end of this scale of emotion, the traditional Japanese tea ceremony involves entry procedures meticulously designed to engender the calm and harmonious mood appropriate to the occasion. These are described in Soshitsu Sen's book *Chado* (1979):

'The purpose of the tea setting is to strip the individual of his worldly cares and transpose him into an environment where, through participation in a tea gathering, he can cleanse his thoughts of the mundane and unimportant, undergoing an experience that is almost spiritual in nature. The mood is one of quietude and peace, and the setting helps to evoke this in all who participate.... Going into the genkau *(entryway), they remove their* zori *(thonged sandals) and go into the* yoritsuki *(changing room), where they deposit their outer wraps and parcels. In the* machiai *(waiting room) they admire the decorations and sip hot water before proceeding to the* koshikake machiai *(sheltered waiting arbor) where they sit and admire the* roji *(garden path). It is here that the*

The typical layout of a traditional Japanese tea house in its garden. (From Soshitsu Sen – Chado, 1979.) The nijiriguchi *(crawl door entrance) is illustrated on p. 64.*

host finally comes to greet them, silently inviting them into the tearoom. The guests then proceed through the garden, passing through a small gate, and wash their hands and rinse their mouths at the tsukubai *(stone water basin), after which they enter the tearoom through the* nijiriguchi *(guest entrance). It is here that the actual tea gathering takes place.'*

This prolonged exposure of the guests to the 'in-between' is essential to the preparations for the tea ceremony. The stages of the process, framed by the architecture of the tea house in its garden, take the guests through a series of doorways and gateways, each of which gives them a stronger and stronger sense of being taken away from the ordinary stressful world outside.

The sensuality of entrance

It may be that the power of entrance is affected by many things that are beyond the control of architects when designing buildings. Even so, awareness of the sensual possibilities of passing through a doorway, together with their associations and evocations of memories, can influence how an architect might think of the role a doorway plays in the experience of a building, room, garden, city…. In the above examples, all the transitions described depend essentially on the generation of a '*solution de continuité*',

a seam in experience created by a door- or gateway.

Huxley's 'tank of warmth, perfume and colour' depends on the wall of the garden as well as the art of the gardener. Chandler's humid greenhouse is made possible by the glass walls and roof, and its entrance made more tantalising by the 'air-lock' doors designed to retain as much heat as possible. And Pushkin's interloper depends on the compartmentalised house with its many doors for his sense of excitement and trepidation.

But there are also powerful dimensions of memory and metaphor in the above examples. As both Pallasmaa and Bachelard imply, these are dimensions in which the architect can deal too. Architects can, through sensitivity to their own lived experiences, create experiences for others that will persist in the memory, or evoke the equivalent of narrative metaphor. The walled garden in *The Romance of the Rose* is the metaphor for love and paradise; the cloister in Allende's *Eva Luna* is a metaphor for the controlling 'prison' of organised religion. These, as we can seen in the walled garden at Edzell Castle, and in the cathedral at Cefalù, are not only represented metaphorically in architecture but are manifest in the settings it creates for people to experience, and to which they relate themselves.

The thermal baths at Vals were built in the 1990s to the design of the architect Peter Zumthor. Vals is a village high in a remote Swiss valley, and the drive to stay in the hotel attached to the baths is long and winding. When you arrive you deserve to enjoy the pleasures the baths offer. There are many. They cater for all the senses.

The plan of the baths is on the opposite page. The entrance is at the top right of the drawing, along a long tunnel that brings you from under the hotel. You can change in one of five changing rooms, with doors arranged at opposite corners (so that you cannot see directly into the main pool area from the approach corridor). When you have changed you walk through onto a raised walkway, like a guest in a chat show, and have to descend slowly down a shallow stepped ramp to the level of the pool area.

There are two larger pools where you may soak, one inside and one outside. Though the two pools are not connected, you can swim into the outside pool from inside the building along a narrow channel and by pushing through a plastic curtain that just touches the top of the water. As you go through this doorway in the water you are aware of having to push the material out of the way. But you are also aware of other changes: the temperature of the air; the light; the sound of your surroundings.

Sometimes when you reach the outside pool and it is snowing, you get that curious sensation of being in warm water with snowflakes melting as they touch your skin.

Inside the building there are many smaller pools; most enclosed in chambers within the heavy stone pillars that appear to hold up the roof. In each case the water fills the chamber from wall to wall. You immerse yourself in each by going through a doorway and down a few steps into the water. Some-

The thermal baths at Vals in Switzerland

times there is a submerged shelf around the wall under the water, for you to sit on. Or there might be a rail just at the surface, for you to hold onto.

Different dark doorways take you into different sensual experiences.

One of the small pools (G on the plan) is usually empty. You step into the water and realise why; the water is icy. No one stays in there very long.

The other pools are warm. One (B) has flower petals floating on it so you walk into a small cave full of perfume.

Another pool (A) is divided by a very thick wall; you have to walk in the water through a narrow passage into an inner chamber. Inside there are people leaning against the bar around the walls. Once you have settled into your place you become aware that there is a subtle and deep noise filling the chamber. You realise it is your companions humming. So you join in, enjoying the resonance of the high rock-lined space.

Vals plays with all your senses. In the chamber marked D on the plan there is a place where you can taste the spa water. In H you can lie on a bed in the dark and listen to the sound of distant cow bells. In I you can stand under torrential showers dropping on your back from a great height. And in F and E you can steam yourself in Turkish baths, in your bathing costume or naked.

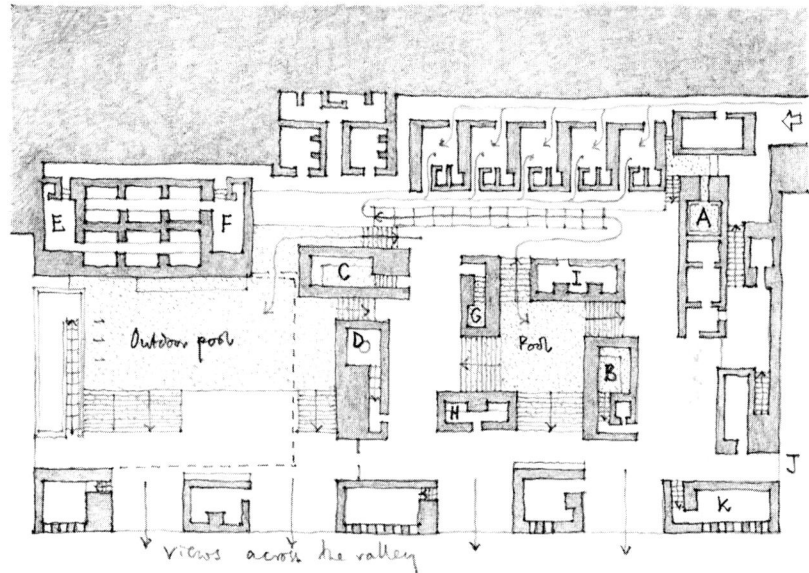

The doorway, entrance, to each chamber is handled carefully. Each stimulates a different degree of trepidation and discovery. I have already mentioned the distinctive way in which you reach the echoing pool A; it is like a cave in an adventure movie or a children's story, where magical things happen.

C is a simple warm pool and its entrance is straightforward. But to enter the cold pool (G) and the perfumed pool (B) you have to go around a corner so, if you have not visited the baths before, you do not quite know what to expect. In the water-tasting room (D) not only do you have to go around a corner but you have to negotiate four shallow steps; the passage is dark and the floor slightly slippery, so you approach

The thermal baths have a number of different sorts of pools: some large, some small; some outside, some inside, some hidden in the structure of the building; some are warm, some cold; some are perfumed, others make you want to sing.

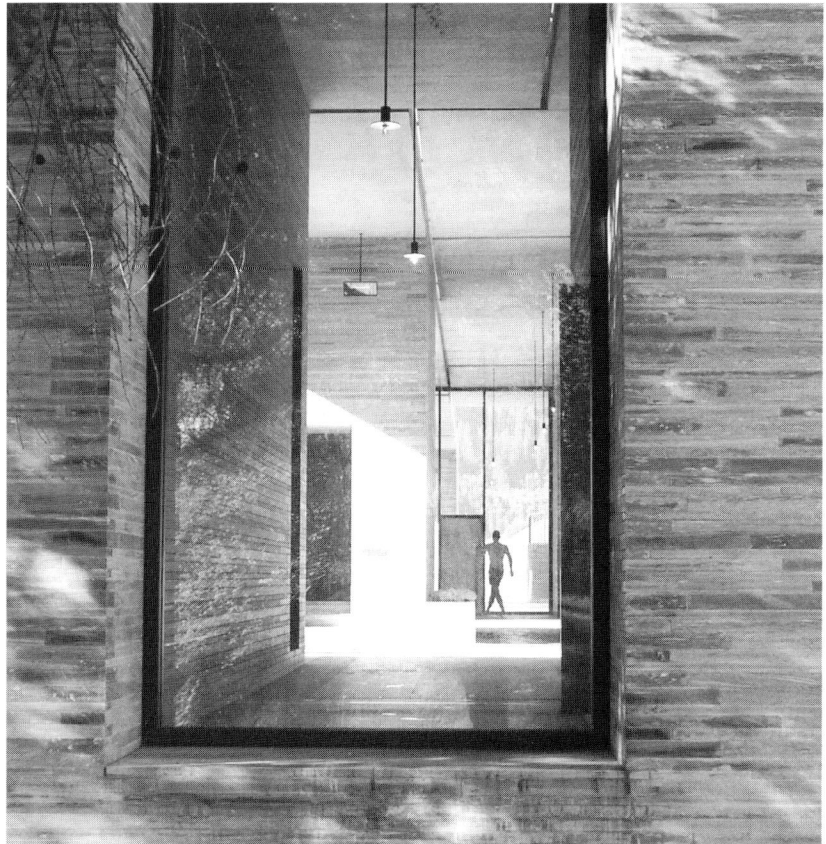

the well cautiously, trying not to slip or stub
your toe, steadying yourself with your hand
against the wall, forced by necessity to feel
the texture of the stone.

At Vals, Zumthor has made a labyrinth
of experiences designed to stimulate all our
usual senses – sight, touch, hearing, smell
and taste – and many emotional senses too.
All are provoked by the mode of going
through doorways as well as by the climate
of the chambers you enter. Entrance from
the changing rooms stimulates either a
sense of selfconsciousness or exhibitionism.
Entrance into one of the small pools provokes a slight sense of trepidation as you
go around a corner and encounter the eyes
of others; but then, when you have found
yourself a place in the pool, you can relax as
if you are back in the womb.

LINDISFARNE CASTLE (a story of entrance and the senses)

Lindisfarne is an island off the north east coast of Northumberland. It is a place apart, mysterious and sacred. It has been the site of a monastery, now ruined, for many centuries. Its most powerful feature is Lindisfarne Castle (right), which stands on top of a rocky crag dominating the rolling moorland of the island. You can see the island and its distinctively sited castle from some miles away on the mainland. It is there that the route to the interior of the castle begins.

Lindisfarne is also called Holy Island. It is linked to the mainland by a causeway which, at high tide, is under water. This adds to the numinous quality of the island. You can only reach it by car or foot at limited times of the day when the causeway is clear of the tide. As you cross you are at the level of the water with wide expanse of sea at either side, and the island ahead. There is a chance you might be marooned, trapped on the island until the tide ebbs.

Once on the island you drive along the shore under a big sky. From this approach you cannot see the castle. After a couple of miles you reach a small village, where there are shops and hotels. Parking, and then walking through the village, you get another view of the castle; your first since you have come onto the island. It is still quite far off. The castle is dramatic, towering above the land and sea.

From the village you walk to the castle. You stroll for about a mile along a winding path, skirting a small bay, gradually getting closer. After leaving the shelter of the village you are exposed to the breezes that blow more or less constantly, though at varying strengths, across the sea. The sky is big again, and the castle (your goal) retains your attention.

As the path reaches the lower slopes of the castle it starts to rise as a ramp around the sea-facing side of the crag. The ramp takes you about a third the way up the slope, from which point you have a broad view over

Lindisfarne Castle was refurbished by the English architect Edwin Lutyens in the early years of the twentieth century.

139

the North Sea. You also realise that the crag and castle are nowhere near as large as they seemed from a distance. The scale of the buildings on the top of the crag exaggerates rather than diminishes the grandeur.

Even though the rock is not as high as you had expected, the climb requires some effort. Breathing a little more heavily you can taste the sea in your throat. At the end of the ramp the path turns through almost 180 degrees and becomes a steeper, stepped path, up to the door of the castle. Entering this you immediately realise that the climb is not over. You turn right and up stairs within a short tunnel. As you do, you are enclosed and rising towards the light of the sky. The stairs are dark and the sound of the sea and seagulls is muffled for a few moments as you walk up the steps.

At the top you find yourself outside again, on a gun platform (though the guns have gone), with another fine view, across the North Sea and back to the mainland. You feel the breeze more strongly, and the sun on your head. Now you feel detached, elevated, separated from the lower world.

You wander to the walls around the edge of the gun platform to survey the panorama, sea and land. You look to the south and can see a much larger castle (Bamburgh) a few miles away on the mainland. There is also a strange obelisk just across the water.

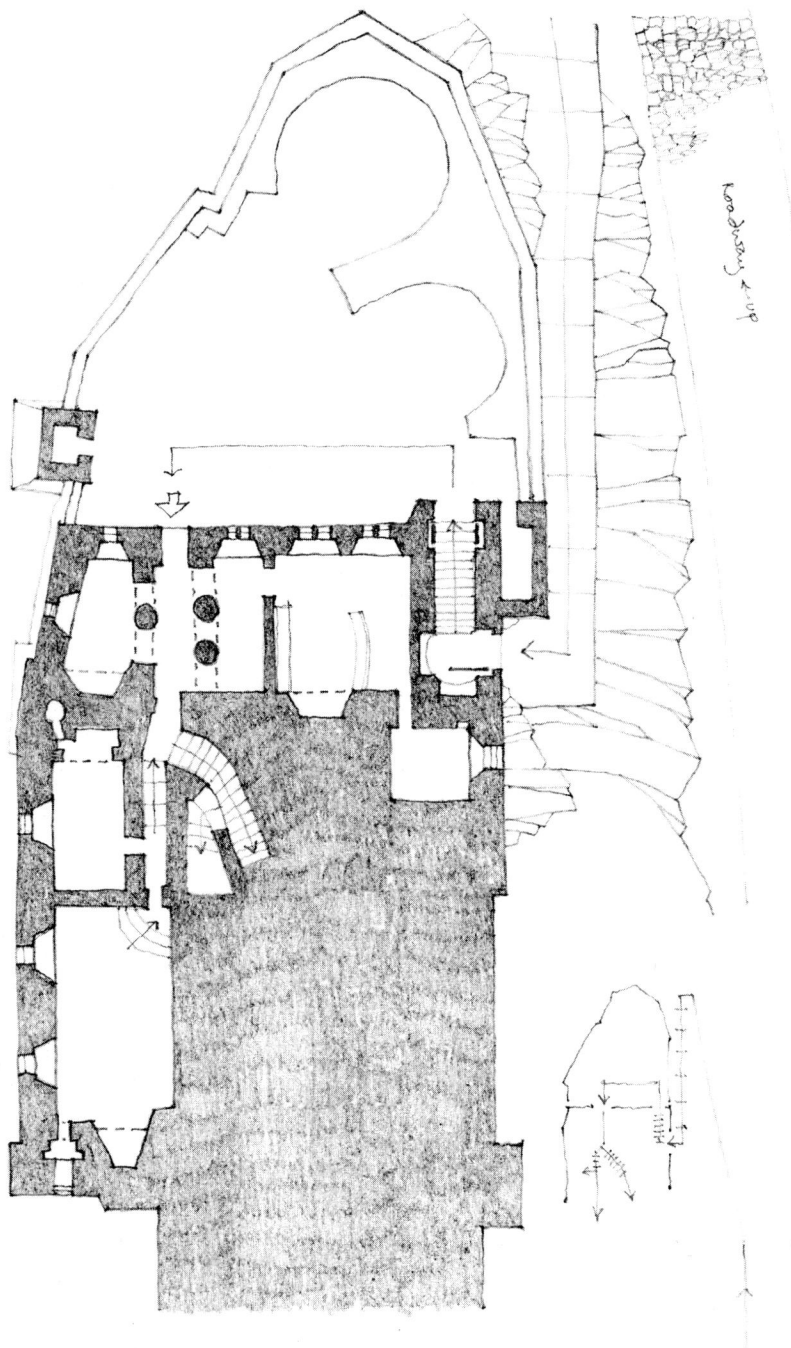

You gaze around, relating where you are to its surroundings. Then you remember there is a castle to explore. So you go to the door and step into a hallway with massive pillars. Beyond them you see a narrow passage leading down (into the heart of the crag) and irregular steps leading upwards. You feel as if

This is the plan of the entrance level of Lindisfarne Castle. It charts the last part of the route, up the stepped ramp, in through the first door and up the tunnel of steps, out on to the gun platform and into the pillared hall.

you have entered a warren, or a subterranean labyrinth. All is tight and dark.

You are now inside the castle you first saw as a fairytale image from the mainland. Inside, the stairs and passageways lead to small chambers with tiny windows looking out in all directions across the island and the sea.

The journey you have made in travelling from the mainland and then approaching and entering the castle has involved all your senses: your eyes, ears and nose, your mouth too when you tasted the sea air. It involved your skin when the sun struck your head and the breeze brushed the hairs on your arms. It involved your muscles in walking along the path and climbing the ramps and steps. It involved your sense of location when you surveyed the surrounding sea and landscape. It also involved your senses of fantasy and history: the strangeness of the island; the fantasy of the fairytale castle; the history of the gun emplacements; the ghosts of passing ships in times gone by.

And at each juncture a doorway – the causeway and village as well as the more orthodox doorways of the castle – propels you into a new situation where your senses are stimulated and exercised anew. The whole composition of the journey turns architecture into the frame of a story, a narrative in which the doorways are the breaks between paragraphs or the conjunctions and prepositions between the phrases of the sentences.

It is a story that is never told in the same way twice: the light changes, from sun to cloud, day to night; the tide changes; the temperature changes; the breeze changes; your mood changes; your companions change; your choice of routes through the labyrinthine passageways changes; history moves on. The frame is there to be interpreted and experienced in as many ways as there are visitors and occasions they visit.

Clockwise from the top left:

– the stepped ramp up to the castle;
– the door into the castle;
– the pillared entrance hall;
– the steps in the tunnel up to the gun platform.

141

ORGANISING SPACE

DOORWAY PLACES

'Blessed is he who shall encounter thee at daybreak, seated before the threshold of thine abode.'

Gilbert of Swineshead (d.1172, *Third Treatise on Asceticism*)

We have seen on p. 94 that Thoreau enjoyed sitting in his doorway musing on life and letting time pass. One suspects that human beings have spent time sitting by their doorways since time immemorial.

The photograph below shows the entrance of Cathole cave on the Gower peninsula in south Wales. It was lived in around 30,000 years ago. The cave is set half way up a cliff with a level platform in front of it. (See the drawing on the right.) It is not hard to imagine the cave's inhabitants sitting just outside the cave's entrance on a sunny evening, cooking their food and talking.

There is something timeless about sitting by a doorway. It is a special place; one where you can be part of the world outside but also withdraw at a moment's notice into the shell of your home. It is a place where you can sit chatting to your neighbours or just while away some time watching the world go by.

In some parts of the world people still live in caves. Cappadocia in central Turkey is a rocky landscape carved into strange formations by the weather. The rock is soft enough for people to have excavated homes for themselves over thousands of years. Many of these have been deserted; erosion has made them unsafe or people have moved to more modern houses. But some are still inhabited.

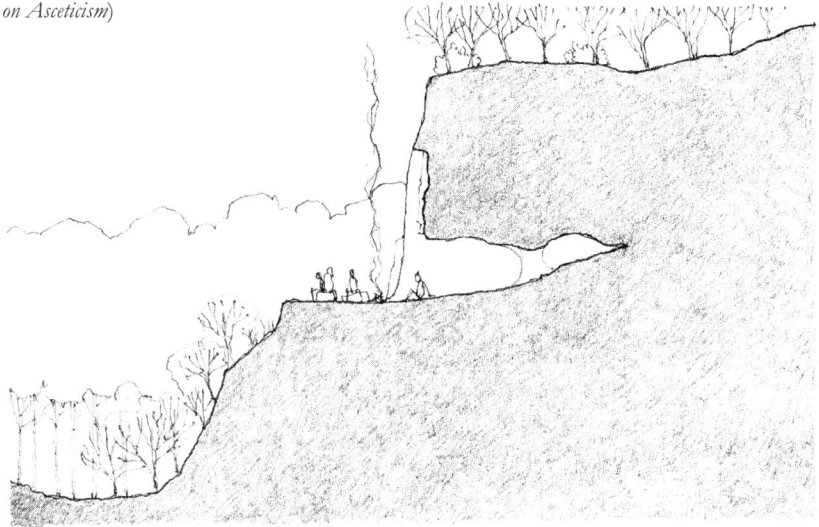

Cathole cave was lived in 30,000 years ago.

The house in the photograph on the right is in the town of Avanos. Its front has been neatly carved from the solid rock. Before it, is a space like a room with bench seats around the perimeter. The architecture, produced by excavation rather than building, provides a place where the inhabitants can live outside and still be at home. It is a place where they can be part of the public, communal part of the town but still attached to their base, the centre of their domestic lives.

Places of privilege and judgement

The attraction of doorway places, especially in warm climates, goes back a long way. In the ancient world of Homer's *Odyssey*, the portico of a *megaron* – the king's quarters at the heart of a palace, adjacent to the central courtyard – was where the king would hold court, confabulate with his princes, and judge cases. The portico was where guests would be provided with a bed for the night, where they could enjoy the cool night air, and not intrude into the private quarters inside, where the king himself would sleep.

The following passage describes Odysseus' son Telemachus staying with King Nestor at Pylos (the palace is on p. 56):

'Nestor arranged for King Odysseus' son Telemachus to sleep at the palace itself, on a wooden bedstead in the echoing portico…. The king

himself retired to rest in his room at the back of the high building…. When tender Dawn had brushed the sky with her rose-tinted hands, Gerenian Nestor got up from his bed, went out, and seated himself on a smooth bench of white marble, which stood, gleaming with polish, in front of his lofty doors…. His sons came from their rooms and gathered round him.'

What Nestor did is what any of us would do. Near a doorway, under a porch is a natural place to settle. Neither closeted away nor at large, by a doorway you can sit in the shade and enjoy the air.

In the ancient walled cities of the Biblical middle east, the gateway was where the elders would sit, where kings and judges would hear petitions, where political speeches

Doorway places may be made intentionally…

were made and where goods were sold. Here are four examples from the Old Testament:

> 'Her husband is represented at the city gate, where he takes his seat among the elders of the land.' (Proverbs 31)
>
> 'Dressed in their royal robes, the king of Israel and Jehosophat king of Judah were sitting on their thrones at the threshing-floor by the entrance of the gate of Samara.' (I Kings 22)
>
> 'Hamar and his son Schechem went to the gate of their city to speak to their fellow townsmen.' (Genesis 34)
>
> 'Elisha said: hear the word of the Lord. This is what the Lord says: about this time tomorrow, a seah of flour will sell for a shekel and two seahs of barley for a shekel at the gate of Samariah.' (II Kings 7)

These examples suggest that from ancient times the gate or doorway was recognised as a definite, not an arbitrary, place. As such it presented a reliable location for political gatherings, the judgement of criminals and the sale of produce. The gate too would be the natural place for transactions between citizens and outsiders.

Appropriating places at doorways

Doorway places are not always so formally incorporated into the architecture of an entrance. Sometimes, as in the photograph above (which was taken in the town of Hania

… or happen informally.

on the island of Crete), they are made when the occasion arises, by taking a couple of chairs and a table out of the house. In this example, the space outside the house, which is made by a small group of houses together with the shade provided by the trees, suggests a pleasant cool place to read the paper or sit with a drink.

Often the appropriation of places adjacent to entrances seems opportunistic or fortuitous rather than planned into their architecture. Such places seem to come into being by use rather than design. A greengrocer piles up his fruit and vegetables by the doorway to his shop as a way of attracting customers; the proprietor of a café arranges tables and chairs on the pavement so that her customers may sit in the sun, or in the shade on the edge of a piazza.

There seems to be some subtle chemistry or good configuration of conditions and use which allows such entrance places to flourish. The doorway in itself is just one factor, though a significant one. There are however many doorways that are not adopted as places, maybe because there is not the necessary space near them, maybe because they are dark and dismal, maybe because there is no impetus of use. The success of a doorway place is not merely a matter of decision.

Successful entrance places hold a poetic fascination, a gravitational attraction. We enjoy them. They seem to celebrate the union or symbiosis of life and architecture. Doorways in themselves can pull people towards them, and entrances places grow from the seed of that attraction.

The unknown architects who have built towns and villages in countries across the globe, together with the inhabitants of those towns and villages, seem to have had an innate sense of how such entrance places work and how they can be cultivated. Some entrance ways (such as that in front of the rock-cut house in Cappadocia illustrated on p. 146) seem consciously to have been conceived and arranged to provide a simple place to sit or display goods.

In warm climates, cafés commonly have sitting places outside their doorways.

A 'stage-set'

Some architects have tried to emulate such unselfconscious doorway places, and elaborate them. Such examples can be attractive, but they can fall short, symbolising the idea of a doorway place rather than actually successfully achieving one; perhaps because the essential ingredient of adoption by life is not forthcoming.

On p. 123 we looked at Schinkel's design for Schloss Charlottenhof at Sansoucci as an example of a building acting as a threshold (between the park and its own formal garden). Schinkel designed other buildings in the park, one of which was a

house for the head gardener (right). For this house he designed an elaborate entrance place which you can see depicted in the engraving alongside. It consists of an irregular composition of elements shaded under a pergola intended to support grapevines. There are places for plants, but there is also a table with bench seats to give the impression that this place could be used by people for an *al fresco* meal on a sunny summer evening. It has the air of an elaborate stage set for a preconceived drama, rather than the immediate engagement with life that one finds in unselfconscious doorway places.

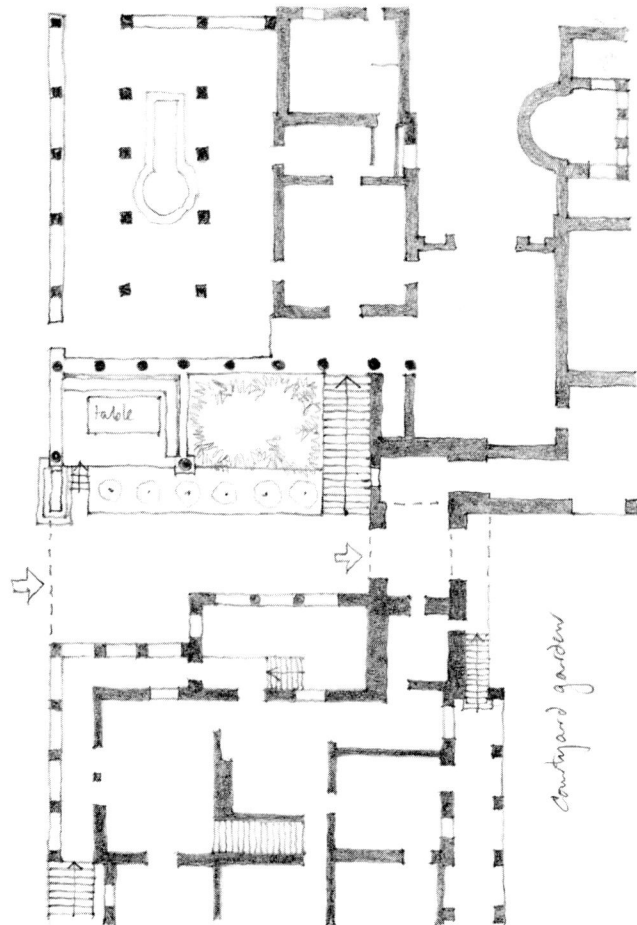

A doorway is where an inside meets the outside. As such, all thresholds are to some extent points of contact, overlap and interaction between different states of being, paradigms, social categories. The doorway of a house, for example, is an interface between the private world of the family and the public world outside. In the chapter on 'doorway places' we saw that this point of interface provides the impetus for in-between places where people can be both at home and in the world. The doorway place becomes a point of contact, a place of meeting, encounter, intercourse, negotiation…, a symbolic arena of personal interaction. In some cases architects have elaborated these points of overlap to make them into places of interaction and intercession.

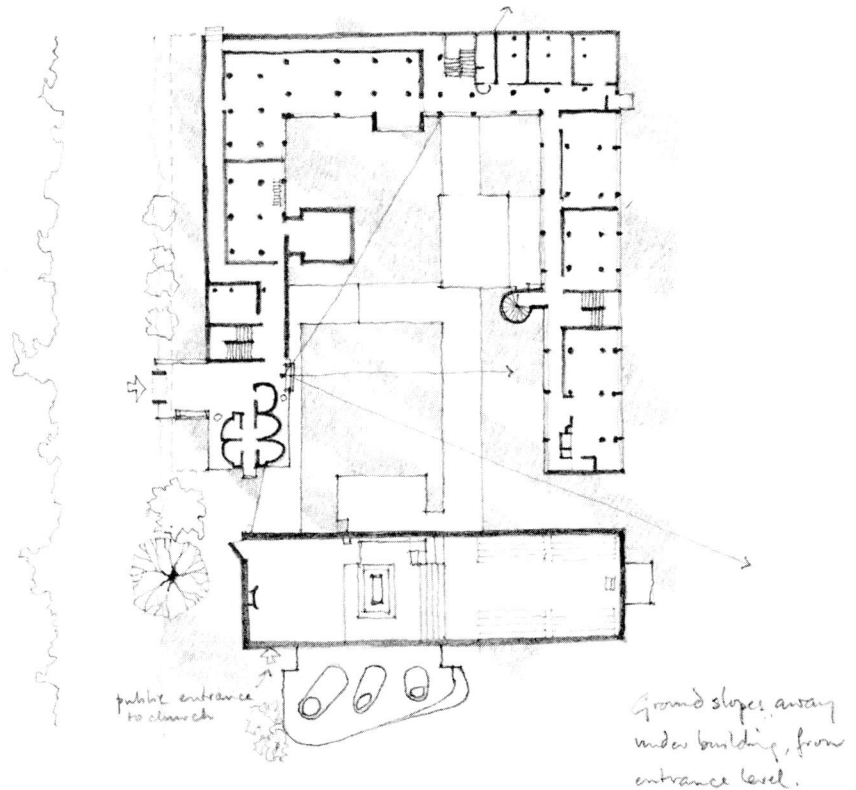

La Tourette

The monastery of La Tourette in southern France (right), designed in the 1960s by Le Corbusier, provides an example of an overlap between worlds occurring at the entrance to a building.

Here, lay visitors cross a small bridge to enter the monastery, which is moored like the decks of an ark along the hillside. An enlargement of the entrance area is shown in the drawings opposite. At the landward threshold of the bridge the visitor passes under a square concrete arch-frame (right), reminiscent of the simple *propylon* (gateway) of the *temenos* (sacred precinct) around an ancient Greek temple. As you enter you can see into the cloister – the enclosed area between the buildings of the monastery – which in this case is not like the traditional cloister of a medieval monastery but falls away as the ground of the hill slopes down towards the distant valley. You can also see glimpses of the surrounding countryside through the spaces between the buildings.

The propylon *at the entrance of La Tourette. (Photograph – Helen O'Connor)*

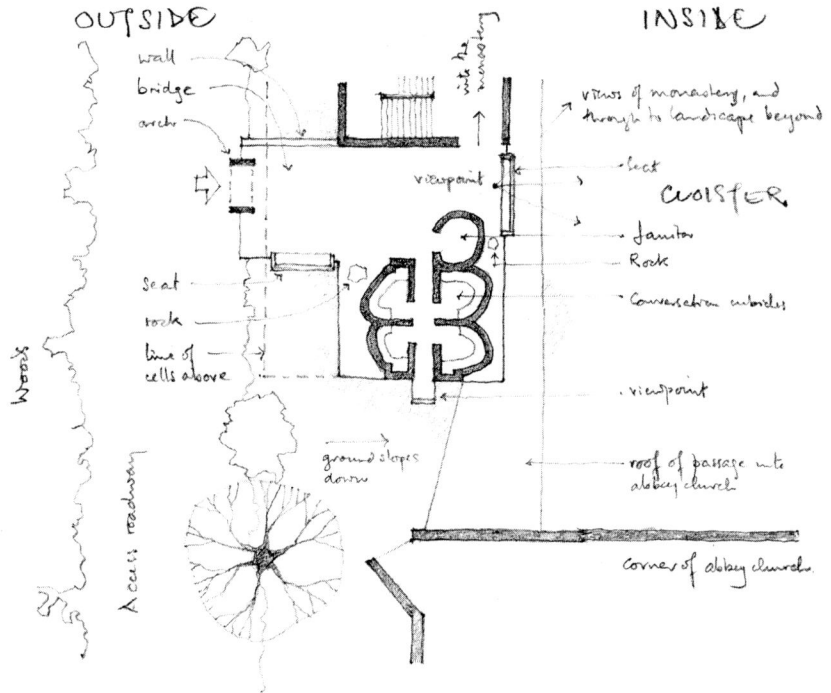

OUTSIDE   INSIDE

wall
bridge
arch
                                    views of monastery, and
                                    through to landscape beyond

                          viewpoint   Cloister

Seat   Janitor
rock   Rock
line of   Conversation cubicles
cells above
                                         viewpoint

                          ground slopes
                          down   roof of passage into
                                               abbey church

                                         corner of abbey church

Access roadway
Woods

At this entrance place there is a small almost circular janitor's lodge and two concrete bench seats, where you might sit for a moment speaking with one of the monks. There are four, more enclosed cubicles, attached to the janitor's lodge, with walls that do not stretch up to the soffit of the floor above, where you could have a more private conversation. These are not rectangular spaces, and have benches around their edges, presumably to suggest a fraternal rather than formally structured relationship between visitor and brother.

The entrance place sits between the main body of the monastery and the large abbey church on its right, though it does not give access to the latter. The entrance was not a place beyond which lay people – non-brothers – could go without permission and invitation. The entrance was therefore a place of meeting, of coming together, a junction and link between the sequestered life of the monks and the world outside. Visitors were not kept completely outside, but neither were they allowed completely inside. Their interaction with the monks took place in an overlap zone, between inside and outside.

Points of confluence

In some instances, more than two worlds meet at a doorway. In the case of a country

house, in which a wealthy family would be served by a coterie of servants, two internal worlds meet the outside world at the front door. In such cases the requirement was that servants could answer the front door from their own backstage region but without the presence of the backstage being apparent to visitors.

In such society there were proper ways of presenting oneself at another's house, and allowing the owners time to prepare themselves to be sociable, or pretend to be away on business. In *The Presentation of Self in Everyday Life* (1967), Goffman describes the appropriate manners:

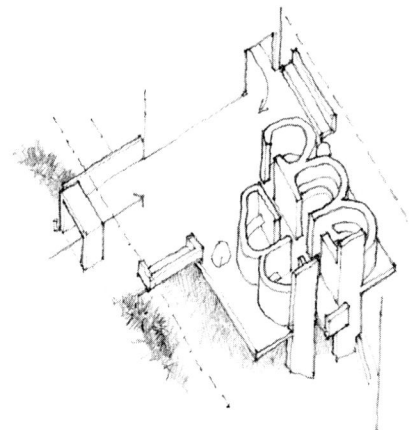

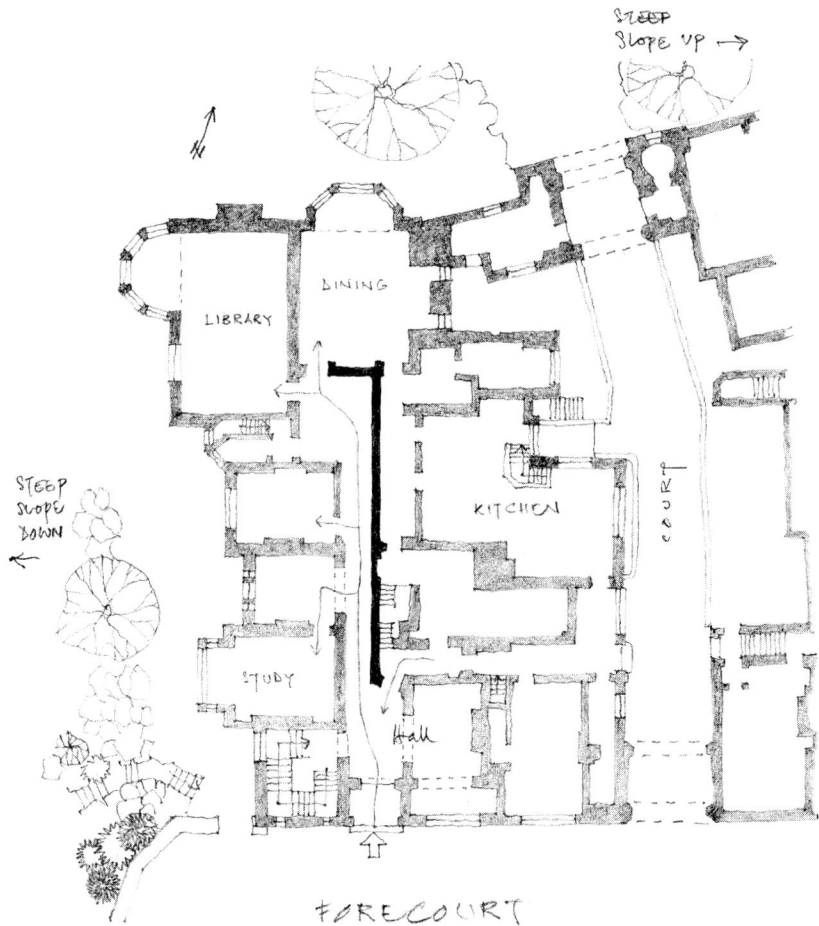

'In presenting oneself to a stranger by means of a letter of introduction, it is thought proper to convey the letter to the addressee before actually coming into his immediate presence; the addressee then has time to decide what kind of greeting the individual is to receive, and time to assemble the expressive manner appropriate to such a greeting.'

Such houses, which were designed for entertaining and impressing guests as much as for living in, would have a warm and welcoming entrance hall where visitors could wait to be welcomed by the owner of the house and where farewells could be taken. It was usual too that there would be a business room or study adjacent to the entrance, hall, into which visitors with estate business could be ushered.

One example of this arrangement is Cragside in Northumberland (right), which was designed by Richard Norman Shaw in the 1870s and 1880s. Here the division between the servants' backstage region and the family rooms is a clear and simple wall (shaded darker in the plan above). At the far end this terminates at the Dining Room, so that there is direct access from the Kitchen just where it is most needed. But at its other end it terminates at the Hall, where there is a doorway from which the butler would emerge to open the front door to visitors, who would be shown into the Hall to await reception by the family, or, if they had come on business, be shown into the adjacent study. In this corner too is the main family stair to the upper floor. This internal entrance place is a key element in the way the house works, especially with regard to visitors. It links with the forecourt where motor cars would pull up. It is easily accessible from the servants quarters, and leads to either the family rooms or to the business room, or to the upstairs where, in this house, there are further living rooms as well as bedrooms.

Something similar happens in most hotels. The realm of the guest and that of

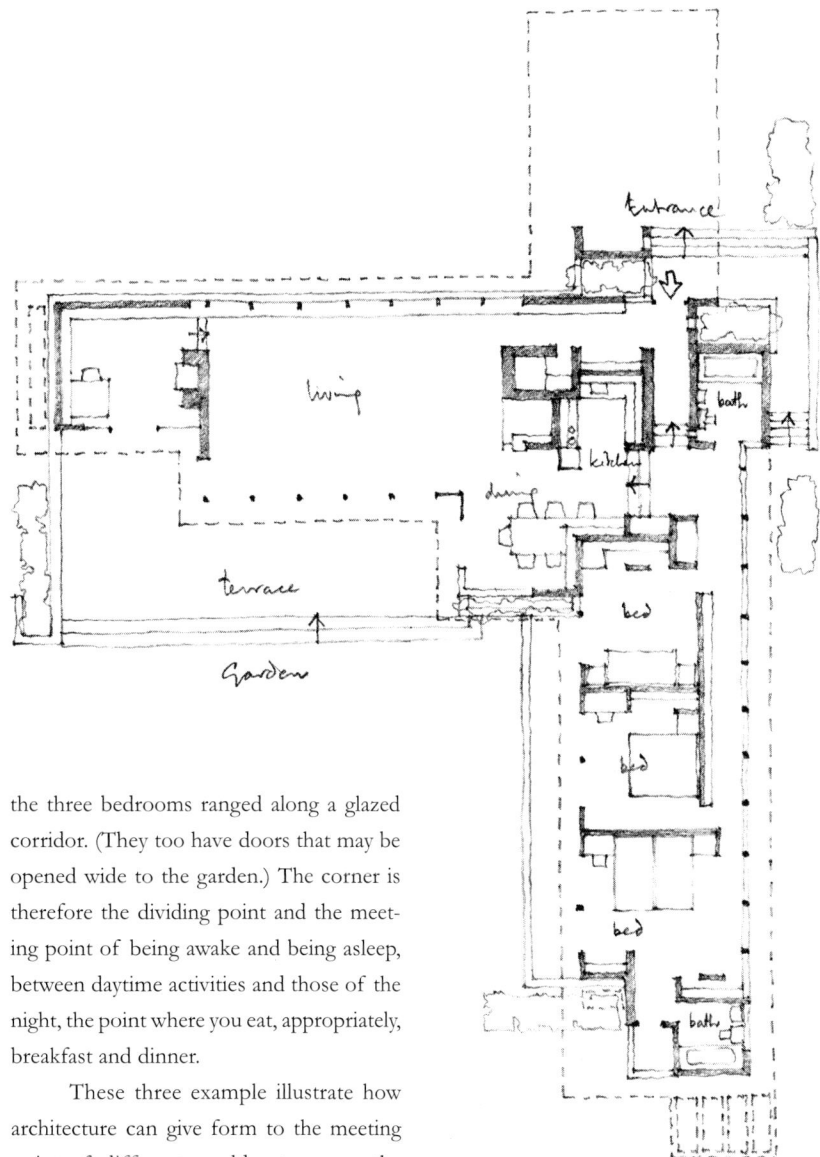

The entrance of Wright's Rosenbaum house is the meeting place of the domestic realms of day and night.

the management, which is hidden away in a backstage world, touch each other at the Reception desk positioned near the front door.

Other sorts of 'worlds' can meet at a front door. The entrance of Frank Lloyd Wright's Rosenbaum House (right) is at the meeting of the worlds of day and of night. The plan of the building has the shape of an 'L', with the entrance at the outside corner. The 'L' corners the garden and forms a trap for the sun from the south and south west. Under the *porte cochère* (the overhanging roof under which motor cars can come close to the entrance) you approach the front door down a few steps. Once you step through the doorway you are faced with two passageways, one leading straight ahead down three more steps but with the view blocked by a wall, and the other leading to the right into a brightly lit living room. (The wall of this room that faces the garden can be completely opened; in the drawing I have shown it without the doors.) These two passageways are formed between the outer walls of the house and the small service rooms, cloakroom and cupboards that are clustered at this corner where they are convenient for access from the front door. The kitchen and dining space are also at this knuckle of the plan. The passageway that had been straight in front of you as you entered leads, past a chicane, to

the three bedrooms ranged along a glazed corridor. (They too have doors that may be opened wide to the garden.) The corner is therefore the dividing point and the meeting point of being awake and being asleep, between daytime activities and those of the night, the point where you eat, appropriately, breakfast and dinner.

These three example illustrate how architecture can give form to the meeting point of different worlds at or near the entrances of buildings, and not just between an inside world and an outside: in Cragside there is an internal division between the world of the family and that of the servants; in most hotels that is a division between the management realm and that of the guests; in the Rosenbaum House there is a division between the accommodation used during the day and that used at night.

ADMITTANCE AND DEFENCE

If there is need for a wall (to keep things in or out) then a break in that wall in the form of a doorway is a point of weakness.

Robert Frost's poem 'Mending Wall' (1915) contains the lines:

'Before I built a wall I'd ask to know
What I was walling in or walling out,
And to whom I was like to give offence.'

An equivalent test can be applied to the wall's counterpart, the doorway; we only need to invert the ideas in Frost's lines:

Before I built a doorway *I'd ask to know*
What I was allowing *in or* allowing *out,*
And from *whom* (or what) *I was like* to
need defence.

These questions draw attention to the positive and negative aspects of any doorway. On the one hand a doorway allows access through a wall; on the other it is a point of weakness to be defended. A doorway can be defined by what it admits and what it has to be defended against.

We can apply our inversion of Frost's questions to the doorways that we have encountered in the early pages of this book.

We have seen that the doorways of an ordinary house admit people and sometimes air (and light). They are defended mainly by their doors against cold, rain, stray dogs, the intrusion of strangers.... These are the purposes of most doorways and doors. And we can play with them, changing how our spaces work and how we use and relate to them.

There are other dimensions to the issues of admittance and defence. The identity of a soccer goal for example (pp. 20–21) derives from the ball and from the goalkeeper (and the defenders in his team). For each team the portal of the opposition goal is the doorway through which the ball *must* pass; for their opposition it is the portal through which the ball must *not* pass. This is the nub of the game. Simple though it is, a goal carries these opposite significances. They are shared to some degree by all doorways. When your brother is in the bathroom he has the door locked, but after some while you might be desperate to get in. To a deposit bank the vault doorway is a portal that must not be violated except by those authorised; to a thief it is a challenge.

In the case of the dell (pp. 11–12) we make a doorway in our minds by making sense of the topography and positions of trees. In doing so we are formulating an interpretation of the setting that allows us into and out of the natural room amongst the rocks and trees. We are giving ourselves permission to enter the place and we recognise that the entrance accommodates us: our size, our mode of movement (walking) and maybe also our identity as an accepted member of the group that might be occupying it. This doorway links and separates the

dell to and from the woods. In our story-telling imaginations we might picture ourselves, like the goalkeeper, defending this interface against an enemy; but what the doorway actually defends is the knowability of the identifiable place from the uncertainties of the indefinite and incomprehensible woods outside. All doorways have this dimension of interpretation too. We assess whether they are allowing us in or keeping us out. Of all the houses on the street where we live there is only one doorway that admits us as members of our family. If we want to join a monastery we might have to change our identity (our beliefs and commitment) before we shall be allowed through the door.

The doorway Masai hunters build into their night camp (p. 13) links them to and separates them from the general danger of predatory animals roaming the land. It is a narrow gap in a spikey brushwood wall that must be plugged effectively to protect the hunters from this threat while they sleep. The spikey brushwood plug keeps out the animals. Only the hunters know how to remove it to allow themselves in and out. The doorway and its rough door are an instrument of discrimination in favour of hunters and against predatory animals.

Doorways are often used as instruments of discrimination. In apartheid South Africa and the southern states of the U.S.A.

signs reading 'NO BLACKS' were placed at the doorways of 'whites only' establishments. In concert halls, cinemas and theatres we have to show that we have paid by presenting a ticket at the door.

And a gentleman will get into trouble if he goes through a door marked 'LADIES'. Public lavatories offer an apt (if unsavoury) example of the dichotomies associated with doorways. In the photograph above we can see doorways that admit air for ventilation but which can be barred with gates to defend them against vandals at night. There may be occasions when one of the doorways is a portal we *must* go through urgently but if the gate is locked we shall be frustrated. According to our gender we interpret, from the signs, which doorway we are allowed to go through – 'WOMEN' or 'MEN'. Each doorway discriminates against one sex; and the third doorway on the right discriminates in favour of people with disabilities.

All doorways to some extent carry these dimensions of conflict, identity and discrimination.

The doorways of a public lavatory pose questions of identity and are instruments of discrimination.

DOORWAYS, DOORS AND CONTROL

'Shut the gate! Don't let Arafat out.'

Madeleine Albright (during Middle East peace discussions, 2000)

Think of the different ways you use doors. You close the front door of your house to keep thieves from stealing your belongings or stop your cat from escaping. You close the door of your bedroom to keep out the noise of the television so that you can get on with some work or go to sleep. Sometimes you close a door to stop other people overhearing when you want a private conversation; sometimes so that other people will not see what you are doing.

Opening and closing doors allows everyone, to some extent, to be architect of the rooms they use. Doors allow small but significant variety and change. Sometimes doors are used as signals. From inside or outside, a room with its door open is a different place from one with its door closed. A room with its door ajar sends out different messages from one with its door wide open or firmly shut. When you slam a door in someone's face or as you storm out of a room you are trying to communicate something.

These few examples illustrate just some of the subtleties of how everyone uses doors to control their space. But often when designing buildings, architects arrange entrances (and exits) with particular types of control over various things in mind. The following words are useful in categorising these types of control: SWITCH, FILTER, GUARDING, TESTING, LOCK (not as in

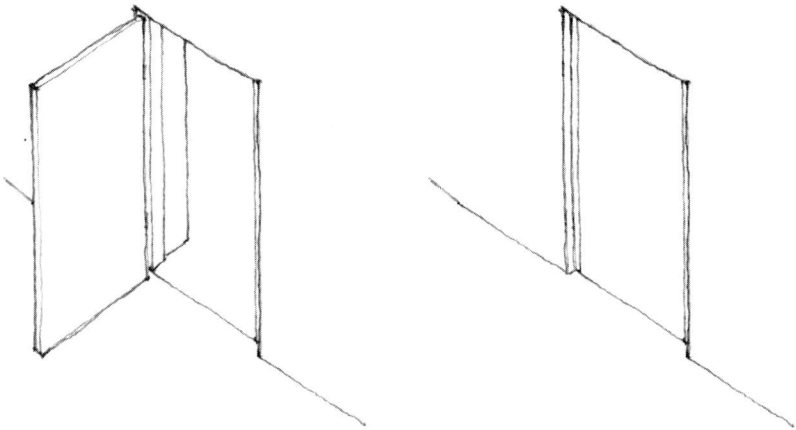

'lock and key' but as in the sort of lock you find on a canal), VALVE and TRAP. We are subjected to these mechanisms repeatedly every day.

Door as switch

The obvious and most basic purpose of a door is to act as a switch. With a door you can switch access through a doorway 'ON' and 'OFF'. As architectural verbs (in the common language of architecture), walls keep things apart; doorways, on the other hand, let things through. As such, a doorway contradicts the wall by allowing passage for things the wall was intended to keep out (or in). A movable door allows the resolution of this contradiction by allowing the doorway sometimes to

The obvious principle of a door is to act as a switch that can turn a doorway 'ON' and 'OFF'.

'What is a door? A flat surface with hinges and a lock constituting a hard terrifying border line? When you pass through a door like that are you not divided?'

Aldo van Eyck (*Team 10 Primer*, 1968)

be open and sometimes closed. When a door is closed the doorway effectively becomes part of the wall.

Just as someone a long time ago invented the wall and doorway, someone sometime also invented the door. Maybe the first door was like that clump of brush with which the Masai huntsmen close the protective circle of their night camp (p. 13). When fences were made of paling or hurdles, the door or gate was probably a loose section tied in place with strips of leather or plant fibre. Someone would have noticed that to get through she needed to untie the strips on one side only and swing the loose hurdle open; so the hinge was invented. Technological development over thousands of years has produced doors and opening mechanisms of many kinds – hinged doors, sliding doors, folding doors, swing doors, kissing gates, batwing doors, one-way doors, automatic doors, glass doors, louvred shutters, curtains, portcullises, drawbridges, gates, up-and-over garage doors, roller-shutter doors…. Always the purpose is the same: to act as a switch, preventing and allowing passage.

A door that acts like a switch represents a 'YES' or a 'NO'. The person who controls the door controls who or what is allowed through. All doors are used to allow some things through while excluding others. We may use the doors of our houses to keep strangers and thieves out but we open them to let our friends and family in. We use them sometimes to keep the rain and wind out, but at other times we open them to allow air to pass through for ventilation. The gates of sheep pens keep the sheep in one place until the shepherd wants to let them free. The gates of fortresses keep the enemy out when under attack but are opened when it is safe. Modern passport controls allow some people to enter a country whilst excluding others without visas.

The control of doorways is an essential factor in the management of space, and therefore life. We use doors to switch on an off the passage of people, air, sound, heat, cold…. We can also use doors to include and to exclude, to imprison and to abject.

A culture without doors

Earlier in this book I mentioned the traditional way of life of Australian Aborigines in a landscape without doors. (The opening of the screen to allow the initiate through in the Engwura ceremony described on p. 110 is a rare example in Aborigine culture of anything approaching a doorway.)

In his novel *The Songlines* (1987), Bruce Chatwin explores how Aborigines make sense of their world and its creation. In his book, Chatwin describes an encounter between a 'Pom' (an Englishman) and an Aboriginal girl working as a secretary. In a tangential way, the passage illustrates how the door, which we tend to think of as ubiquitous, can be a culturally specific device.

> ' "Well, if you look at it their way," (Arkady) grinned, "the whole of bloody Australia's a sacred site." He was on the point of explaining when an Aboriginal girl came in with a stack of papers. She was a secretary, a pliant brown girl in a brown knitted dress. She smiled and said, "Hi, Ark!" but her smile fell away at the sight of a stranger. "This is a Pom," he said to the secretary. "A Pom by the name of Bruce." The girl giggled, diffidently, dumped the papers on the desk, and dashed for the door.'

At the centre of this brief and seemingly inconsequential incident there is an Aboriginal girl who has a general air of cultural displacement or uncertainty. Living with a tribe in the traditional way on the land she would not have been wearing a 'brown knitted dress' but little or nothing. She is uncomfortable with strangers and formality. As a 'secretary', she has been given an identity within a hierarchical Western management structure which would seem anathema to a society organised according to tribal associations with spirit ancestors, ruled by male Elders, and with a conservative attachment to arcane and enigmatic rituals.

Significantly in Chatwin's description, the girl enters and exits through 'a door', the image of which provokes a dramatic contrast with that of a way of life roaming wide and free across land without compartments. Without being overly emphasized in Chatwin's passage, this door and the room to which it gives closure compounds the air of cultural displacement surrounding the girl.

The power of the door as an element alien to such people accustomed to life on open land is evident too in the following anecdotes. I was told them by a social anthropologist working with Aborigine tribes living in traditional ways across Australia.

First, he told of an Aborigine friend who, on being given a lift home, would neglect to close the car door behind him, not out of any impoliteness or intention to annoy but just because the act of closing a door, since less necessary than opening it to get out, was outside his usual way of behaving.

Second, and more concerningly since this example illustrates the excluding and isolating power of doors, he told of instances of Aborigine women being beaten to death by their men behind closed doors whilst relatives in the next room stood by without intervening. In traditional life in the open air, the relatives would have pulled the man away before fatal harm could have been done. But even though they undoubtedly heard the violence in the next room, the closed

Warm air platform

Igloo with low entrance (and raised benches around the edges) to stop warm air escaping.

(but not locked) door prevented them from breaking it up; it had 'switched off' their access. What was happening behind the door seemed to be in another world and none of their business.

A door stands between and in place of many subtleties of the interaction between people. It replaces immediate interpretation of a situation and interpersonal relationship with a blank sheet of material. To 'close the door' on someone metaphorically is to exclude them, to shut them up or out.

Doorway as filter

We all use doors in their doorways as filters. We allow some things and people in whilst closing other things and people out. But many doors and entrances are designed to do this for us, so that we don't have to keep opening and closing them. These display different degrees of ingenuity.

A fine mesh screen door on a house in a warm climate is a literal filter. It allows air to ventilate the house, but excludes small insects, especially mosquitoes. A locked barred gate (top right) filters out people who do not have the key, whilst allowing cats to pass in and out freely. Catflaps (middle right) also filter out people and large dogs (but unfortunately, unless fitted with some magnetic recognition system, do not filter out strange cats who want to come and steal the food of those who live in the house).

Some doorways work as filters in different ways. Like the threshold of a hay barn keeping the valuable grain on the threshing floor, the threshold of a bathroom may keep water from spoiling a carpet (above); or the low doorway of an igloo, which allows people access whilst preventing too much warm air from escaping.

Many troglodyte houses of Cappadocia, in central Turkey, have doorways cleverly designed to keep out animals whilst allowing people through (bottom right). They have a high sill, some two feet high, into which a vertical central slot has been cut. People can enter by putting one leg at a time through the slot, but animals (other than domestic cats and dogs) cannot enter. This device allowed the people who lived in the cave dwellings to keep their doorways open for light and ventilation in the hot weather.

159

The doorways of some village houses in Africa (above) do the same thing in a different way. They use a combination of a doorway and a low wall, as described by Paul Oliver in his book *Dwellings* (2003):

> 'Usually measuring less than 1m high, the doorway opening requires that one stoop down, proceed into the dark interior in this position, then stand up halfway to stride over a small semi-circular wall.'

Stiles, kissing gates, a cattlegrid (top right)... are filters in that they all control thresholds by letting some things through whilst stopping others. Electronic fob or card entry systems are designed only to allow through those people who are authorised. Ticket systems filter out those who have not paid from those who have. Locks filter out those without a key. There are too many examples and variations to list them all.

But sometimes doorways act as filters inadvertently. If the doorway of your house is too narrow to carry a settee through it, you have a problem. A flight of steps at a doorway effectively prevents people in wheelchairs from entering. A heavy door will filter out those without the strength to push it.

Guarding and testing

Sometimes filtering at doorways is best done by people. A guard at the entrance to a castle or a palace is there to filter out friends from enemies. A porter or janitor of a public building keeps an eye open to check that

A cattle grid filters livestock from traffic.

A guardsman filters friends from enemies.

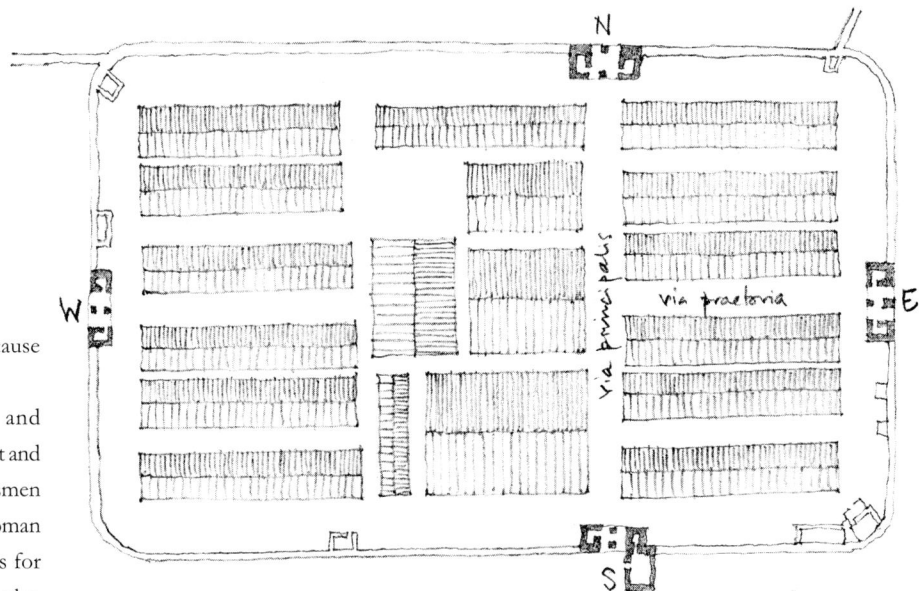

The fortress of Housesteads on Hadrian's Wall accommodated a garrison guarding a northern entrance into the Roman Empire.

undesirable people cannot come in to cause disruption.

People who guard doorways and entrances need their own places to sit, wait and watch. In Britain, at royal palaces, guardsmen have sentry boxes (opposite page). In Roman times, forts had gatehouses with rooms for guards. (The drawing on the right is a plan of Housesteads Fort on Hadrian's Wall in the north of England. Typical of Roman fortresses it has an entrance in the middle of each of its four sides. The one to the north led out of the Roman Empire into the land now known as Scotland.) At the entrance to a factory there may be a special booth or office near the door occupied by a janitor who will check the papers of those who wish to deliver or take away goods. If you go to see the Managing Director of a business or the Vice Chancellor of a university you will find the office guarded by a posse of secretaries. Most office buildings will have a receptionist sitting at a counter near the door. Some apartment blocks have porters or concierges, provided with their own living accommodation on the ground floor. Reception desks of hotels are positioned to greet and interrogate guests as they come in.

Going through most doorways involves passing a test of some kind. To get into your own house or office you have to pass the test of having (and remembering) the right key. To be allowed into your friend's house you have to be recognised as your friend's friend. In your gang as a child you probably invented secret passwords for entry into the garden shed, to filter out those who were not members. At border crossings, the 'doorways' into and out of countries, you have to show your passport to gain entry; people without the requisite visa are filtered out. In hotels you have to give your credit card details to the receptionist before being given the key to a room. At the cinema you have to first buy a ticket and then show it at the door to gain entry. Many of these tests have their architectural requirements and consequences. The people who sell you tickets, question you to ascertain that you are who you say you are, search through your bags...; all need places to do these things, and places to sit and wait.

They might also need a mechanism to help them sort those who may enter from those who may not.

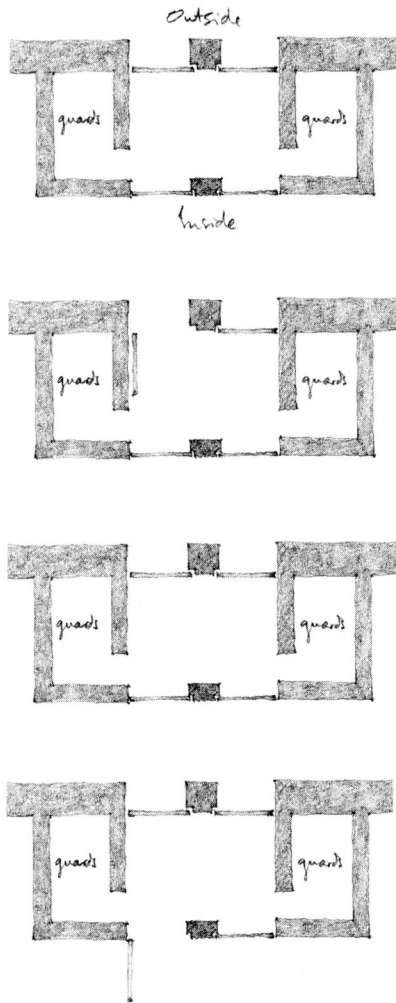

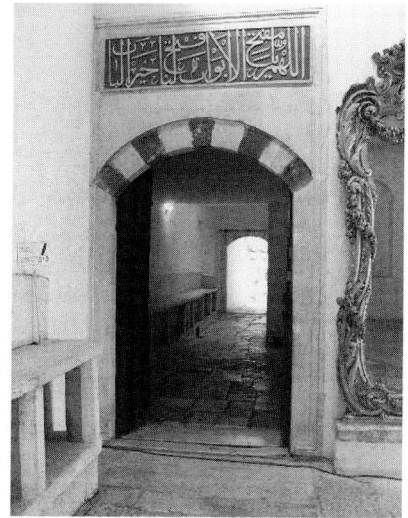

Entrance as lock

One way in which the guards of Housesteads Fort were helped to sort those who may enter the empire from those who could not was by the design of the gatehouse in which they worked. It was designed with two sets of doors with a holding space between (above). As strangers approached from the north the outer door could be opened so that they could be admitted, maybe one at a time, into the holding space. There, their identities could be checked. Before the inner door was opened to allow the people through, the outer door would be closed so that there could be no surprise insurgence.

This is the principle of the lock. It is the same principle that allows canals to go up and down hills without losing excessive water. It is the principle behind the double sets of doors at the entrances of public buildings, which allow people to enter without too much heat, or cooled air, being lost to the outside. (The quotation from Chandler's *The Big Sleep* on p. 133 describes a lock entrance into a greenhouse.) The revolving door (above) applies the lock principle in a different way.

The lock is used particularly for entering capsules in inhospitable environments. Submarines have lock entrances that allow divers to exit and re-enter whilst preventing water from flooding the vessel. Space ships have airlocks that allow astronauts to leave the vessel without the air inside escaping.

There is an example of a lock entrance in the harem of Topkapi Palace in Istanbul (right). The harem was where the Sultan accommodated his many wives. No man, other than the emasculated eunuchs, was allowed to see the wives. When food was brought, by men, from the kitchen it had to be left in the space between two doors. While door A in the photograph and plan (right) was opened to allow the kitchen

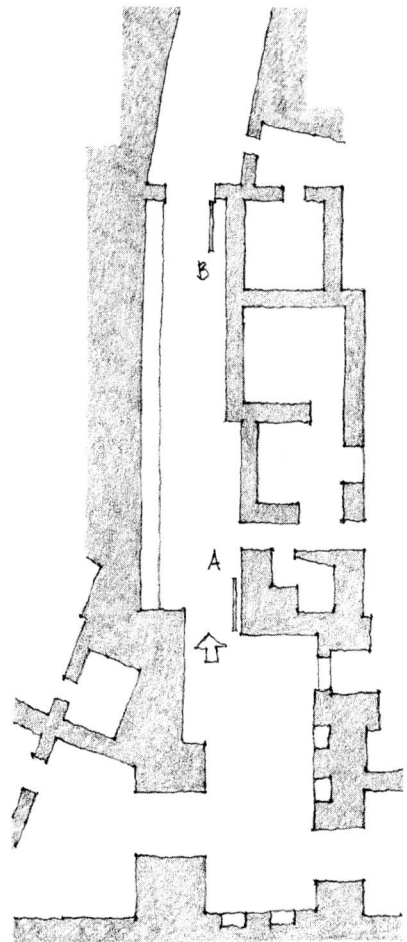

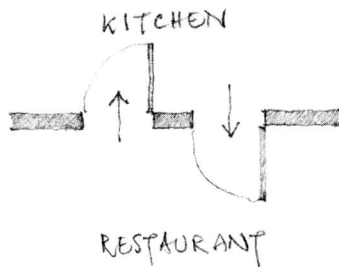

KITCHEN

RESTAURANT

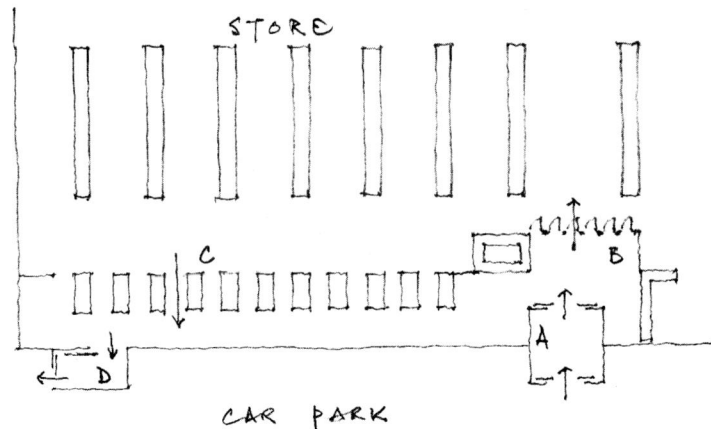

STORE

CAR PARK

servants to deliver the food, door B was closed. After leaving the food on the shelf provided, door A would be closed and door B opened to allow the women to collect their meal. In this way men from the kitchen could provide food without setting eyes on the Sultan's wives.

Door as valve

Valves allow things through in one direction only. Some doors operate as valves. They are not often used in the domestic setting (though it is possible to buy catflaps that can be adjusted to keep a cat outside once it has exited, or *vice versa*.) Often they are used in restaurants, between the kitchen and the dining room (above). 'IN' and 'OUT' doors prevent waiters and waitresses crashing into each other.

Valve doors are used to control large volumes of people. Turnstiles at sports grounds are valve doors because they only allow you to pass in one direction and thus obviate the chaos that would be caused if someone decided to go in the wrong direction.

Valve doors are used in supermarkets too. The drawing above shows a typical arrangement. A on the plan is a 'lock' door, but it is also a valve in that it is intended only to allow you into the store. At B there

is a range of swing gates that open inwards only. Then you explore the store and buy your provisions. At C, the check-outs, you pay; but they are valve doors too, since the check-out people will only let you pass in one direction. And D, another 'lock' door, allows you to pass out of the store only. This arrangement of valve doors is partly intended to keep a smooth flow of people through the store, but it also helps ensure that people pay for what they take off the shelves, since everyone is manoeuvred into passing through a check-out position.

Airports and train stations too are designed with numerous valve and filter doors, arranged to take travellers step-by-step through the sequence of operations involved in getting on a plane or a train.

Trap

Traps usually depend on valve doors; they allow you into a situation from which you cannot escape. You might feel that the arrangement of valve doors at the entrance of supermarket traps you inside the store so that you will spend some money, but traps are usually used in mortal situations.

A mouse, rat, tiger... can be caught in a trap from which is cannot extricate

Sometimes doors act as valves, allowing you to pass through in one direction only.

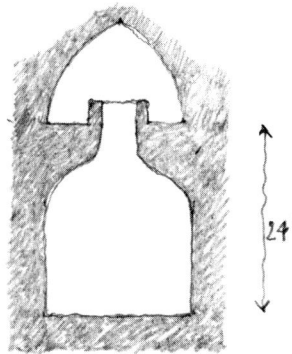

Some spaces have entrances that allow things in but not out again.

itself. When a lobster crawls in through the entrance of a lobster-pot it cannot get out (above left). A similar principle to the lobster-pot was employed by the builders of the 'bottle' dungeon at St Andrews Castle in Scotland (above right). As a prisoner you would have been unceremoniously dropped down the hole in its roof. This is its only doorway. It is more than twenty feet deep. As you fell you would probably have broken some bones, left with no more thresholds to cross, and to die in pain.

Military designers like to engineer traps for the enemy. The ancient Arcadian Gate into the city of Messene (right) dates from the fourth century BC. Here the gate was fortified, but if attackers managed to breach its doors they found themselves trapped in a circular enclosure surrounded with walls on top of which defenders could stand to rain down spears and arrows on the trapped attackers. The press of their own comrades continuing to try to get through the gate would prevent those in the trap from escaping.

Entrance traps in storytelling

The trap is a frequent theme in films and novels. Sometimes the trap is framed as a series of circumstances that culminate in the victim finding himself in a situation from which he cannot escape. Although narratives almost always accentuate the human dimensions of such situations, they almost always have an architectural dimension too. The times when they do not, the trap is a psychological one. But otherwise the victim, whatever

The Arcadian Gate as Messene was designed to trap attackers inside the gate so that they could be slaughtered.

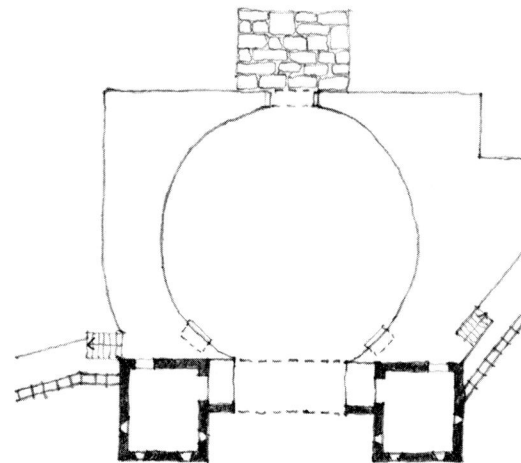

PLAN

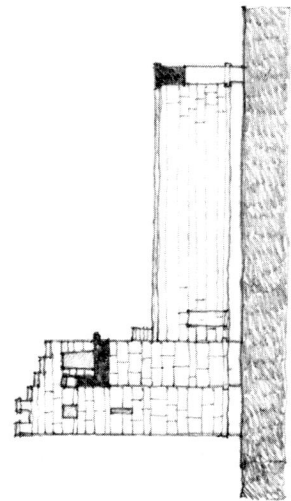

SECTION

FRONT ELEVATION

other difficulties he might find himself in, is trapped physically as well as psychologically: by finding himself in a dead end street or corridor; in a room with barred windows; or even (to think of architecture in a negative sense) in an open landscape without cover or hiding place. When Saddam Hussein was captured, after the Iraq War in 2003, he had effectively trapped himself in his own hiding place, a small pit in the ground.

In *The Seven Samurai* (Akira Kurosawa, 1954), villagers, threatened by marauding bandits, under the direction of the Samurai who have come to help them, deal with and defeat some of the attacking bandits by letting their guard down and allowing them, a few at a time, into the heart of the village. By opening the gates in their defences and allowing the bandits to enter, the villagers trap them in a place where they have them surrounded and are vulnerable. The entrance is made into a one-way valve that allows the enemy in but not out. The barrier built to keep the bandits out helps to defeat them by trapping them once they are inside. Outside the village the bandits are unknown and unknowable, and hence more dangerous.

Inside, they become knowable, and, being reduced in number, vulnerable to the villagers and their Samurai helpers.

In another Japanese film *The Woman of the Dunes* (Hiroshi Teshigahara, 1963), an academic who has been collecting insects in the sand dunes by the sea misses his bus home at the end of the day. Wondering what to do, some local people offer him lodging with an old woman in a strange house, which is at the bottom of a large pit in the sand. The 'old' woman turns out to be an attractive girl whose husband and child have, at some indeterminate time in the past, been 'swallowed by the sand'. The academic descends into the pit by climbing down a rope ladder, and spends the night in this chronically sand-threatened house. The next day he finds that the rope ladder has been removed, and by entering the pit he has become trapped with the girl. In this impossible situation, he must help the girl keep back the encroaching sand, which constantly threatens to engulf the house. He also, of course, like Odysseus by Calypso, becomes trapped by the girl's sexual attractiveness. It is a metaphorical, and may be also a slightly misogynist film.

DUNNOTTAR CASTLE (an aggressively defensive entrance)

Dunnottar Castle on its rocky promontory.

In our own houses we use the external doorways as points of discrimination between those people and things we want to let in and those we wish to keep out or defend ourselves against. In fortresses defensive entrances can be elaborate. Because they are dealing with issues of life and death the architects of the entrances into fortresses have to be ingenious. There are many examples. Here is just one.

The photographs on the right are of Dunnottar Castle on the east coast of Scotland. It stands dramatically on top of a high and rugged promontory linked to the land by a narrow neck of rock. On the opposite page is a sketched plan of the entrance.

The only doorway of the castle (A on the plan and illustrated in the bottom left photograph) is fitted with a heavy wooden door that would have been bolted against enemies. Even so it would still have been a point of weakness and the focus of attack, so the doorway is further protected by various defensive arrangements and devices: 1. it is approached up long steep and tiring steps (B) so that heavily-armed attackers would be out of breath by the time they reached it; 2. unpleasant things would have been dropped on enemies from the battlements above as they approached the door; and 3. there are loopholes in the wall to the right (C on the plan, and just visible in the bottom left

The only door into the castle; at the top of steep steps and defended from the right by loopholes.

The loopholes facing intruders, and the irregular steps.

photograph) through which muskets could be fired at anyone approaching and trying to break down the door.

If the enemy under attack from the defenders managed to breach the door they would be faced with more muskets aimed at them through four loopholes in the wall directly ahead (D on the plan and clearly visible in the bottom right photograph). Dodging these they would have had to negotiate an intentionally complicated arrangement of steps (E), and even then they would not have known what awaited them around the corner (F). Additional defenders would have waited to attack invaders from chambers on both sides (G).

As the nub of attack and defence, the doorway of Dunnottar Castle is a good example of the conflict afflicting all doorways, though usually in less dramatic ways. In time of war, the destiny of the place and the authority it represented would have been concentrated into that one spot.

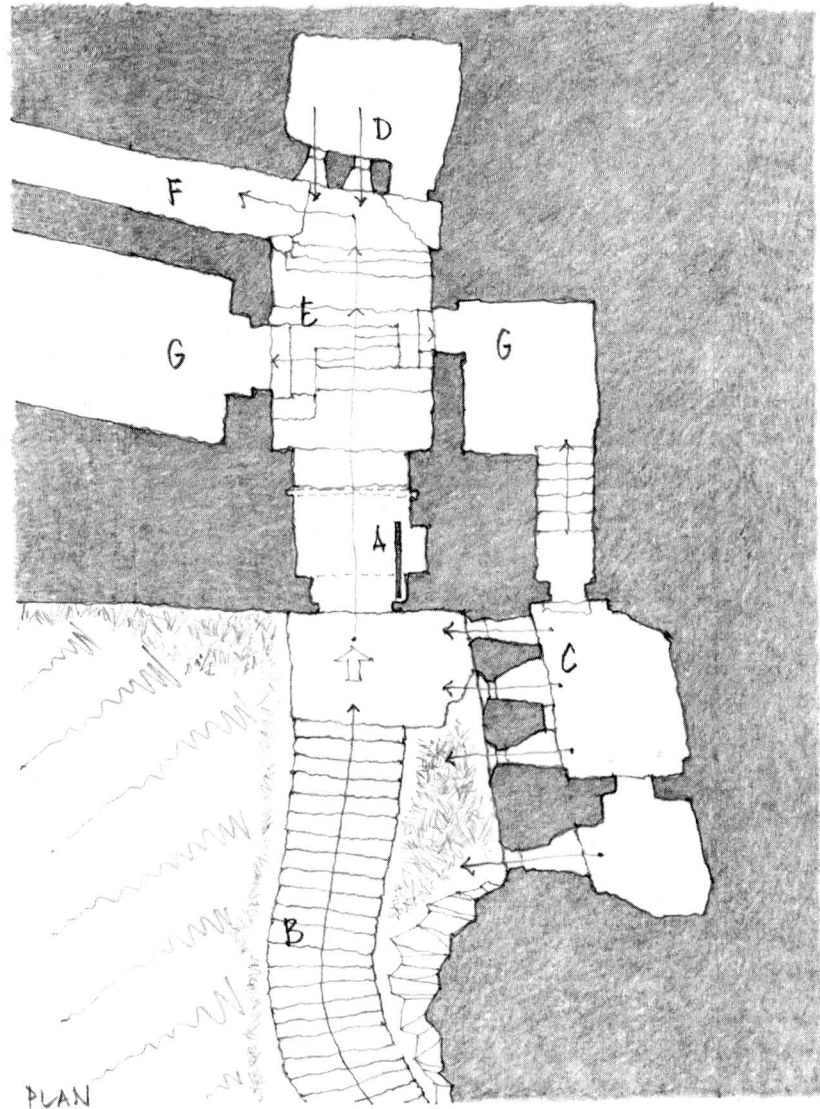

PLAN

A HOTEL TERRACE DOORWAY (variable climatic defence)

The following example is less dramatic than that of the defensive castle entrance but illustrates the ingenuity we apply to the design of doorways to deal with conflicting circumstances; to allow some things through whilst defending against others.

In cold climates it is common to have more than one set of doors between inside and outside, often with a small lobby between. In this way, working like an air-lock, warm air can be kept inside while someone is coming in. The two doors, and the space between, increases the separation (and the insulation) between outside and inside at the point where it is most vulnerable.

In hot climates the circumstances are different. Even so, layers of division between inside and out are often used in different permutations to deal with differing conditions.

In the example in the photograph alongside, the doorway between an Italian hotel bedroom and its terrace is fitted with three layers that can be opened or closed. These are, from the outside: louvred shutters; glass doors; and fabric curtains.

The things the doorway must allow in or out are: people; light; air; and the view.

The things the sets of doors and curtains might have to prevent coming in or allowing out are: warm air; cool air; bright sunshine; light; rain; the view into the bedroom; intruders; and troublesome insects.

A hotel terrace doorway in a warm climate.

The layers are used in a variety of combinations to deal with different circumstances. For example:

– closing only the glass doors allows a view out, lets light in, and keeps cool air-conditioned air inside; the doors also keep out mosquitoes, rain and intruders;

– closing only the shutters shuts off the views both out into the landscape and into the bedroom, providing privacy and security; the louvres allow ventilation, let in a little light but neither bright sunshine nor rain; but they do not defend the room against insects;

– closing only the curtains also shuts off the views out and in; they allow in hardly any air or light; and they might keep out some of the mosquitoes but are no good against rain or intruders.

The other permutations are of course to have all three layers open or closed, or to close: glass doors and shutters; glass doors and curtains; or shutters and curtains. Each permutation adds subtlety to the ways admittance and defence can be managed. Getting the combination right for particular circumstances is a matter of experience and judgement.

The layers between inside and outside can be used in different permutations: glass doors only; louvred shutters only; curtains only; or any combination. Sometimes the number of permutations is further increased by the provision of a second set of curtains of a light net.

THE DOORWAYS OF A HOUSE

We can learn something about what door-ways contribute to the architecture of a house, and how we use them and how they affect us, by looking at and thinking about doorways we know well.

On this page there is a sketch plan of the ground floor of our house. It is not a large or unusual house but the ground floor has more than fifteen doorways including the gateways into the front garden and driveway and some doorways I have made with shrubs in the rear garden.

Some of the things these doorways do are obvious: they allow people in and out of the house and its rooms; most of them are fitted with doors so that they may be opened and closed, switched *off* and *on* to manage access to different spaces. The external doors keep the weather and stran-gers out and children and warmth in; the internal doors may be closed to provide privacy and block out noise (I close door D when I am working in the study). The front doorway (C on the plan) is the beginning and end of our private domain and where we greet visitors and receive deliveries: it has a door-bell, letter-box and light; with its number on the door it identifies the house; it is where we are sometimes engaged in discussion by political canvassers or religious missionaries; in the summer this doorway is adorned with flower pots and hanging baskets, at Hallowe'en we might hang a pumpkin under the porch, and at Christmas we pin a wreath of holly on the door. The garden gateway B is where we wave off visi-tors when they leave, and watch as they drive away down the road and disappear around the corner.

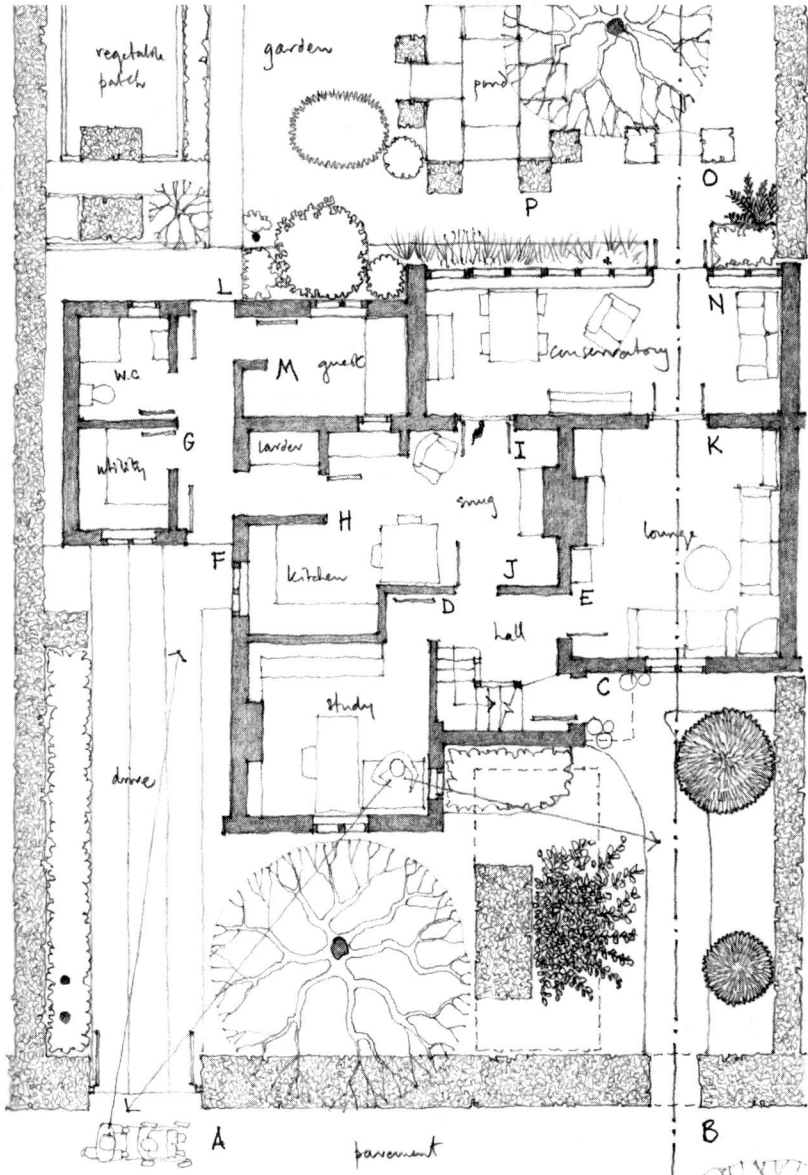

The ground floor plan of our house.

The doorways play more subtle roles too. They play an important part in the routes into, through and within the house. The hall is a key space: even though it is one of the smallest rooms in the house it has the most doorways: four plus the stairs – the 'doorway' to the upstairs. The hall acts as a distribution space giving access to other parts of the house.

Some of the doorways form into sequences, like punctuation points in a sentence. For example: when I come home I walk from the pavement (at the bottom of the drawing) through the arch in the high beech hedge (B) into the front garden; then I walk up to the front door (C) and open it with my key. I step into the hall where I take off my coat, and then through the door (J) into the 'snug'. I have then passed through three doorways and been in four 'rooms' (including the street and front garden) as I walked from the pavement to the heart of our house. At each doorway I feel progressively more separated from the world outside, more deeply embedded in my family's private world. And at each my demeanour changes slightly.

From the snug I can follow another sequence of doorways which takes me first (through I) into the conservatory and then (through N) into the rear garden where I am back outside but in a special small

'paradise' buffered by the house from the world outside.

The front garden arch in the hedge (B, above) is aligned with the lounge window and glazed doors K and N as well as a pair of bushes that form another doorway in the garden (O), so that as I enter the front garden I have a glimpse straight through the house to the garden at the back. The indirect route I take to get through to the garden is punctuated by a total of five doorways and takes me through six rooms each with a different character.

When small children come to visit, another linked sequence of doorways comes into play. The children run circuits through doorways I, K, E and J, enjoying the strangeness of entering each room repeatedly from the same direction (the architectural equivalent of chanting a circular sentence – the snug leads to the conservatory leads

The front garden gateway, B on the plan. The front door is open, and a glimpse of the rear garden visible through the aligned windows.

to the lounge leads to the hall leads to the snug…). Eventually the children change direction, deviate from the circular route (through doorway N into the garden perhaps) or are stopped abruptly by a parent.

When visitors approach, it is good to be able to see who is coming, and whether they are friends or strangers. From inside our house it is easy to see when people approach. When we are in the lounge, conservatory or even the garden we can see people coming to the front door (along the alignment of doorways N, K, the lounge window and gateway B). When in the kitchen we can see if someone comes to the back door (F). And when I am working in the study I can see both approaches. In these ways we can see who is coming and prepare before opening the door. (From the study I can also observe one of the ways that doorways stimulate distinct behaviour patterns. When people walk past gateway A they almost always turn their head to glance into our driveway. As a passer-by it is hard not to be curious about what one might see through a doorway. We all do the same if a doorway is open as we walk down a street.)

Specific doorways play their parts in the zoning of our house too. Door H for example separates off a small back area of the house, where there is a larder, a utility room, a shower room and a small guest

room. This door works in two different ways: in the normal running of the house it screens off piles of laundry and the noise of the washing machine from the rest of the house; but when we have a guest staying, the utility room door can be closed, and the guest can feel they have a part of the house to themselves.

Doorway I, between the snug and the conservatory.

We use the doors to manage visitors' access to different part of the house too. When some sorts of visitor arrive at the front door (C), we close doors D and J. We allow them only into the hall and through doorway E into the lounge. In this way we can keep them out of the sometimes less tidy parts of the house and thus hope to give the impression that our domestic lives are represented by the more tidy lounge.

And finally, the doorways and doors of the house (external and internal) play an important role in the different ways we use the house in different seasons of the year. In the summer the threshold of doorway I is a step from the cool shade of the snug into the warmth of the conservatory; in the winter it is a step from the fire-warmed snug into a cold conservatory and hence much less used. In the warm weather of summer we open nearly all the doors of the house allowing a fresh breeze to pass through most rooms. The front garden becomes a sitting room and the back garden becomes a dining room. By contrast, in the winter all doors are closed and, with the fire lit, the snug accommodates dining room and sitting room all in one. It is by the doors that the house expands in summer and contracts in winter.

These are a few of the parts doorways and their doors play in the architecture of a house. They illustrate something of the range of things that doors do. As well as being like punctuation points in the experience of a house they can be like the keys on a musical instrument, enabling different 'tunes' to be played on a house in different social circumstances and in different weathers.

The alignment of doors and lounge window, looking from the rear garden.

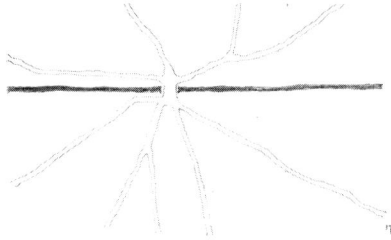

Doorways draw together pathways. They make fixed points. Before and after them, where space is open and fluid, we can wander; but a doorway defines a specific point of access through a wall or across a divide. Part of the charm of Sottsass's 'Doorway to enter into darkness' (p. 16) is that it defines an exact point at which to cross the line of shadow. Even though there is nothing to stop you crossing into the shadow at other places, the doorway invites and symbolises the idea of a transition from light into dark by specifying, quite exactly, a point at which to make it.

Like phrase marks in a piece of music, full stops in a paragraph or chapter divisions in a book, doorways articulate various threads of movement, bringing them together for a moment of coincidence and reflection before moving on. Like pegs holding down a rope, or the hoops in a game of croquet, doorways anchor routes at specific points. They pin down fluid space and provide points of reference.

Stroma

Stroma is an island in the Pentland Firth, between the far north of Scotland and the Orkney islands. Nowadays Stroma is deserted and the houses of the fishermen who once lived there stand in ruins.

The island provides a simple example of how doorways provide anchorage points for routes. The coast of Stroma is almost completely lined with cliffs. But at a few places there are small inlets with pebbled beaches (above) where small boats can be launched or hauled in from the sea. These inlets are the doorways on to the island. They are the junctures between the land and the open sea, across which fishermen wander in search of fish. As you can see in the map of the island (right), these inlets, one of which was developed into a harbour, provide the starting points for the simple network of paths that cross the island. The inlets pin the ends of the paths in place.

The same is true of any room with more than one doorway, field with more than one gateway or city square with more than one point of access. The doorways identify the end points of routes across them. So that in my office (right, which we also saw on pp. 58 and 80) there is an implied route between

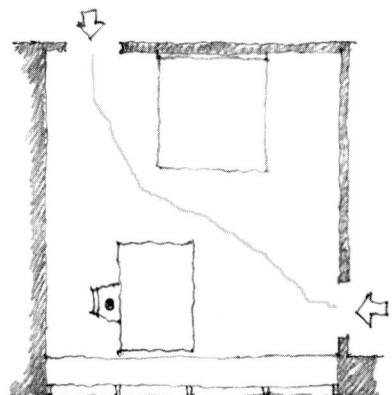

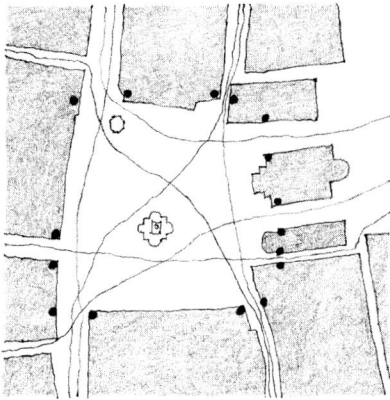

the two doorways, which conditions how I position the furniture. And, like the pockets on a snooker table, the junctions where the streets meet a town square (above) define the end points of the different routes people take across the space.

The same happens for whole settlements. The gateways of a walled city, for example, do not only define the points of entry, but also the end points of the routes across the city. For example, in Urbino, in northern Italy (right), the routes stretch from gateways in the northern wall to one at the southern tip of the city, and from a gateway in the western wall to one in the eastern. Where the major cross-city routes meet, there is a piazza, which recognises and takes advantage of the crossing. Where streets meet the piazza they are like doorways into a room at the heart of the city. (In the plan these 'doorways' are marked by black dots.)

The skeleton of the plan

The routes and doorways of a plan provide the framework for understanding how to use the building. In his book *The English Gentleman's House* (1864) Robert Kerr wrote:

> *The relation of the rooms to each other being the relation of their doors, the sole purpose of the thoroughfares is to bring these doors into proper system for communication.... The Corridors*

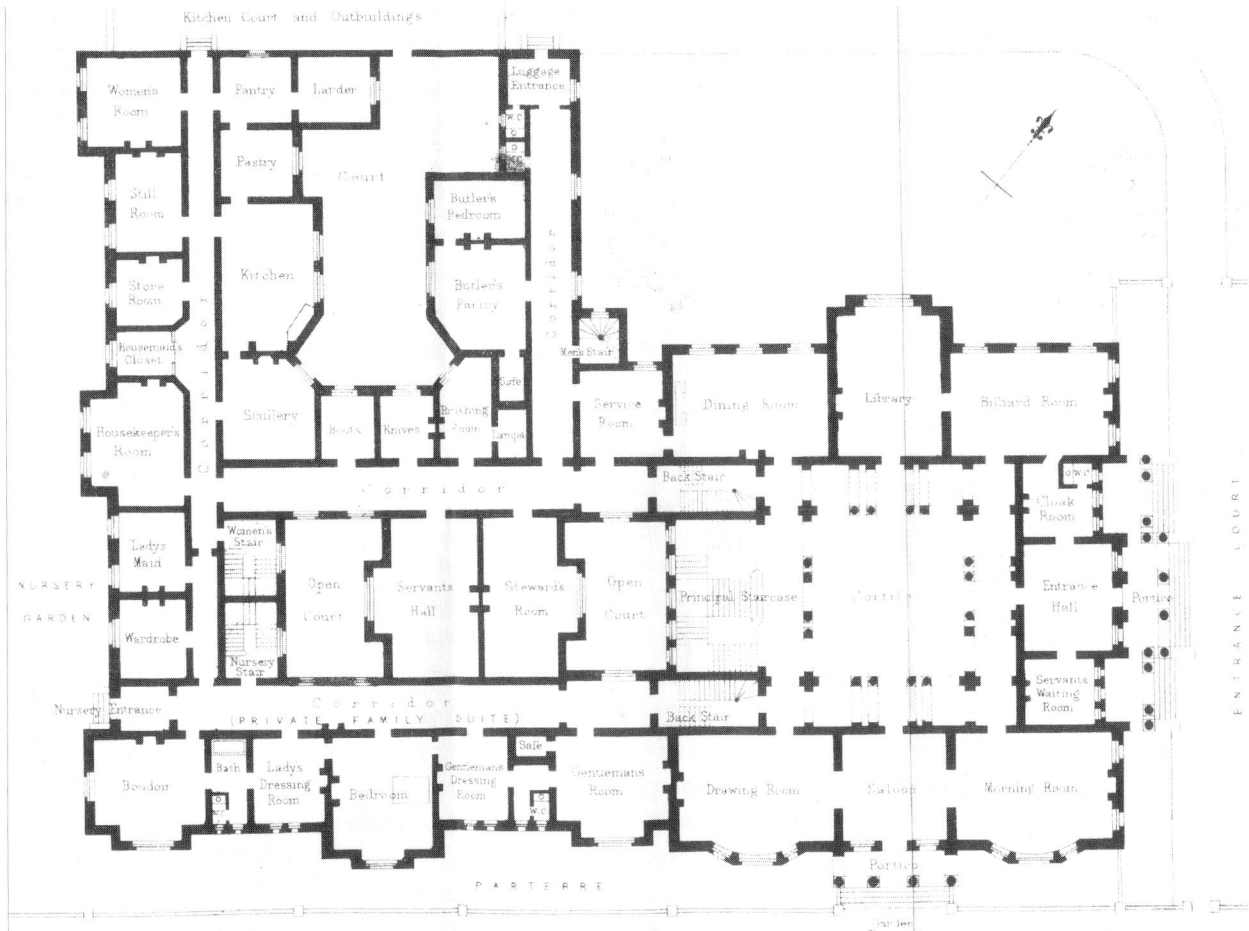

and Passages of a house… are the Skeleton of its Plan; because the relations of the rooms to each other are in fact the relation of their doors; and accordingly, every one can call to mind instances where those thoroughfares and this relation of doors is so contrived that one appears to understand their system instinctively, and others, on the contrary, where one is always at a loss.'

The plan above is one of Kerr's own designs, though it was never built. In it he uses various devices to establish a clear circulation 'Skeleton'. The diagram of this skeleton is given on the right. From the Main Entrance on the right of the plan the route leads into a cortile (an interior courtyard) which, with its surrounding cloister, provides a distribution and datum space that gives

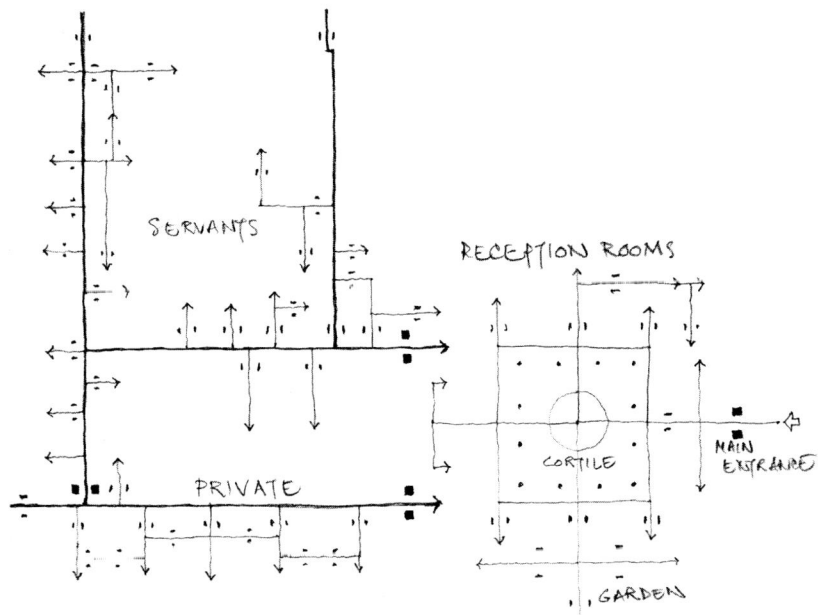

access to the doorways of all the major rooms arranged around it.

By contrast, the rest of the house is organised by corridors. From the bottom left corner of the cortile a doorway gives access into the private realm of the family rooms ranged along their own corridor. And a doorway in the top left of the cortile leads from the servants realm, itself organised by three corridors. Each of the three main realms is divided from the other two by doorways, as of course is each of the main rooms from the cortile. The result is a finely structured composition of spaces, divided by doorways into zones belonging to different sections of the house's community, and with different characteristics.

Doorways and philosophy

Kerr's house is composed of many rooms, and each necessarily has to have its own doorway. The house has a Library, Drawing Room, Dining Room, Morning Room, Billiard Room, Bedrooms, Dressing Rooms, Boudoir… and more bedrooms upstairs. There are also kitchens, rooms for cloaks and for servants to wait, a scullery and a pantry, and even separate rooms dedicated to boots and to knives. The corridors and doors form the backbone of the house and organise the way in which it is to be used.

This house is an extreme example of compartmentalisation. It was produced by a society that valued discipline, order, and intricate organisation of functions; it was a society that also compartmentalised people into classes and occupations. In this book I have alluded to the idea of a world without doors by evoking the usual image of the life of Aborigines in the Australian outback. The culture of the Victorian English gentleman was starkly different (maybe diametrically opposed) to that of the Australian Aborigine. This was a culture with a strong organisation and hierarchy, based on possession of land, space and people. Whereas the image of Aboriginal culture in Australia evokes the idea of a landscape unfragmented by ownership, which does not know or need compartmentalisation with walls, that of the Victorian English gentleman relished the use of the wall as an instrument in the rigorous and implacable management of space. Set in its walled estate, and supplemented by its walled gardens, the country house was composed of many rooms, each with its place within a carefully structure hierarchy. The English gentleman's house stands as a prime symbol of this highly structured, regimented, possessive, and class-sensitive culture.

The relationships between all those rooms, and the division of the family from the servants' realms, are defined by the

'You walk through a series of arches, so to speak, and then, presently, at the end of a corridor, a door opens and you see backward through time, and you feel the flow of time, and realize you are only part of a great nameless procession.'

John Huston (1906-1987)

doorways between them. These articulate the circulation system that allowed it to work. They are the switches, valves and locks in its mechanism. You can look at the plan of such a house and see the overall pattern of its organisation but you also know that your experience of it in reality, whether as a servant or a member of the family, would have been one of doors, door after door after door, each with its own identity determined by that of the room into which it led, and maybe (in the servants' realm) labelled: 'BOOTS', 'KNIVES', 'LARDER'…; doors between places where one could behave in one way and others where one should behave differently; doors into private realms; doors that granted privileges and doors that excluded; doors that divided a dominant class from another that served them.

According to Kerr's argument, in a good house plan, as in a good philosophical argument, you would know where you are and where you are going at all times. In short, you would 'know your place'. The alternative would be to be lost and confused.

Finding your way

Because they are like pegs holding down rope-like routes, doorways are important elements in finding your way through a building.

Remember going for an interview (for a job, or a place in university…). You have been given the address in the letter of invitation that arrived through your letter box. A few days later, you travel to the building where the interview will take place. You approach its entrance. Like Theseus approaching the Labyrinth you must find your way to the office of the interview panel who will test you. Going through the doorway you look around.

There's the desk with a receptionist. 'Good morning.' You ask the way. 'Take the lift to the second floor; turn left as you step out of the lift; go through the double-doors in front of you and around the corner to the right; go through the second door on the right and up the stairs in front of you, doubling back on yourself; walk along the gallery to the door at the end; go through that door and you will find the office you are looking for on the left. I'll ring ahead.' 'Thank you.' You take the lift, step out to the left, go through the double-doors, turn right, take the second door on the right, go up the stairs (doubling back on yourself) and along the gallery. As you see the door at the end, someone emerges smiling sympathetically. 'Hi.' 'Hi. Would you mind waiting here for a moment; they've not quite finished with the person before you.' You sit down. Now you feel nervous. Ten minutes pass.

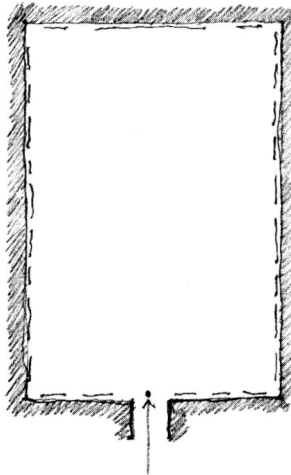

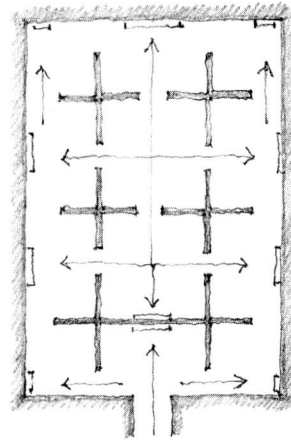

Doorways entice; they draw you through from one room to the next.

Eventually the same door opens again and you're invited through. (You wonder what happened to the person who was interviewed before you; where did they go?) You go through the door at the end of the gallery and then through another door on the left. In front of you is a table with three people silhouetted against a window; they are smiling with their mouths but scrutinising you with their eyes. You have reached the lair of the Minotaur through a labyrinth of doorways.

Channelling movement

The orientation of doorways, perhaps aided and abetted by valve doors, can be used to manipulate the ways in which people experience the spaces of a building.

The entrance to a store near my home is laid out like this (below). As in the store

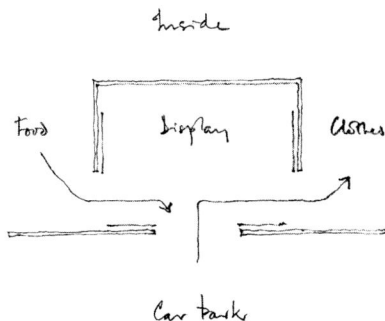

plan illustrated on p. 163 this is a 'lock' entrance, which helps keep draughts out and warm air inside in cold weather. But its architect has designed it to do other things too. This is a store to which people come mainly to buy food, but the owner wants to sell clothes too. So, as you go through the front door, only the automatic door on your right, which leads to the clothes area of the store, will open. The doorway from the food area is 'exit only' and opens only when approached from inside. The entrance makes you pass the clothes before you can buy your food.

Doorways attract. Like magnets their mystery invites you forward to see what is through and beyond them. They can be used to orchestrate experience.

Manipulating movement is part of the art of designing galleries and museums. Doorways play an important part in this manipulation. The curiosity they stimulate draws people through from room to room. Imagine going into a large open room lined with paintings (above). You would see them all from the doorway as you entered. To look at them in detail you would have to walk around the edge of the room. Now imagine the same room divided with partitions (above right). In this case as you enter

179

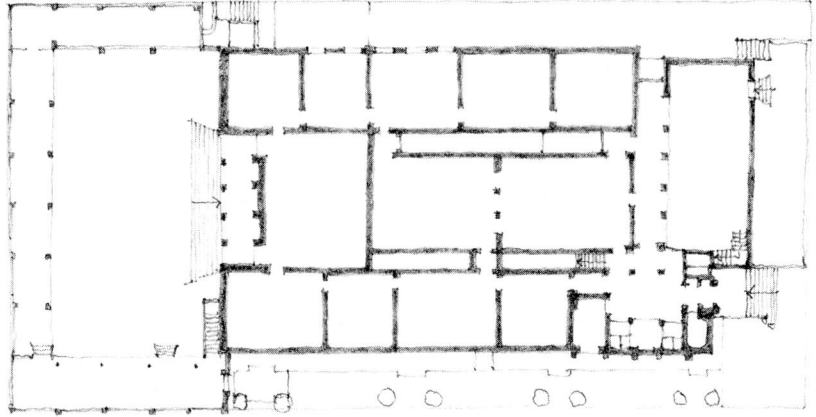

you cannot see the whole room. Not only do the partitions provide extra wall space so that more paintings can be exhibited, they divide the space into rooms; and the doorways entice you from one room to the next. The doorways also provide opportunities for framing particularly important works on doorway axes (above), increasing the pull from room to room.

The plan above right, which is typical of nineteenth and early twentieth century gallery layouts, is of the Liljevalch Art Gallery in Stockholm, designed by Carl Bergsten, and built in 1916. It is composed of a sequence of rooms with doorways aligned *enfilade* so that a visitor can see through from one end of the building to the other. Although there are some choices of route to be made and some back-tracking involved, the doorways lead visitors through the sequence allowing them to view the exhibits in manageable groups.

Progression and procession

Doorways play their part in articulating definite lines of movement through buildings. They may define steps in a hierarchical sequence.

In the Broch of Gurness on Orkney, which is a fortified village built about two thousand years ago, there is a clear path

that leads from the main gateway over the defensive ditch, between the dwellings, and up to the thick-walled circular broch at the heart of the village. The doorways define stages in the progress from the outside world into the heavily defended core of the settlement. The doorway into the broch has a guard chamber alongside. One can imagine that if the village was attacked its inhabitants would take refuge within the thick circular walls of the broch.

Doorways are staging points on a route, and can frame the line of a procession.

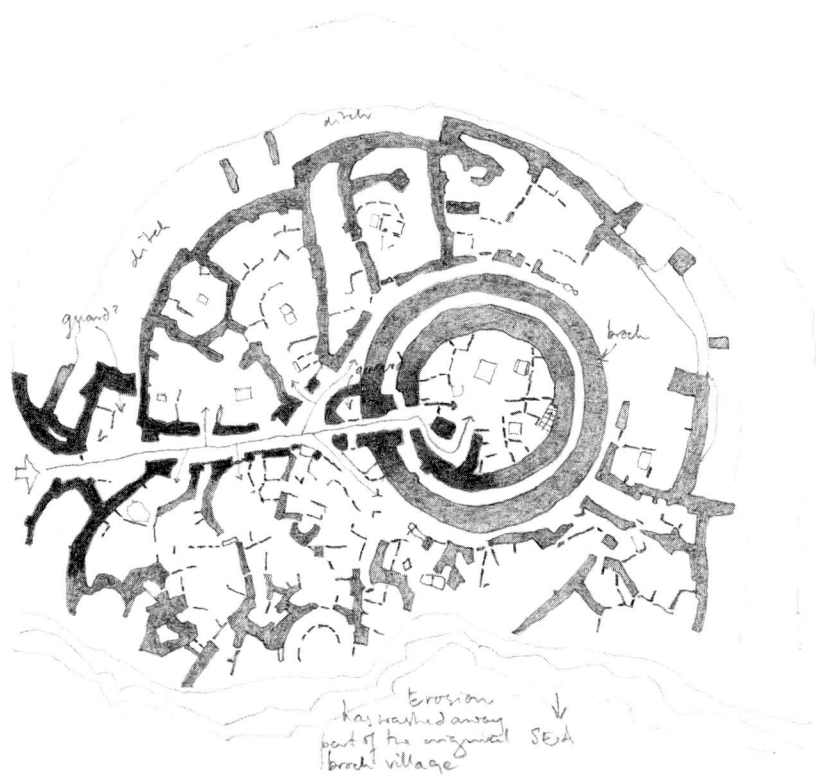

Gurness suggests a hierarchy of stages of defence and protection. Doorways can define stages in hierarchies of mystery or sacredness too.

On p. 40 we saw that the builders of the temples in Malta some five thousand years ago recognised the power of a sequence of doorways aligned on their shared axis. The sequence of doorways establishes thresholds which imply stages of initiation into or understanding of mysteries. The doorways draw the person from one to the next, establishing a sense of movement and progression. Although the size of the doorways, their occasional high thresholds and the relatively short length of axes from entrance to altar suggest that the Maltese temples may not have been used for formal processions, the dynamic of the sequence of doorways is a typical architectural device in buildings that are.

The ancient Egyptian palace temple of Rameses II (right) dates from nearly two thousand years later than the Maltese temples. Like the temple palace of Rameses III shown on p. 101 it has a doorway of appearance visible on the left side of the first courtyard. The main part of the temple has a much longer sequence of spaces than the Maltese temples, punctuated by many more doorways. Here there are seven creating a grand axis that at one point ascends a stair.

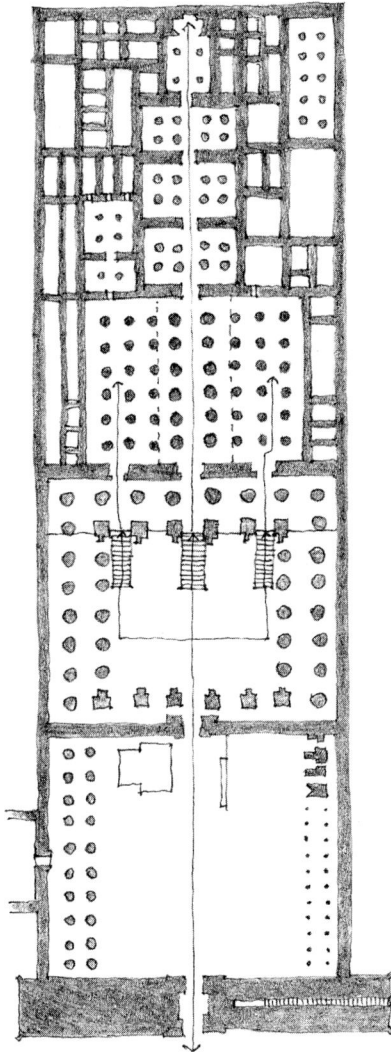

The palace temple of Rameses II has an axial sequence of seven doorways, culminating in an eighth, which is a false doorway.

There was another 'doorway' in the sanctuary at the culmination of the axis, a false door that no one but the spirit of the pharaoh (when dead) would be able to use. It seems certain that this grand axis was designed to orchestrate the formal event of a procession, with the doorways dividing it into sections and providing sequential opportunities for the pharaoh to appear.

CRYPT UNDER (out flow)

Because of our experience of wedding and funeral processions in churches, our first assumption might be that in the Egyptian example the procession would progress in the direction of the sanctuary. But an alternative, and probably more accurate interpretation, is that the route in Rameses's temple was intended to progress in the opposite direction. The Egyptians were concerned with resurrection; there are carved images of pharaohs emerging from false doorways. The suggestion therefore is that the sequence of doorways in the temple of Rameses II were intended to punctuate stages in the dead pharaoh's journey back to life as well as the ascending approach of priests to the sanctuary.

The association of such processional routes with ascent is common in architecture – as in the church shown in section above – and it is also common that the doorways, whether actual doorways from outside to in, or symbolic doorways such as the arch into the sanctuary, are positioned at each change of level. The combination of steps and doorway accentuate the transition from one stage of the route to the next, manifesting progressive detachment from the mundane.

Doorways mark the 'capital letters', 'commas', 'colons', 'semi-colons' and sometimes even the 'full-stops' of a route through a building. This is a sketched (and therefore no doubt inaccurate) section through the Crichton Church in Dumfries.

LABYRINTH ENTRANCES

Sometimes doorways are arranged to confuse, disorientate or merely hide the interior to which they give access. The labyrinth entrance is an extended instance of the avoidance of the directness of a simple doorway or of an axial sequence of door-ways. It substitutes concealment and uncertainty for clarity.

The Romanian philosopher of reli-gion, Mircea Eliade, has speculated on the meaning of labyrinths. In his book *Patterns of Comparative Religion* (1958) he wrote:

> 'Without being over-hasty in deciding the origi-nal meaning and function of labyrinths, there is no doubt that they included the notion of defending a "centre". Not everyone might try to enter a labyrinth or return unharmed from one; to enter it was equivalent to an initiation. The "centre" might be one of a variety of things. The labyrinth could be defending a city, a tomb or a sanctuary but, in every case, it was defending some magico-religious space that must be made safe from the uncalled, the uninitiated. The military function of the labyrinth was simply a variant on its essential work of defending against "evil", hostile spirits and death. Militarily, a labyrinth prevented the enemy's getting in, or at least made it very difficult, while it admitted those who knew the plan of the defences. Reli-giously, it barred the way to the city for spirits from without, for the demons of the desert, for death…. But often the object of the labyrinth was to defend a "centre" in the first and strictest sense of the word; it represented, in other words, access to the sacred, to immortality, to absolute reality, by means of initiation. The labyrinth rituals upon which initiation ceremonies are based are intended for just this – to teach the neophyte, during his sojourn on earth, how to enter the domains of death without getting lost. The labyrinth, like any other trial of initiation, is a difficult trial in which not all are fitted to triumph.'

The Necromanteion

In western Greece stand the ruins of the Necromanteion. The plan is shown above. This strange building is thought by archae-ologists to have been built about two and a half thousand years ago as a place where people could go to speak with the dead – a building that gave access to the underworld,

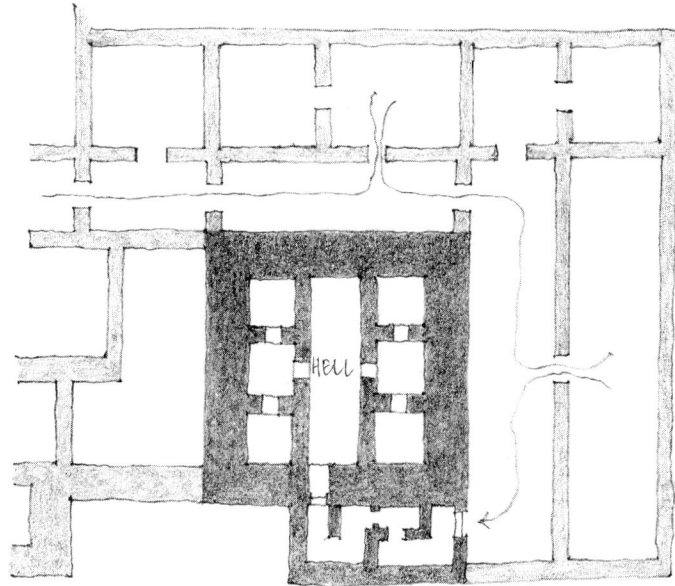

The Necromanteion has a labyrinth entrance intended either to prevent spirits escaping from within or to confuse visitors wishing to speak to the dead.

HELL

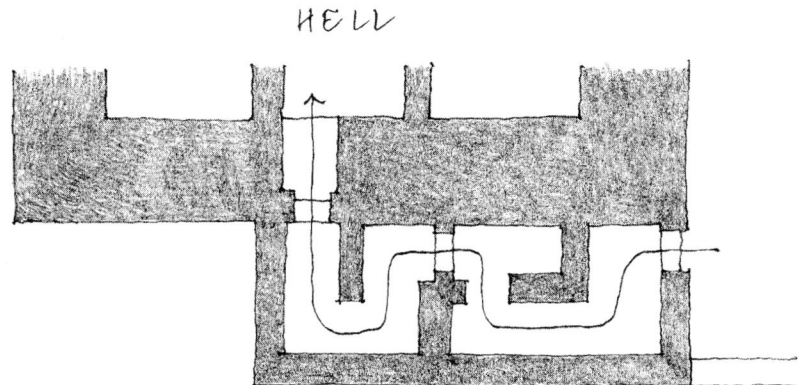

the home of Hades and Persephone. It is located in the place where Odysseus is described by Homer in *The Odyssey* as having spoken with the dead. The Necromanteion comprised a complex of buildings, including the accommodation of the priests who would minister to the visitors, as well as rooms in which the visitors would be prepared for the experience of talking with their ancestors. It is thought that visitors wishing to talk to the dead would have to prepare over a few days, eating special foods and maybe being given hallucinogenic drugs, before they were allowed into 'Hell'. The culmination of the complex is a four-square building, with very thick walls, divided geometrically into nine equal parts, the central three of which form a hall, from which there is access to three secondary chambers on each side. The hall is built over a vaulted subterranean chamber. Access to this large cellar is by a rectangular hole in the floor of the hall, very near the doorway, which is positioned not on the central axis of the hall but in the corner. Nowadays there is a metal ladder down into the subterranean hall; presumably in ancient times there was a wooden ladder, or maybe a rope ladder that could be pulled up to leave a terrified visitor marooned in the Hall of Hades. Pieces of machinery have been found in the ruins; these are thought to have been parts of contraptions used to lift or move

ghostly puppets in the dim light, as apparitions of the dead.

As appropriate for such a portentous building, the entrance is handled in a way that frames and contributes to the experience of the visitor, as well as having some symbolic purposes too. The approach to the square core is made nearly as long as possible, passing, from the main entrance of the complex, through corridors along two sides of the thick walls. Along these corridors were the rooms for preparation. Walking along these corridors it is unlikely that one would realise that the walls on your right were those of the central core of the complex. The building is designed for the direct experience of visitors, rather than for their appreciation of its overall layout; indeed, its mystery would be enhanced by the difficulty of assimilating its plan. Eventually, after the days of preparation and probably in a drugged state, visitors would be led to the end of the corridor, to the entrance of the square building (though they would have

The plan of the inner core of the Necromanteion in north western Greece shows the labyrinthine entrance passage.

The doorway into 'Hell'.

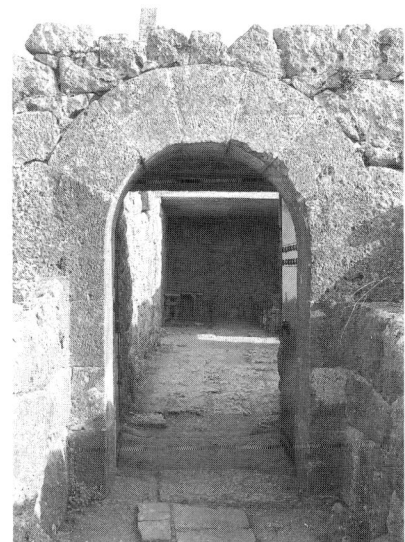

DITCH

BRIDGE

no way of knowing that it was square). Here there is not a simple doorway, but a short labyrinth, with seven turns. The exact purpose of this labyrinth is unclear, but its effect would surely be to disorientate the already confused visitor. It may well also have been intended not so much to protect the 'centre' (as Eliade discusses in the passage quoted at the beginning of this section) but to prevent the spirits from Hell escaping to cause havoc in the outside world.

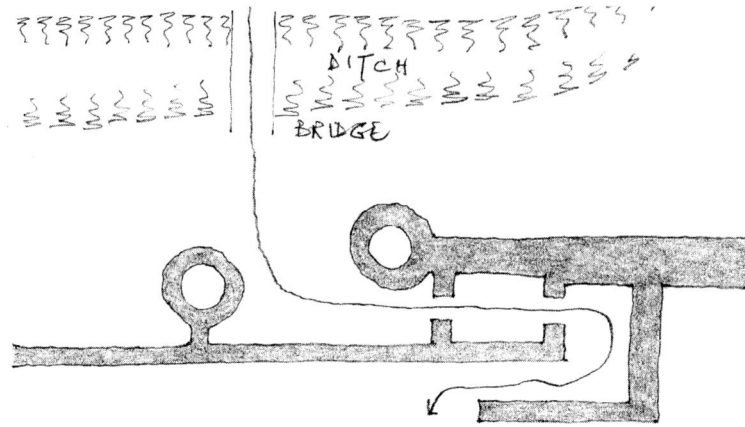

Labyrinths for defence

The labyrinth entrance can be an aid to defence. On pp. 166–67 we saw how in Dunnottar Castle the entrance was designed to confuse invaders. In the ancient city of Mantinaeia (top right) the gateway was designed to slow down and confuse any of the enemy who breached it, so that they could be attacked more easily. And in the fortress of Chanquillo in Peru (lower right), which dates from around 400 BC, the entrances are provided with simple labyrinths designed either to slow up invading forces or to prevent spirits from escaping from a sacred interior. In this instance, archaeologists seem unsure which was the intention.

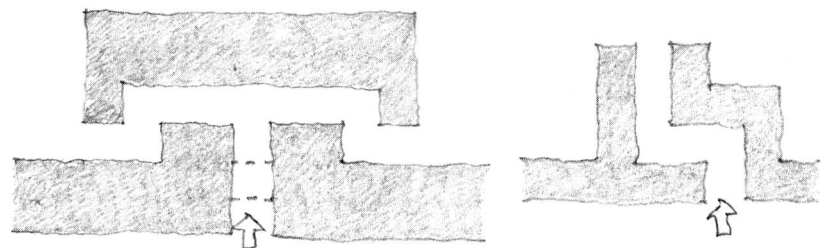

The same principle of confusion and disorientation was used by the East German authorities between the mid 1960s and the end of the 1980s when Germany was divided into East and West. The border crossings between the two halves of Germany were laid out as huge labyrinths through which those who wished to cross had to drive. The tortuous route slowed them down, and prevented them from seeing the end – the way out. If they had tried to 'make a break for it', they would have quickly got lost, and easily caught (or worse) by the border guards.

Entrances for privacy

Houses in Muslim countries are designed to provide complete privacy. They have few

Labyrinth entrances have been used in fortresses, to confuse and slow down invading forces.

185

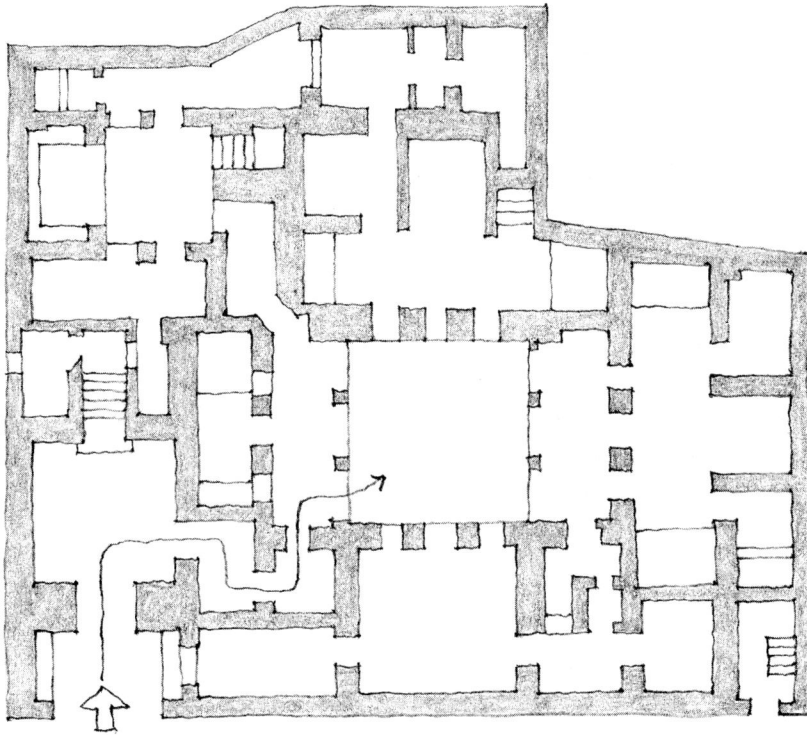

Traditional houses in Muslim countries have labyrinth entrances to preserve the privacy of the courtyards at their hearts.

But probably the most frequently encountered labyrinth entrances are those of public lavatories.

windows on the external walls, and their interiors are lit by courtyards. By using labyrinth entrances (above) the privacy of the courtyard is preserved from the street and from occasional visitors.

But probably the most frequently encountered labyrinth entrances in western countries are those into public lavatories. All such conveniences are provided with entrance arrangements that prevent people outside seeing those inside. The extravagant example on the right is from the motorway services at Durham in the north of England.

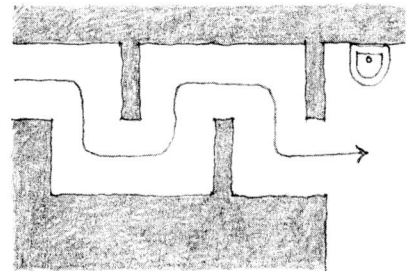

ST PETER'S CHURCH, KLIPPAN

> *'Though it was full of doors, they all opened from the inside, and could not even be seen from the outside.'*
>
> **George MacDonald** (*The Golden Key*, 1867)

Between pp. 47 and 51 I gave an account of approaching the Roman Catholic cathedral in Cefalù on the island of Sicily. Here is a description of approaching and entering a another church, of a different denomination, in a different country and from a different period of history. It is a building that gives a contrasting account of the relationship between religion and the congregation it serves. An aspect of this contrast is evident in the different ways in which one finds one's way to and into the two churches.

In the 1960s, the Swedish architect Sigurd Lewerentz designed two emotionally intense churches in Sweden, one at Björkhagen in the suburbs of Stockholm, and one in Klippan, a small town in southwest Sweden, about six hours on the train from Stockholm.

I was once in Stockholm, teaching. I knew of Lewerentz's work, and so went to see the church in Björkhagen, St Mark's. I wanted too to visit the church in Klippan, but was resigned to not seeing it because of the distance. St Mark's astonished me, and I knew St Peter's in Klippan would be even more interesting. The visit to St Mark's persuaded me to make the six hour train journey to Klippan, without hope of being able to get back to Stockholm in the day. The mission became an architectural pilgrimage; the journey one of anticipation.

I passed the journey in the sociable atmosphere of the smoking compartment of a Swedish train, some of the time talking and some watching the south Swedish landscape. I arrived at Klippan station mid-afternoon. The town is one of those spaced-out rural Swedish communities. Set in clear light and open countryside, there seems no imperative that buildings be crammed close together. The station itself was no more than a platform with a ticket building like a house.

I did not know where the church would be. I did not ask, but wanted to wander. From the station I drifted to the right, along a spacious road. I had an image in my mind of what the church would look like, so I went searching.

I felt I had found it when I saw a hedge; maybe because the hedge seemed to be hiding something in a town that was otherwise so unconcealed. Approaching the hedge I wandered to the right and found a small car park. From this there was an opening in the hedge, a pathway at the end of which I saw the distinctive dark purplish-brown brickwork of a Lewerentz church (which I knew from photographs). I walked towards it.

From this direction, the first recognisable feature of the building was not a door, nor a cross or steeple, but a chimney stack (right). Nothing of the building was more

than one storey high, and although the brick-work seemed severe and uncompromising, the scale and the chimney seemed almost domestic. At the chimney the path formed a 'T'. The right turn led to some municipal gardens; the left to a more enclosed garden with a pool of water. I turned left.

As one approaches any building one looks for the entrance. I looked but saw no immediate clues. From the water garden I saw there seemed to be a 'street' between the buildings of the church, with an open metal gate… an invitation to enter (above). Through the gate I saw the street had a right-angle turn. (The plan of the complex is alongside.) The buildings on my right were ancillary buildings, offices and so on. I knew the enigmatic building on my left was the church itself, but could see no obvious entrance. There was a door but it certainly did not invite entrance; it was plain, locked, and I do not think it even had a handle. I turned the right angle in the 'street', with steps down to a subterranean level on my right; they could not be the entrance to the church.

The wall on my left was without any openings. I walked along it, through another gate, and found myself feeling outside again, rejected by the building, on another street, and having found no entrance into the church. I turned left again, keeping the church on my left. I passed a small

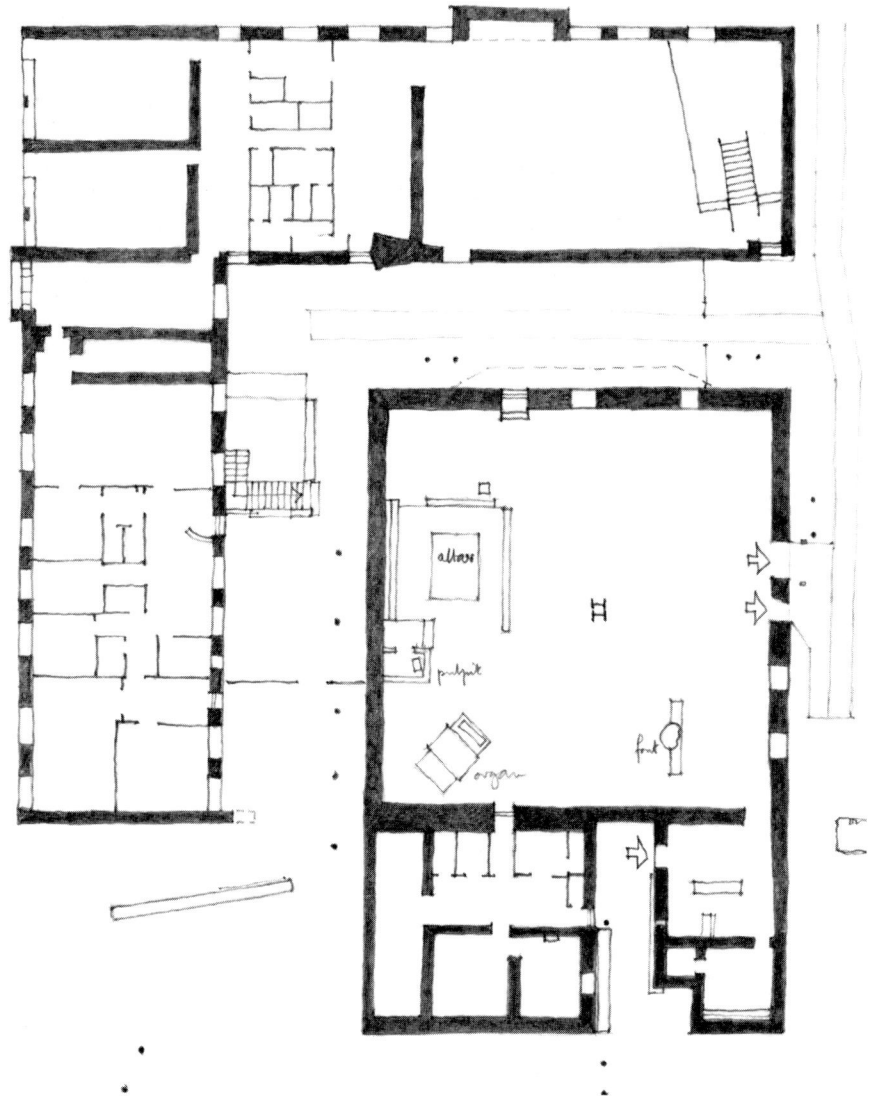

yard, which looked like where the dustbins were kept, though there were no bins there, and turned left again, through an opening between the church and a hedge, finding myself back in the water garden. I had been right around the building and failed to find a way in.

From the pool I looked at the wall of the church and saw that there were two doorways, close together. Neither had a handle, and anyway they looked like they were the doors into the plant room (where

The plan of St Peter's church in Klippan. The chimney I saw as I approached the building is at the top of the drawing; the 'dustbin yard' at the bottom.

the heating boiler might be) or had some other similar utilitarian purpose. They were not the way in.

Being resourceful, and having had some years' experience of finding ways into buildings, I decided that if I could not find the 'front' entrance (there seemed not to be one, but I was, implausibly, prepared to discover that my failure to find one was due to my lack of observation) then I would try to get in by the back way. I returned to the 'dustbin yard' (above). On the left was

a glazed door, locked, but through its glass I could see it was not a way into the church. Lower down in the yard (the brick paving slopes down unevenly), and on the right, tight in the corner, was a plain black door with a simple metal handle.

I opened the door (I cannot remember whether I pulled or pushed it open) expecting to find myself in a place with buckets and brooms and ladders. Instead I found myself transported into a mysterious cave. It was like a small cavern built of bricks, lit partly by dim wall lights and partly by daylight filtering down through what appeared deep crevices in the brick-vaulted roof. I could hear the sound of water dripping. I walked the short distance to an opening in the far left corner (below left), and saw the inside of the church, itself like a large brick-built cavern, dark but with glaring white light coming in through uncompromisingly square windows without frames. I could see, dimly, a massive piece of steel structure standing apparently in the middle of the church supporting the roof. I could see the primitive huge brick altar lit by star-like lights hanging over it. And, literally glowing in a patch of sunlight, a giant clam-shell font (right), white, with

The font, made from a giant clam shell.

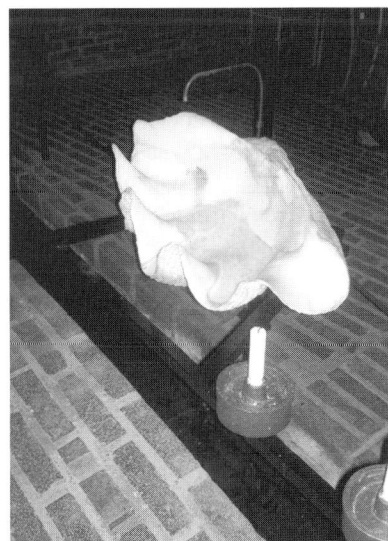

water dripping from its edge into a water-filled crack in the uneven floor (producing the sound I had heard as I came through the outer door). I wandered around the edge of this square cavern, and was there for three quarters of an hour before I realised that, because of its presence, I had not yet felt able to approach the steel structure at its centre. I went to it, touched it with the palm of my hand and then tapped it. In the darkness, it rang like a bell.

After recovering from that, I explored the interior of the church some more. I found that the doors which from the outside I had thought were those into the boiler room were in fact doors that could be opened at the end of the service to allow the congregation to emerge from the dark cavern into the water garden – an oasis of calm.

Like Lewerentz's much earlier building – the Chapel of the Resurrection (pp. 59–60) – St Peter's offers a transformative experience architecturally and spiritually, managed by its doorways.

In contrast to the self-proclaiming and dominant cathedral in Cefalù, the Klippan church is almost secret and hidden. It is not a building that projects its axis out into the world. It is more like a pagan cave shrine enclosing a mystery. St Peter's conceals a centre that must be discovered, and perhaps not where expected. When one does find the way into Lewerentz's church it is not to stand on the axis of an image of a remote and judgemental God, but to come into the presence of a symbol of strength standing in the midst of the congregation and holding up the roof.

The doorway exiting from the church into the water garden.

ARCHITECTURE
WITHOUT DOORWAYS

DOORWAYS AND DENIAL

As we approach the end of this book we can consider if architecture could exist without the doorway as one of its key elements.

We have seen that the doorway is a function of separation even though primarily a device for linkage and communication. If a doorway (like that of Sottsass on p. 16) were to be erected between two people standing in the middle of an open field it might link them with its axis but it would also separate them into distinct halves of the field; they would feel more separated from each other than without the doorway. Doorways provoke, as well as are made necessary by, walls that divide – that separate space from space or enclose a specific space so that it is isolated from everywhere else.

It follows that architecture without doorways can take two diametrically distinct forms: 1. walls, enclosures, cells… which have no access through or into them; or 2. open space or loose compositions of elements that do not enclose space in ways that completely separate it from its surroundings.

Such is the abiding symbolic power of the doorway and its symbiotic antithesis (the wall) that the first of these is almost always associated with the denial of life, by incarceration, absorption or death, whilst the latter is often associated with liberty of movement, the fluidity of space and the affirmation of life. Enclosures and cells

without doorways, or a solid block of matter into which it is impossible to gain entry, deny space, existence, movement; whilst more open groupings of elements suggest a state of being in an environment free of definite thresholds of demarcation and their connotations. The second of these alternative architectures without doorways is discussed in the next chapter.

Buildings without doorways

Enclosed spaces with no means of escape always terrify. One remembers the story of the black cat trapped within a wall in Edgar Allan Poe's story; the two riveters reported to have been trapped to die slowly within the double-hull of the S.S. Great Britain; the desperate crew of an unsavable submarine; miners trapped in a tiny pocket of air deep underground; asylum seekers found dead in a locked transportation container…. All provoke the asphyxia of claustrophobia.

The implacably enclosed volume of space, with no access or escape, is easily seen as a symbol and reminder of death. It has been so through the history of architecture.

In ancient Egypt the pyramids were intended as tombs that would be closed, like the lives of those whose bodies they contained, for eternity. Even so, as has already been noted on p. 54, their bases

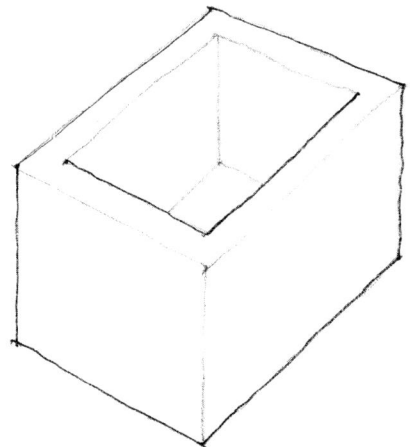

An enclosure with no doorway evokes the tomb.

No doorway can access the interior of solid matter. Some ancient civilisations, such as that of the Nabateans of Petra (now in Jordan), believed that gods – Djinns – inhabit rock, and carved blocks as their homes.

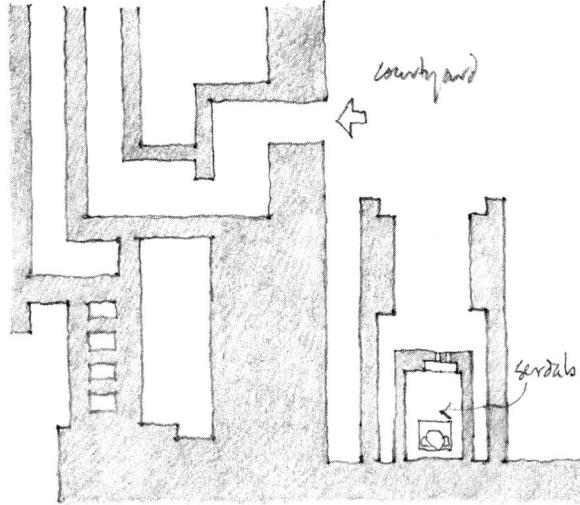

were provided with false doorways, hidden away deep within mortuary temples, through which the soul of the dead pharaoh could pass in and out (below).

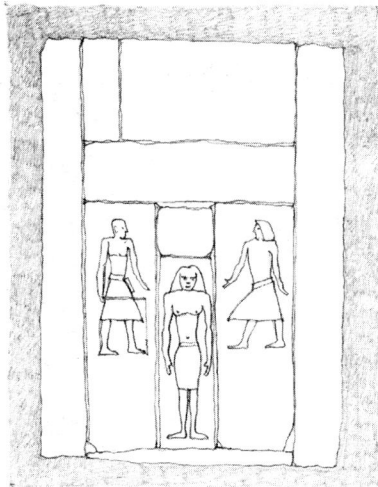

The tomb chamber itself was to be left with no means of human access. In some cases pyramids were provided with other rooms with no doorways. The Stepped Pyramid of Zoser for example has a *serdab* near the entrance of its mortuary temple (top). This was a small cell containing a statue representing the *ka* or soul-double of the dead pharaoh. The cell had no doorway but there were two holes at eye level so that the *ka* could watch people as they came and went. The statue's entombment within the cell echoed the soul's unreachability beyond the wall of death. But with its two watching eyes the *serdab* must also have been an unnerving reminder of the pharaoh's abiding presence.

A serdab stood at the entrance of the mortuary temple at the base of the Stepped Pyramid of Zoser. It contained an effigy of the dead pharaoh's soul, who could watch the entrance through two eye holes. (Note too the labyrinth entrance of the mortuary temple, indicated with an arrow.)

Caisteal Uisdean on the Isle of Skye became its builder's tomb.

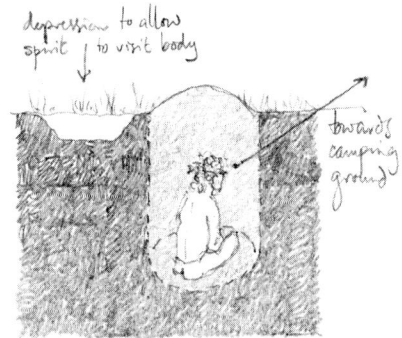

The sign over the gateway to Dante's Hell read 'Abandon all hope, ye who enter here'. The grave has no doorway through which one may come and go. And to find oneself trapped in an enclosed place with no doorway is to find oneself alive in one's own grave. We saw one such place on p. 164 – the 'bottle' dungeon at St Andrews Castle in Scotland, which offered its prisoners no hope of escape unless a rope was dangled from the opening in its roof. Another mortal enclosure was Caisteal Uisdean (opposite), also in Scotland, on the Isle of Skye. This is a tower, now ruined, with no doorway. Its story is that its builder, having been disloyal to his laird, was walled up inside and left to die.

Such is the fear or frustration at the finality of death that people, as did the ancient Egyptians, sometimes give its physical symbolisation as a wall, a doorway; architecturally implying an other side on which the dead still live, and through which they might, like St Simon on p. 67, one day return.

This desire to ameliorate the wall of death is common to many cultures. The Arunta tribe of Aboriginal Australians, for example, made graves in which the dead were positioned sitting up and facing the tribal camping grounds (above). Alongside the grave a depression was made in the ground, as a doorway through which the soul of the dead person could pass in and out to visit the body it had inhabited in life.

Many Christian graves or memorials, following the ancient example of the Egyptian pharaohs, take the form of a doorway or have a doorway depicted upon

Traditional graves of the Arunta Aboriginal tribe in Australia have a depression alongside to be used as a doorway by the soul.

Many Christian graves take the form of doorways.

them. (The example on the previous page is from the wall of St Machar's Cathedral in Aberdeen.)

And the Mausoleum at the Dulwich Art Gallery, which contains the tombs of the benefactors who enabled the gallery to be built, is built like a grand porch with three blind doorways, one on each side (right). The gallery and its mausoleum were designed by John Soane and built in the early nineteenth century. Around the same time, the poet and artist William Blake depicted death as a doorway (below).

The Mausoleum at Dulwich Art Gallery in the south of London is built as a grand porch complete with blind doorways.

THE REDUNDANCY OF THE DOORWAY?

Around the time of end of the First World War (c.1918) the German philosopher and theoretician of history Oswald Spengler wrote a series of books under the title of *The Decline of the West*. The underlying thesis of this huge and erudite work was that human civilisations through history have been and will continue to go through distinct phases of development, apogee and decline. These theories were discredited soon after their publication, and Spengler's reputation suffered by association with the growth of Fascism in Germany between the wars. But some of his ideas were especially influential amongst contemporary architects in northern Europe and America, because they involved human relationships with space.

One of Spengler's ideas was that the spatial patterns of organisation evident in the architecture produced by a civilisation were evidence of the underlying 'culture idea' – the distinguishing intellectual character – of that civilisation. Ancient Egypt, Spengler suggested, was a civilisation focused on the pathway leading to eternity, as evident in the pyramids with their causeways and mortuary temples, culminating in their great geometrically regular mountains of stone (the pyramid of Chephren on p. 53 is a good example). According to the same theory: ancient Greece was a civilisation focused on the body in space, evident in the temple set as a distinct object in the wide landscape; Byzantine civilisation was one of enclosed space, evident in the cave-like basilica, which Spengler likened to a Greek temple turned inside out like a glove; and Chinese civilisation was one of wandering through a maze, as evident in the complex patchwork of spaces of a traditional Chinese house.

Spengler's writing is powerful for architects because, notwithstanding his ideas about the mechanics of history, they reveal architecture as a potentially philosophical medium that may be used to explore and manifest ideas, propositions and beliefs about life, culture and society through the handling and organisation of space.

This understanding of architecture – as philosophy through space – holds interest whether or not any particular civilisation might be defined by a single distinguishing idea. But the idea that Spengler ascribed to 'the West' was particularly intriguing for architects. The distinguishing culture idea of Western civilisation, Spengler claimed, had been, for some centuries, its fascination with infinite space. This was architecturally manifested in its interest in breaking free of enclosure; in the striving for more and more expansive glass walls in Gothic cathedrals. 'The West' was a civilisation that refused to be contained; it strove to reach for the horizon and beyond into space.

Whether or not Western civilisation could be summed up by this one defining idea, it was a claim that intrigued architects who encountered it in the 1920s. It was an idea that challenged fundamental orthodoxies of the architectural organisation of space restricted by structure and based on the unit of the room. Whether or not it held the authority of history, it was an idea that opened up (literally as well as metaphorically) architecture to reinvention.

Eric Gunnar Asplund the Swedish architect, who was made Professor of Architecture in Stockholm in 1931, referred to Spengler in his inaugural speech. After reviewing Spengler's theories of culture ideas and their expression in architecture, Asplund put the case for a 'modern conception of space':

The characteristic of today's architecture is the dissolution of the room…. Across the world, provoked by the demands of reality, one is witnessing a move away from (the conception of the enclosed room), because it works against the satisfaction of real needs, and one begins to see emerging the principle of the dissolution of the room, a principle which is natural to our present time and to our actual conditions, and behind which we can also glimpse new formal architectural values. According to this conception, architectural space does not try to shut itself off like an isolated, architecturally complete unit, but opens itself to some degree to the sun, to nature, to human life and movement.'

This movement for a reassessment of the ways in which people occupy space and define it for their activities, and to which Asplund by the above speech pledged his allegiance, had radical consequences not only for the wall – its enclosure of rooms, courtyards, streets, town squares… – but also for the doorway. Spaces that were open 'to the sun, to nature, to human life and movement' should not need doorways or doors. Doorways and the barriers they provoke were part of the old regime.

Gradual entry

Entrance is not always a clear cut matter of crossing a distinct and incontrovertible line. Sometimes the transition from clearly being outside to being clearly inside is not the matter of a moment, but drawn out, taking time. A complete process of entrance often goes through a series of stages, through a series of doorways, taking you from the most public or open to the most private or closed. But gradual entrance can be more subtle, with spaces blending one into the next, gradually becoming more and more internal, like the spatial equivalent of a gradual crescendo in the performance of a piece of music.

Take for example the following description, taken from Georges Perec's series of short essays under the title *Species of Spaces* (1974, trans. Sturrock 1997):

'You began by following a gently winding path to the left of which there rose up, very gradually, with an extreme nonchalance even, a slight declivity that was oblique to start with but which slowly approached the vertical. Bit by bit, as if by chance, without thinking, without your having any right at any given moment to declare that you had remarked anything like a transition, an interruption, a passage, a break in continuity, the path became stony, that's to say that at first there was only grass, then there began to be stones in the middle of the grass, then there were a few more stones and it became like a paved, grassy walkway, while on your left, the slope of the ground began to resemble, very vaguely, a low wall, then a wall made of crazy paving. Then there appeared something like an open-work roof that was practically indissociable from the vegetation that had invaded it. In actual fact, it was already too late to know whether you were indoors or out. At the end of the path, the paving stones were set edge to edge and you found yourself in what is customarily called an entrance-hall, which opened directly on to a fairly enormous room that ended in one direction on a terrace graced by a large swimming pool.'

Or this from W.G. Sebald's novel *The Rings of Saturn* (1995, trans. Hulse 1999):

'In particular, (Somerleyton Hall) was famed for the scarcely perceptible transitions from interior to exterior; those who visited were barely able to tell where the natural ended and the man-made began. There were drawing rooms and winter gardens, spacious halls and verandahs. A corridor might end in a ferny grotto where fountains ceaselessly splashed, and bowered passages crisscrossed beneath the dome of a fantastic mosque. Windows could be lowered to open the interior onto the outside, and inside the landscape was replicated on the mirror walls.'

In some situations there are no clear and stable thresholds.

We can represent the idea of a gradual, progressive or an imperceptible process of entrance in diagrams. If you passed the point of a pencil across the drawing below, you would know when the point was right inside and when it was right outside the area of shade; you might also be able to suggest when the point was about a half or a third the way in or out; but it would be difficult if not impossible to determine when it crossed the threshold between outside and inside.

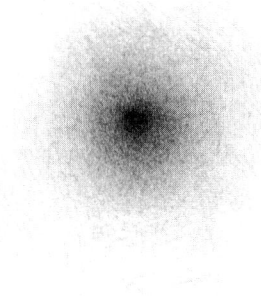

You can do the same with walls. The diagram on the right shows the plan of a composition of walls. Again you could easily tell when you were inside the composition and when outside, but deciding on the exact point of entry would be difficult. This drawing, as it happens, is not just a diagram, but the skeletal plan for a house that was never built. It is known as the 'Project for a Brick House'. The architect was Mies van der Rohe.

You can do the same with the ink spatter alongside, which is also like the plan of a section of fairly densely wooded forest. You know when you are deep within the 'forest' of spots (there are a few points you might choose as most inside) and when you are outside, but it is difficult to tell exactly where you make the transition.

If the Brick House had been built it would have actually had quick clear boundaries between inside and outside; these would have been defined by walls of glass rather than the brick walls in the skeletal plan. You can see these in the more complete plan on the next page; the glass walls are shown as solid single lines closing the openings

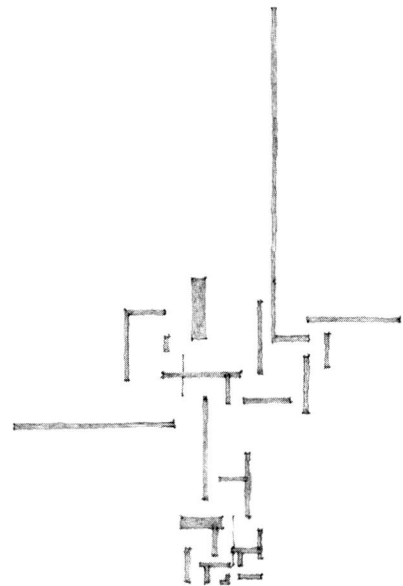

Spatial compositions that have 'insides' but no distinct threshold.

between the brick walls. The dashed lines mark the extent of the outline of the roof of the house. And it is interesting to note that, unlike in many conventional houses where the edges of roofs and the lines of the walls are more or less contiguous, here there are

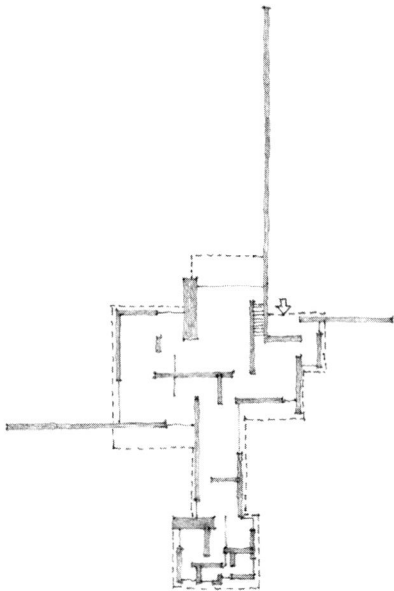

portions where the walls project beyond the extent of the roof and the roof oversails the walls, further blurring the division between outside and inside.

The most celebrated building in which Mies van der Rohe explored these ideas is the Barcelona Pavilion (above), a display pavilion built for the international exhibition that was held in Barcelona in 1929. Some of Mies's writing suggests that he, along with his contemporaries, read Spengler; and the pavilion in Barcelona can be read as a temple to dissolving precise divisions between inside and out.

The Barcelona Pavilion building is an exquisite example of an architect exploring an intellectual and spatial idea. The composition can be deconstructed into the layers

Mies van der Rohe's Barcelona Pavilion. Reflections and glass walls confuse distinctions between inside and out.

of different elements that go to make it up. The building is a very pure composition of the clear basic architectural elements of platform, pit, wall, glass wall, column and roof (right). The aggregation of elements is illustrated by the drawings that follow.

The first element of the building is the platform (1). In itself this element has a very clear boundary – its edge – and a very clear entrance – the steps up to it from the general level of the large square in Barcelona, on the edge of which the pavilion stands.

The next elemental layer of the building consists of the two pits that are built into the platform (2). Both of these are quite shallow but they are also both filled with water. They have very clear boundaries too, and unless you want to get your feet wet, these define places where you, as a visitor and the mobile centre (the point of the pencil) within the building, cannot go. So far, with the platform and the two pools, the building is very much like a formalised and geometrically pure and organised landscape of land with two lakes, in the smaller of which stands the statue visible in the photographs on pp. 191 and 201.

The next elemental layer imposed on this elemental 'landscape' consists of the walls (3, top of opposite page). Some of these do seem to reinforce the perimeter border established by the platform, but

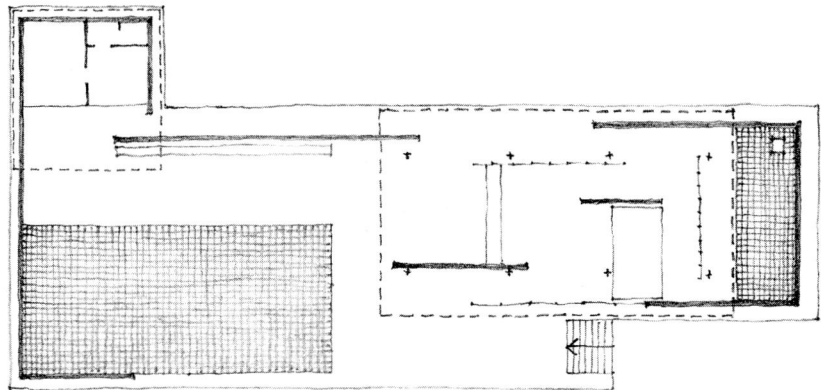

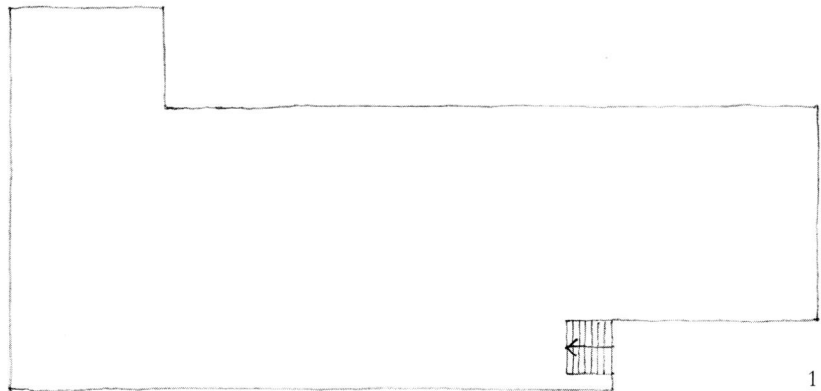

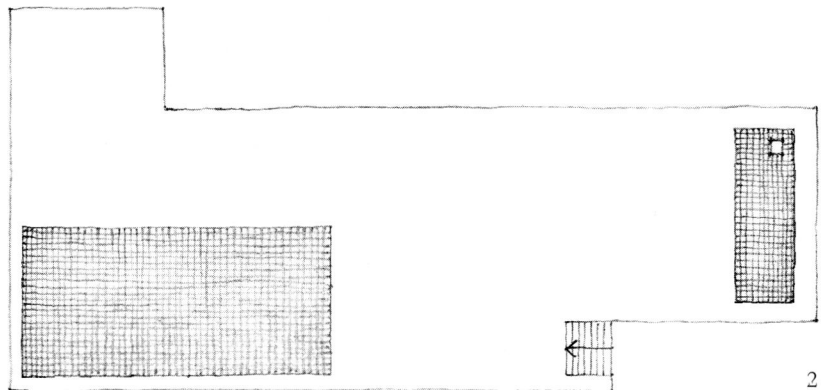

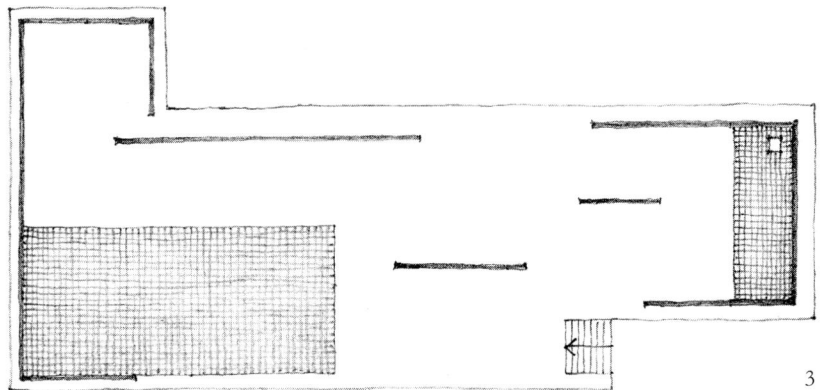

3

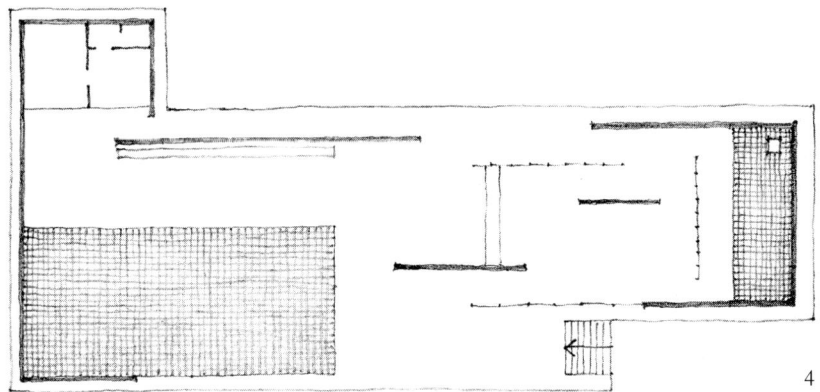

4

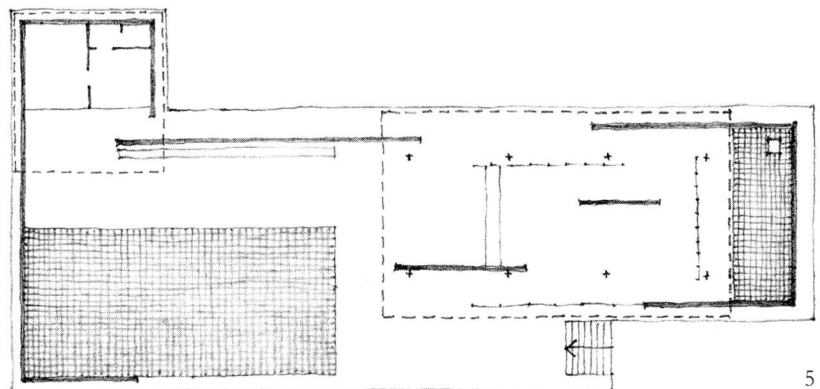

5

others float on their own terms within the 'landscape'. There are the beginnings of a sense of 'inside', but no clear definition of where the threshold is. Some of the walls are plain, but others are built of richly figured stone.

The next layer consists of the subsidiary walls and a bench (4). There are a variety of these, which could be further subdivided into their own layers, but that would need too many analytical drawings. Briefly, there are the thin partition walls and the glass front wall of the small administrative block in the top left corner of the plan. Then there are the more important glass walls that contribute to the composition of the major part of the pavilion to the right of the plan. Some of these are of clear glass and some of cloudy translucent glass. (One set of these, the pair of parallel glass walls close together near the centre of the plan, are of the cloudy glass, but the space between them has a roof light above, so they give out an ethereal glow.)

The last-but-one elemental layer comprises the roof, which is visually supported by the eight cruciform polished metal columns (5); the roof also gets support and stability from some of the walls. Just as in the Brick House project, the edge of the roof plays its own game – it is a pure rectangle echoing those of the pools in the platform – without always following the line of the walls. The complexity of the building is compounded by the transparency of the glass and the reflections in the polished materials and water.

The result of all these layers is a subtle architectural composition. But there is one more layer, which may be seen in the full plan above. This last layer – a black carpet (6) which I have shown white to avoid the confusion of having an apparent block of solid matter in the heart of the plan – identifies the closest thing to a 'centre' that the building possesses. This is the place where the king and queen of Spain held court when they visited the pavilion. The journey from the outside to this heart is not a matter of passing through a clear doorway, as it was for ambassadors visiting the sultan in Topkapi Palace (pp. 54–5); it is a matter of going through a progression of spaces that gradually become more and more internal; first onto the platform, then under the roof, and then between the glass and solid walls.

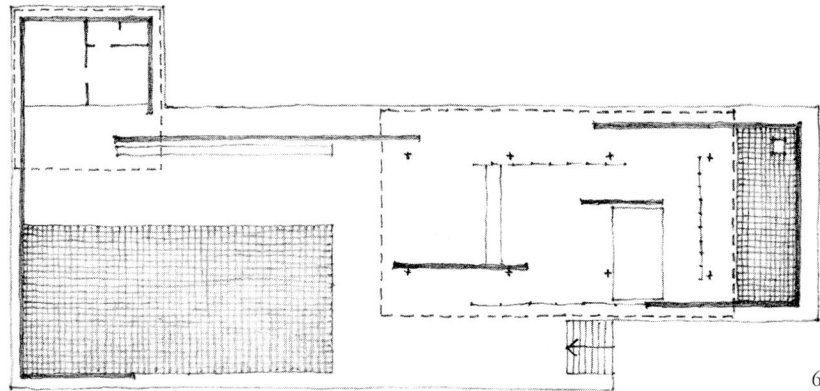

But as you reached the black carpet you could not have avoided the decision whether or not to step across its precise threshold.

In its original form, when first built in 1929, the Barcelona Pavilion had no doors. After the exhibition the pavilion was demolished. The pavilion as it stands in Barcelona now is a reconstruction built in the 1980s. Ironically, for security, it has now been given doors, positioned at the two narrow points between the walls under the roof and giving the building the precise thresholds that its architect made efforts to avoid.

THE WAY OUT

'(to mock the simplicity of his guest, the King) bade him enter the labyrinth, where he wandered, humiliated and confused, until the coming of evening, when he implored God's aid and found the door.' **Borges** (*The Aleph and Other Stories*, 1949)

Hopefully this book has shown that a doorway is more than merely a hole in a wall through which we get from outside to inside or from one room into the next. A doorway is more than a practical necessity brought about by our predilection for dividing up the space of the world by building walls.

A doorway is an instrument for the management and nuancing of space; it is also a punctuation in our experience of the world, and has psychological effects on how we see the world and how we behave. As such a doorway can have poetic and philosophical dimensions and be used to manipulate people's perceptions, relationships and sense of identity. By positioning people precisely and taking them along predetermined routes, doorways can orchestrate impressions and even cultivate certain beliefs. They can seduce as well as repel.

A doorway is a locus of opposites and contradiction. It links spaces on either side of a barrier but it also divides those spaces. It creates a sense of otherness in places and between the occupants of those places. A doorway discriminates between those who may pass through and those whom are excluded. Often they are guarded and kept under surveillance. Usually they can be locked shut.

A doorway hides more than it reveals, and controls what may be seen. Passing through a doorway may be a challenge but it is also often a reassurance, the attainment of a place of safety and privacy.

By our doorways we measure the world – a doorway establishes the scale of a building in relation to physical and psychological dimensions.

By doorways we also measure time. Doorways are staging points, punctuations, in our experience of space: whether in the landscape, where we pass from fieldgate to stile to a ford across a stream…; in the city, where we pass from city gate to archway to passageway…; or in our own houses, where we pass from garden gate to front door to room doorways…. In all, the threshold is the metaphor and crystalisation of the moment, the altar of arrival and departure.

Doorways are fixed points. A doorway can establish a datum to which we relate and by which we know where we are. Doorsteps provide points of view, from where the world can seem a different place. Doorways are where worlds encounter their neighbours; where we meet our friends, and sometimes battle with enemies.

As in-between places, doorways are where we can be in a state of being neither here nor there, in limbo, a transitional state of becoming rather than being. Often we cross a threshold in the blink of an eye, but sometimes we linger.

Doorways are where we present our selves to others and display our identities; they are where we introduce ourselves and ask others who they are.

We read doorways like we read faces; they tell us whether we are welcome or might be in jeopardy. Sometimes they lie to us and lure us into situations we would rather avoid. It is at a doorway that we change, not only where we are, but who we are. Doorways are switches in our minds as well as in our management of space; as we pass through we might smile or hold out a hand in greeting, we might grimace or even collapse with horror. We live in a symbiotic relationship with our doorways. We determine and manipulate them, and they affect and challenge us.

And finally, it is at doorways that we say goodbye, return to our private world or wander off into the sunset.

'And now the Soul stands in a vague, intense
Expectancy and anguish of suspense,
On the dim chamber-threshold... lo! he sees
Like a strange, fated bride as yet unknown,
His timid future shrinking there alone,
Beneath her marriage-veil of mysteries.'

Sarojini Naidu ('Past and Future', in *The Golden Threshold*, 1916)

ACKNOWLEDGEMENTS

Thank you…

… Gill for encouragement and tolerance; Mary, David and James for their amused interest in Dad doing a book on 'doors' (and for providing a few of the photographs); my friend and travelling companion Alan Paddison for providing many examples, quotations from esoteric texts and company on some of the journeys that contributed to the research for this book; Graeme Hutton, Head of the Dundee School of Architecture, for his support and patience; Dean Hawkes for long term encouragement and friendship; Tony Aldrich, especially, for the drawings and photographs of the Lychgate at Rame; Peter Blundell Jones for suggesting some of the sources; Marlene Ivey for telling me about Sottsass's doorways in the desert and her own work; Kathryn Findlay for some of the Japanese examples; Peter Sutton for his insights into Australian Aborigine culture; Calum Pallister for telling me about his experiences of the Mongolian *gher*; Charlie MacCallum for material relating to St Bride's, East Kilbride; Gabrielle Rivers for material on Presteigne courtroom; Daphne Kaufer for information on biblical instances of city gateways; Jenny Millar and Seaton Baxter for telling me about the research into children and precipices; Helen O'Connor for remembering to take a photograph of the entrance of the monastery of La Tourette; and Lorens Holm for speculating on why he hesitated at my threshold.

Thanks too, for general moral support and good humoured gibes, and for offering examples for which space in the book was unfortunately not found, to Adam Sharr, Flora Samuel, Juliet Odgers, Liza Raju Subhadra, Mary Wrenn, Monique Massie, Nathan Crilly, Neil Verow, Tracey McConnell-Wood and Samuel Penn.

Special thanks to Caroline Davidson for her constant support and acute criticism as the project developed; and to Caroline Mallinder, Georgina Johnson and Ben Woolhead at Routledge for seeing the project through to realisation.

And finally, thanks too to all those many others who, when told I was writing a book on doorways, spontaneously offered the best, or most memorable, examples from their own experience. Perhaps they are now more conscious of doorways and what they do.

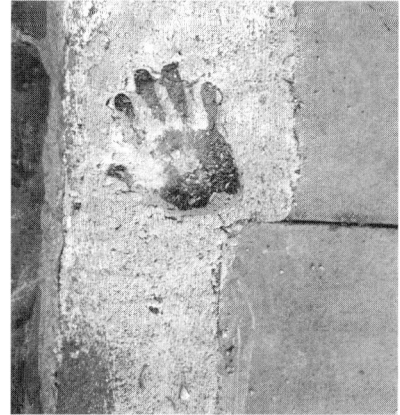

BIBLIOGRAPHY

This is a list of the books and other publications mentioned in the text:

Isabel Allende (trans. Peden) – *Eva Luna*, Penguin, London, 1989

Gaston Bachelard (trans. Jolas) – *The Poetics of Space* (1958), Beacon Press, Boston, 1964

Nicholas Black Elk (as told through Neihardt) – *Black Elk Speaks*, University of Nebraska Press, 1932

Peter Brook – *The Empty Space* (1968), Penguin, London, 1990

Jorge Luis Borges (trans. Hurley) – *The Aleph* (1949) *and Other Stories*, Penguin, London, 2000

Anthony Burgess – *Earthly Powers* (1980), Vintage, London, 2004

Titus Burkhardt – *The Art of Islam*, World of Islam Festival Trust, 1976

Albert Camus (trans. Laredo) – *The Outsider* (1942), Penguin, London, 1983

Raymond Chandler – *The Big Sleep* (1939), Penguin Books, London, 1973

Mircea Eliade (trans. Sheed) – *Patterns in Comparative Religion* (1958), Bison Books, New York, 1996

Mircea Eliade (trans. Trask) – *The Sacred and the Profane* (1957), Harvest Books, London, 1968

Robert Frost (ed. Hamilton) – *Robert Frost: Selected Poems*, Penguin, London, 1990

Erving Goffman – *The Presentation of Self in Everyday Life* (1959), Penguin, London, 1990

Homer (trans. Rieu) – *The Odyssey*, Penguin, London, 1946

Ted Hughes – *Tales from Ovid*, Faber and Faber, London, 1990

Aldous Huxley – *Crome Yellow* (1921), Penguin, London, 1936

Michael Huxley and Noel Witts (eds.) – *The Twentieth Century Performance Reader*, Routledge, London, 1996

Franz Kafka (trans. Muir and Muir) – *The Trial* (1925), Penguin, London, 2000

Robert Kerr – *The English Gentleman's House*, John Murray, London, 1864

Guillaume de Lorris and Jean de Meun (trans. Horgan) – *The Romance of the Rose* (C13th), Oxford U.P., 1994

George MacDonald – *The Complete Fairy Tales* (C19th), Penguin, London, 1999

Gabriel García Márquez (trans. Grossman) – *In Evil Hour* (1962), Penguin, London, 1996

Gabriel García Márquez (trans. Grossman) – *Living to Tell the Tale*, Penguin, London, 2003

Herman Muthesius (trans. Seligman) – *The English House* (1904), Crosby Lockwood Staples, London, 1979

Kiyoyuki Nishihara (trans. Gage) – *Japanese Houses: Patterns for Living*, Japan Publications, Tokyo, 1967

Michael Ondaatje – *The Conversations: Walter Murch and the Art of Editing Film*, Knopf, New York, 2002

Juhani Pallasmaa – *Eyes of the Skin: Architecture and the Senses* (1996), Wiley, Chichester, 2005

Georges Perec (trans. Sturrock) – *Species of Spaces and Other Essays* (1974), Penguin, London, 1997

Edgar Allan Poe – *Tales of Mystery and Imagination* (C19th), Dent, London, 1975

Philip Pullman – *The Subtle Knife*, Scholastic, London, 1997.

Aleksandr Pushkin (trans. Chandler, Chandler and Meerson) – 'The Queen of Spades' (1834), in Robert Chandler (ed.) – *Russian Short Stories from Pushkin to Buida*, Penguin, London, 2005

Barbara Radice (ed.) – *Design Metaphors*, Rizzoli, New York, 1988

Vincent Scully – *The Earth, the Temple and the Gods*, Yale U.P., New Haven and London, 1962

W.G. Sebald (trans. Hulse) – *The Rings of Saturn* (1995), Vintage, London, 1999

Soshitsu Sen – *Chado*, Weatherhill, New York, 1979

Alison Smithson (ed.) – *The Team Ten Primer*, MIT Press, Cambridge, Mass., 1968

Oswald Spengler (trans. Atkinson) – *The Decline of the West* (c.1918), George Allen and Unwin, London, 1952

Henry David Thoreau – *Walden* (1954), Bantam, New York, 1981

H. Clay Trumbull – *The Threshold Covenant* (1894), Impact Christian Books, Kirkwood, Minnesota, 2000

Simon Unwin – *Analysing Architecture*, Routledge, London, 2003

Simon Unwin – *An Architecture Notebook: Wall*, Routledge, London, 2000

C.F.A. Voysey – *Individuality* (1915), Lund Humphries, London, 1979

R.D. Walk and E.J. Gibson – 'A Comparative and Analytical Study of Visual Depth Perception', in *Psychological Monographs* 75, 1961, p. 519

INDEX

eBooks

eBooks – at www.eBookstore.tandf.co.uk

A library at your fingertips!

eBooks are electronic versions of printed books. You can store them on your PC/laptop or browse them online.

They have advantages for anyone needing rapid access to a wide variety of published, copyright information.

eBooks can help your research by enabling you to bookmark chapters, annotate text and use instant searches to find specific words or phrases. Several eBook files would fit on even a small laptop or PDA.

NEW: Save money by eSubscribing: cheap, online access to any eBook for as long as you need it.

Annual subscription packages

We now offer special low-cost bulk subscriptions to packages of eBooks in certain subject areas. These are available to libraries or to individuals.

For more information please contact webmaster.ebooks@tandf.co.uk

We're continually developing the eBook concept, so keep up to date by visiting the website.

www.eBookstore.tandf.co.uk